YOUTH IN CITIES
A Cross-National Perspective

Whether in the inner-city ghettos of the United States, the barrios of Brazil, or the ethnic neighborhoods of Germany and Lebanon, a growing number of urban youth find themselves marginalized from the social mainstream, facing the familiar problems of fragile families, residential segregation, limited or no access to education, premature entry into the world of work, and involvement in illegal activities. Both rich and poor countries are failing to meet the social and developmental needs of their urban youth as a result of weak institutional frameworks coupled with global economic restructuring that undermines traditional ways of earning a living. This volume compares the circumstances of urban youth from a cross-national perspective, illustrating the formidable challenges faced by young people trying to define their place in a rapidly changing world. Using both comparative evidence and case studies, this volume illustrates the common needs of youth throughout the world, despite the highly varied sociocultural circumstances in which they develop, and makes a case for the role of youth as creative social assets and positive forces for social change.

Marta Tienda is Maurice P. During '22 Professor of Demographic Studies, Professor of Sociology and Public Affairs, and Director of the Office of Population Research at Princeton University. She is coauthor or coeditor of *The Color of Opportunity: Pathways to Family, Work, and Welfare; The Hispanic Population of the United States; Divided Opportunities: Poverty, Minorities and Social Policy;* and *Hispanics in the U.S. Economy.* She is President Elect of the Population Association of America.

William Julius Wilson is Lewis P. and Linda L. Geyser University Professor at Harvard University. He previously taught at Washington State University, the University of Massachusetts at Amherst, and the University of Chicago. Professor Wilson has received 37 honorary degrees and was awarded the 1998 National Medal of Science. He is author of *The Declining Significance of Race, The Truly Disadvantaged, When Work Disappears: The World of the New Urban Poor,* and *The Bridge Over the Racial Divide: Rising Inequality and Coalition Politics.*

THE JACOBS FOUNDATION SERIES ON ADOLESCENCE

Series Editor: Michael Rutter

The Jacobs Foundation Series on Adolescence addresses the question of what can be done to promote healthy development around the world. It views this important question from different disciplines in the social sciences. Economists and sociologists may consider how we can promote human capital over time, specifically an individual's ability to become educated and to develop earning power; demographers and sociologists may analyze development patterns over generations; psychiatrists and psychologists may tackle the problem of how much change is possible in psychological health during the life course and over generations.

Drawing from these different domains of inquiry into human development, the Jacobs Foundation Series on Adolescence examines the potential for change across generations and during the life course in three areas: (1) human capital, (2) partnership behavior, and (3) psychological health and the rearing of children. The purpose of the series is to further the goals of the Jacobs Foundation – to contribute to the welfare and social productivity of the current and future generations of young people.

Youth in Cities: A Cross-National Perspective, edited by Marta Tienda and William Julius Wilson

YOUTH IN CITIES

A Cross-National Perspective

Edited by

Marta Tienda
Princeton University

William Julius Wilson
Harvard University

CAMBRIDGE
UNIVERSITY PRESS

PUBLISHED BY THE PRESS SYNDICATE OF THE UNIVERSITY OF CAMBRIDGE
The Pitt Building, Trumpington Street, Cambridge, United Kingdom

CAMBRIDGE UNIVERSITY PRESS
The Edinburgh Building, Cambridge CB2 2RU, UK
40 West 20th Street, New York, NY 10011-4211, USA
477 Williamstown Road, Port Melbourne, VIC 3207, Australia
Ruiz de Alarcón 13, 28014 Madrid, Spain
Dock House, The Waterfront, Cape Town 8001, South Africa

http://www.cambridge.org

First published 2002

Printed in the United States of America

Typeface Minion 10.5/13 pt.   *System* LATEX 2$_\varepsilon$ [TB]

A catalog record for this book is available from the British Library.

Library of Congress Cataloging in Publication data available

ISBN 0 521 80908 8 hardback
ISBN 0 521 00581 7 paperback

Contents

Contributors

Gary Barker, Director, Instituto Promundo, Rio de Janeiro, Brazil

Mary Carlson, Associate Professor of Psychiatry (Neuroscience), Department of Psychiatry, Harvard Medical School, and Associate Professor of Population and International Health, Harvard School of Public Health, Boston, Massachusetts

Neide Cassaniga, Researcher, Center for Research on Childhood, Universidade Santa Ursula, Rio de Janeiro, Brazil

Louise Chawla, Associate Professor, Whitney Young College, Kentucky State University, Frankfort, Kentucky

Felton Earls, Professor of Social Medicine, Department of Social Medicine, Harvard Medical School, Boston, Massachusetts

Ghada Abu El-Rous, Women's Programme Supervisor, Questscope for Social Development in the Middle East, Amman, Jordan

Wilhelm Heitmeyer, Professor, Director of the Interdisciplinary Institute for Conflict and Violence Research at Bielefeld University, Bielefeld, Germany

Sandy Hobbs, Reader, Psychology Division, School of Social Sciences, University of Paisley, Paisley, Scotland

Jim McKechnie, Senior Lecturer, Psychology Division, School of Social Science, University of Paisley, Paisley, Scotland

Haytham A. Mihyar, Programme Supervisor, Questscope for Social Development in the Middle East, Amman, Jordan

Fred Ogwal-Oyee, Programme Officer, Division of Emergency Programmes, United Nations Children's Fund, Asmara, Eritrea

Deborah Prothrow-Stith, Director and Associate Dean, Division of Public Health Practice, Harvard School of Public Health, Boston, Massachusetts

Mamphela Ramphele, Managing Director, The World Bank, Washington, DC

Curtis N. Rhodes, Jr., General Director, Questscope, Bromley, England

Irene Rizzini, Psychology and Sociology Professor, Center for Research on Childhood, Director, Universidade Santa Ursula, Rio de Janeiro, Brazil

Jill Swart-Kruger, Research Fellow, Department of Anthropology and Archaeology, University of South Africa, Pretoria, South Africa

Marta Tienda, Maurice P. During '22 Professor of Demographic Studies, Professor of Sociology and Public Affairs, and Director, Office of Population Research, Princeton University, Princeton, New Jersey

Robert White, Associate Professor in Sociology and Law, Law School, University of Tasmania, Hobart, Australia

William Julius Wilson, Lewis P. and Linda L. Geyser University Professor, John F. Kennedy School of Government, Harvard University, Cambridge, Massachusetts

Foreword

Whether in the ghettos of the United States, the barrios of Brazil or other South American countries, or the ethnic neighborhoods of Germany, France, or other European countries, a growing number of urban youth find themselves marginalized from the social mainstream, facing the familiar problems of fragile families, residential segregation, limited or no access to education, premature entry into the world of work, and involvement in illegal activities. As the United Nations (UN) Convention on the Rights of the Child testifies, both rich and poor countries are failing to meet the changing social and developmental needs of their urban youth as a result of weak institutional frameworks coupled with global economic restructuring that undermines traditional ways of earning a living.

For this reason I am pleased to present the volume *Youth in Cities: A Cross-National Perspective*, which is the first in the new Jacobs Foundation Series on Adolescence, to be published by Cambridge University Press. The volume is based on a conference, "Youth in Cities: Successful Mediators of Normative Development," sponsored by the Jacobs Foundation of Switzerland at their Communication Center, Marbach Castle (Germany), on October 22–24, 1998. More than 40 international scholars and practitioners of youth programs assembled to portray the circumstances of urban youth throughout the world and to illustrate the formidable challenges young people face as they try to define their place in a rapidly changing world. Documenting the condition of youth living in cities and identifying interventions that are most successful in ameliorating the pernicious effects of urban poverty are the first steps to improving the life circumstances and opportunities of the vast majority of the world population.

In addition to addressing a relatively ignored, rapidly growing, and highly vulnerable population throughout the world, several features of the chapters in the volume are noteworthy. First, assessing youth from both the standpoint of the researcher and the practitioner yields a grounded base from which to draw policy lessons. Stronger than either approach alone, this hybrid tack strikes a balance between theory and application. Second, the use of cross-national comparisons and case studies allows for an analysis of differences and similarities among strategies devised to improve the state of youth the world over. Third, by evaluating the efficacy of an array of interventions, important policy lessons can be culled. Finally, the conviction that the views of young people must be integral to the formulation of policies aimed at improving their life chances is a common thread apparent throughout this volume.

It is my hope that the volume will have the wide acceptance it deserves. Academics from developmental psychology, sociology, political science, and legal scholarship will find novel insights from case studies that either support their prior conceptions or modify them in new ways with concrete evidence from practitioners. Lay audiences, including policymakers and attorneys and practitioners who develop and operate programs to promote healthy youth development, will also find creative ideas to bolster their successful interventions on behalf of youth.

Klaus J. Jacobs, Chairman
Jacobs Foundation

YOUTH IN CITIES
A Cross-National Perspective

I

SETTING THE CONTEXT

1 Comparative Perspectives of Urban Youth
Challenges for Normative Development

Marta Tienda and William Julius Wilson

The share of youth residing in urban areas surpassed 50% by the turn of the 21st century and is projected to rise further because of high fertility and continued rural–urban migration (United Nations, 1993:5). Urban living can alleviate many of the hardships associated with rural poverty and underdevelopment, but in the context of rapid social transformation, it can also increase the challenges of normative youth development.

The consequences of extreme material deprivation are especially harsh for the very young, whose neurological development, physical health, and emotional capacity are permanently compromised by poor nutrition, limited emotional and intellectual stimulation, and inadequate satisfaction of basic human needs, such as safe shelter, clean drinking water, and predictability of social environment. Whether in the inner-city ghettos of the United States, the homelands of South Africa, or the favelas of Brazil, growing numbers of urban youth find themselves at the periphery of city life, facing the familiar problems of poverty: fragile families, inadequate nutrition, limited or no access to education, premature entry into the world of work, and involvement in illegal activities.

Despite bewildering differences in the social and cultural contexts experienced by urban youth worldwide, the developmental challenges confronted by those reared in materially disadvantaged circumstances are strikingly similar. A child born at the beginning of the 21st century has a 4 in 10 chance of living in extreme poverty (UN Children's Fund, 2000:1). About 24% of the world's population lives on less than $1 per day, but in poor countries, the share is close to 35% – the majority of these are women and children (UN Children's Fund, 2001: Appendix).

Among industrialized countries, the highest child poverty rate prevails in the Russian Federation, where more than one in four children was poor during the 1990s, but the United States is not far behind, as one in six young people lived below the official poverty threshold in 1999 (National Center for Children in Poverty, 2000). In Canada, Australia, Israel, and Poland, child poverty rates hover around 15–16% and are just under 10% for France and the Netherlands (Bradbury and Jantti, 1999). These averages conceal appreciable variation within countries. For example, in 1999 child poverty rates in the United States hovered around 30% for minority groups, although they were considerably higher in 1990, before the prolonged period of economic prosperity. Residential segregation further accentuates the pernicious consequences of poverty by limiting interaction between lower and middle classes, thereby perpetuating the cycle of social exclusion that stymies the life chances of even the most industrious youth.

As global economic restructuring alters the sociopolitical and cultural landscape of nation states, governments encounter formidable challenges in satisfying the social and developmental needs of their youth. This is especially difficult for income-strapped countries of the Southern Hemisphere, where the intense pace of urbanization taxes the ability of weak institutional frameworks to meet the changing needs of rapidly growing youth populations (Brockerhoff, 2000). Global economic restructuring also has contributed to the marginalization and social isolation of low-income families in the Northern Hemisphere, thereby restricting opportunities for normative youth development. Moreover, the low-fertility regimes that characterize most industrialized countries do not necessarily translate to higher resources for youth, who frequently find themselves in competition for resources in a rapidly aging population (Preston, 1984).

In both developed and developing societies, poverty takes a devastating toll on young people and rests at the core of human rights violations against them (UN Children's Fund, 2001). The intertwined fate of nations in the global economy has fostered greater awareness of their shared circumstances. The plight of youth reared in material disadvantage throughout the world was the focus of a decade-long international effort to develop guidelines for protecting the rights of children and youth around the world. The product of this effort – the Convention on the Rights of the Child (CRC) – is the first legally binding international instrument to make explicit the full range of rights to which every child is entitled. This holistic treaty, which recognizes every child's right to a standard of living conducive to physical, mental, spiritual, moral, and social development, stands as a unified global commitment to redress the root causes of child poverty and to assuage its deleterious consequences within the resources available to national governments.

The Convention is predicated on the notion that tackling poverty requires a strategic and integrated approach that combines human rights and civil rights law with economic, social, political, and cultural rights. The document also identifies several strategies to promote normative development, including prevention of risky behaviors, protection from physical and emotional harm, as well as enlistment of youth participation in decisions and activities that affect their own destinies.[1]

Partly as a response to the Convention, in recent years policymakers, researchers, and practitioners working in highly diverse urban contexts have been making more concerted attempts to document, understand, and address the worsening condition of the world's growing youth population. However, apart from commissioned studies and annual reports prepared by international monitoring agencies, there has been relatively little exchange among scholars and practitioners – either within or among nations – regarding the status of youth growing up in cities.[2] This is so despite the intense urbanization processes under way in many countries classified as "least developed" by the United Nations.

Accordingly, as a response to the paucity of scholarly and practitioner exchanges, the chapters in this volume synthesize existing knowledge about the status and experiences of youth reared in precarious urban environments from an interdisciplinary and cross-national perspective. In addition to addressing a relatively ignored, rapidly growing, and highly vulnerable population throughout the world, several features of the essays that follow are noteworthy.

First, the chapters build on the experiences and insights of *both* practitioners and researchers, an unusual approach to youth. This twin strategy yields a firmer foundation for drawing practical lessons than either a research or an applied approach alone because it forces an intermediate ground between theory and application. Second, several chapters combine case studies with extensive cross-national comparisons, which are essential

---

[1] The Convention has been ratified by every country in the world except the United States and Somalia. However, by signing the Convention, the United States has signaled its intention to ratify.

[2] United Nations Children's Fund (UNICEF) and the World Health Organization (WHO) are two prominent international agencies that have added to their ongoing assessment of the "State of Children" a dedicated study of the condition of youth.

to identify circumstances that are common to most settings and those unique to particular sociocultural contexts. Third, several chapters attempt to identify both successful and unsuccessful interventions to draw policy lessons with wide appeal that can be practically implemented both to improve the life circumstances of youth and to enhance their opportunities to lead productive and stable lives. Finally, although collectively the chapters cover a broad substantive terrain and many draw extensively on international comparisons, they are unified thematically by their focus on normative development and a limited range of possible mediators. These include physical and emotional well-being, exposure to risky environments and violence, and creative community-level strategies to engage youth in prosocial change.

Volume Overview

Selected sociodemographic indicators of the countries included in the volume as case studies, as well as the corresponding regional development averages for these indicators, are provided in Table 1.1. By most measures, Uganda is the most impoverished setting for urban youth among the countries considered. However, as the regional indicators for the least developed nations reveal, some youth reside in even more precarious environments. More than one in three Ugandan residents lives on less than $1 per day, compared to only 2% of Jordanians, 11% of South Africans, and 26% of Brazilians.

Youth in developing countries are 15 times more likely to die before age 5 when compared to their counterparts in industrialized countries, and those in the least developed countries 27 times more likely to do so. However, there is considerable variation in child life expectancy among developing countries. South Africa's child mortality rate is twice that of Jordan's. In part these differentials can be traced directly to the varying contours of societal underdevelopment, but national differences in income inequality are also responsible. Moreover, boys and girls do not experience similar opportunities to become productive citizens, as is evident in the differentials in school enrollment rates. Gender disparities in educational attainment are especially pronounced in South Africa and Uganda.

Developing nations also differ appreciably in their urban structures: Whereas more than three in four youth in Jordan and Brazil reside in urban areas, only about half of South African youth do so. Fewer than one in five of Uganda's youth resides in an urban area, compared to about half of youth in other developing nations. By contrast, about 80% of youth in industrialized

Table 1.1 Selected Sociodemographic Indicators of Child and Adolescent Well-Being for Regions and Selected Countries Circa 2000

Countries and Regions	Under-5 Mortality Rate 1999	Primary School Enrollment Ratio 1995–99[a] (Net)		Secondary School Enrollment Ratio 1995–97[a] (Gross)		Percentage of Population Urban 1999	Percentage of Population below $1 a Day 1990–99[a]	Percentage of Urban Population Using	
		Male	Female	Male	Female			Improved Drinking Water Sources	Adequate Sanitation Facilities
Industrialized countries	6	96	96	105	107	79	–[b]	100	100
Germany	5	86	87	105	103	87	–	–	–
United States	8	94	95	98	97	77	–	100	100
United Kingdom	6	97	98	120	139	89	–	100	100
Developing countries	90	84	77	55	46	48	26	91	81
Brazil	40	–	–	31×[c]	36×	81	5	89	81
Jordan	35	86	86	52×	54×	74	2	100	100
South Africa	69	88	86	76	91	50	11	92	99
Least developed countries	164	63	54	23	14	28	35	80	73
Uganda	131	92	83	15	9	14	37	72	96
World	82	85	79	61	54	57	24	93	84

[a] Data that refer to the most recent year available during the period specified in the column heading.
[b] – Data not available.
[c] Data that refer to years or periods, other than those specified in the column heading, differ from the standard definition, or refer to only part of a country.

Source: United Nations Children's Fund (2001). *State of the World's Children, 2001,* tables 1, 3, 4, 5, and 6; http://www.unicef.org/sowc01/tables/

nations live in cities and towns. Of course, urban residence implies different opportunities and obstacles for youth residing in industrialized, developing, and least developed countries. In the industrialized world, virtually all urban dwellers have access to adequate sanitation and safe drinking water, but in Uganda, less than three quarters of city dwellers can avail themselves of these urban amenities, and in South Africa, only 92% enjoy safe water. Approximately 20% to 25% of urban Brazilian youth lack access to adequate sanitation facilities.

Against this thumbnail sketch of the social and economic conditions in which youth are reared around the world, one might expect equally diverse developmental needs. Yet, although the specific social and cultural conditions in which youth are reared do differ appreciably, one of the main themes developed in the chapters that follow is the similarity of young people's needs for healthy psychosocial development. All the chapters identify the value of harnessing the creative energy of youth, and the numerous social, community, and familial advantages to treating young people as an asset rather than a societal burden.

Youth as a Force for Social Change

Throughout the world youth represent a source of cultural innovation and dynamism that is seldom acknowledged in countries around the world, much less nurtured. Although several authors stress the importance of tapping the creative potential of youth, the three chapters included in this section emphasize the myriad ways that youth are powerful agents directing the course of social change. Ramphele reminds us that youth are often the harbingers of cultural, social, or economic transitions within and across countries.

Unfortunately, once transformed, society often ignores the condition of its youth and confines them to a marginalized status that undervalues them. One reason is that much of the current literature on youth focuses on an assessment of the negative consequences of maladaptive behavior and the tremendous costs incurred by society in regulating deviant behavior, rather than on the potential of youth for creative change. As Ramphele so clearly shows in her analysis of the positive effects of the South African Black Consciousness Movement on youths, creating high self-esteem among young people increases their empowerment. Inspired by the Black Consciousness Movement, young people set about helping adults in their communities overcome feelings of inferiority generated by years of racism and thereby break the cycle of fatalism.

Developmental psychologists emphasize that successful normative youth development requires intact nuclear and extended families, supportive communities, realistic perceptions of opportunities, and predictable behavior and experiences. However, in many societies, past legacies and the drastic socioeconomic changes accompanying globalization have eroded these resources. Greater numbers of children are growing up in poor, parent-absent households without the support of their extended families in areas where the growth of social capital is hindered by the lack of material resources. Moreover, in rapidly changing social and local worlds, behavior and experiences are exceedingly more random – that is, far less predictable – and therefore youth are greatly more disoriented from their developmental tasks.

Under conditions of greater uncertainty, the answer to normative development lies in risk management – on the level of both the individual and the community. In order to succeed, young people must accept the risks in their environment and develop creative ways to manage them. Ramphele argues that societal institutions not only have to build effective risk-management strategies, but must require leaders able to design appropriate interventions as well. Only confident youth who dare to imagine a better future are able to focus their energy on reaching it. Accordingly, Ramphele concludes that successful interventions in places with low human capital must include steps to raise the young people's self-esteem. Young, confident people will be better equipped to negotiate successfully the risks in the future, to become valuable members of society, and to reach their full potential.

Building on the basic idea that the creativity and energy of youth can be channeled to produce positive social change, Swart-Kruger and Chawla examine the success of participatory programs for children of South African streets and squatter camps. Like several authors in this volume (see especially Earls and Carlson, this volume), they call for a more inclusive approach to solving child-related social problems. A focus on deviance and normlessness, the authors argue, diverts us from attending to the lack of adequate programs that deal with the whole child. To develop their argument, Swart-Kruger and Chawla discuss two concrete programs funded by the Nelson Mandela Children's Fund, Street-Wise and Growing Up in Cities, which are inspired philosophically by the Convention on the Rights of the Child and the African Charter on the Rights and Welfare of the Child. Both programs illustrate outstanding and successful approaches to help children achieve autonomy and self-esteem. Also, both programs require local governments to create social conditions that enable communities to meet the basic needs of youth.

Street-Wise is a comprehensive services intervention program for street boys, and Growing Up in Cities is a long-term community development program for 10- to 14-year-old children living in a Johannesburg squatter camp. Street-Wise, which began as a street school, has become a national program designed to integrate boys into the mainstream society, further attesting to its acclaimed success. A drop-in shelter program, a nutrition program, and a reconciliation program to reconnect boys with their families supplement Street-Wise's basic education program, which emphasizes literacy and job-training skills.

Although different in their details, Street-Wise and Growing Up in Cities share many similarities that are crucial for understanding their success. An important feature of the programs is their strategy to give voice to the views of youth both in shaping and in operating the program. Both programs sought a compromise between the Western individualistic perspective and the collectivistic approach of South African communities in developing strategies to service youth. An important strength of both programs is their ability to provide individualized attention to each child.

Also, both programs recognize that negative perceptions of youth often preclude investments of scarce social resources for their benefit. Therefore, during the start-up phases, both programs sought to change adults' and the general public's perception of street children. Both programs share the goal of creating physically and socially safe environments that nurture children's positive identities. In short, both programs illustrate the need for multifaceted approaches that crystallize over time as program developers learn more about their clientele and consider the most effective means to promote the individual and collective well-being of youth.

Although the idea of well-being is central to the concept of normative development, measuring it poses thorny methodological challenges. After summarizing existing studies about well-being, Earls and Carlson conclude that few satisfactory operational measures exist. Drawing on the work of Sen and Habermaus, Earls and Carlson argue that a deliberative process – one that involves children as major stakeholders in the framing and implementation of research initiatives that explore well-being – has both intrinsic and extrinsic benefits. Intrinsically, children can develop competence and confidence by involvement in the research process, and extrinsically, children's direct involvement in research can help the development of more precise measures of this multifaceted construct. These ideas, which allow children to be collaborators rather than just *subjects*, are inspired by the Convention on the Rights of the Child, which acknowledges that children are able to make deliberate decisions and exercise their rights.

After describing the epistemology of their approach, Earls and Carlson discuss a practical application of their theory of adolescent well-being, namely, a project in Chicago that investigates how young people characterize their own well-being. As paid interns, youth took part in conversations about children's rights. In conversations about well-being, they identified their parents, teachers, and police officers as crucial ingredients. Moreover, the child-initiated discourse revealed that adults must provide structure and motivation for youth development and must maintain a presence to help channel the creative contributions of youth. The process of working with the adolescents draws into sharp focus the importance of civic engagement as a crucial factor in transition to adulthood. This, according to Earls and Carlson, is the highest form of well-being.

Urban Youth Experiences in Cross-Cultural Perspective

As young people grow up, their integration into society is a prerequisite for their normative development and well-being. Imparting a sense of acceptance and belonging is crucial to accomplish integration. Using German cities as illustrations, Heitmeyer investigates how the changing conditions of cities impact on young people's behavior and need to belong. Important mechanisms to integrate youth socially include access to functional social systems (such as education and labor markets), compensatory social policies to combat economic polarization, shared values and norms, stable social memberships, and wide participation in social life. These requirements are even more important for integrating immigrant youth and the economically disadvantaged into the social mainstream.

Heitmeyer contends that conventional socialization mechanisms are failing to integrate a growing number of young people, especially immigrants and impoverished youth. Changed social and economic opportunities and higher levels of cultural pluralism foster greater uncertainty, more responsibility in decision making, more pressure to compete, and less social support – circumstances that individually and collectively undermine healthy, normative youth development.

Rising residential segregation, which often acts as a mobility trap, produces social isolation, resignation from required and optional activities, rejection of mainstream norms, unemployment, and violence. These circumstances accentuate interethnic social distances and further complicate the developmental challenges confronted by urban youth. Heitmeyer warns that unless social policies are implemented to reverse these trends, Germany will witness the creation of an "urban underclass" comparable to that characterizing American segregated cities (Wilson, 1987; Massey and Denton, 1993).

Heitmeyer recommends that municipal governments play an active role in urban migration policy to ensure social integration and to prevent ethnoracial divisions from expanding among urban youth. Unfortunately, just the opposite response appears to be developing, as there is a trend toward greater domination of the market and preference for tougher measures in dealing with noncompliance (see also White, this volume).

With a better understanding of the connection between urban disintegration and maladaptive youth development, urban leaders and social architects not only can attenuate economic polarization among the young, but also enhance their development by creating safe environments conducive to prosocial behavior. Heitmeyer is pessimistic about these prospects, however, arguing that European cities will most likely experience the creation of an "urban underclass" divided by physical, social, and economic space because the incentives to broker on behalf of youth are usually lacking.

Nowhere is this need for a voice greater than among homeless children. The growth of urban poverty and in particular the marginalization of youth have fueled a public debate about the plight of children who are omnipresent on the streets of primary cities in South America. In Brazil, one of the most publicized examples of the existence of street children, the reaction by the authorities to the presence of unsupervised children roaming the streets has been to reduce their numbers by the use of harsh and punitive measures.

Recent media reports about the intolerable conditions experienced by street kids detained in state-operated reformatories and the worrisome numbers of youth who have died while under the care of authorities have led to a public demand for more humane treatment of these youth. The seemingly intractable problems require an in-depth understanding of why children are on the streets in the first place, and what kinds of interventions are best suited to their needs.

Rizzini, Barker, and Cassaniga find hope in the response of Brazil's community-based organizations and nongovernmental organizations (NGOs) to the plight of street children. Preventive programs being created distinguish between working children, who trade their wares on the street and usually return home to parents and siblings with their day's earnings, and homeless children, who spend their entire lives on the street and who have little or no contact whatsoever with family members. However, despite the growing success of programs that target homeless youth, the number of young people who have been fortunate enough to have contact with these interventions remains relatively low.

Rizzini and her colleagues suspect that Brazilians will be more supportive of public expenditures that promote the well-being of *all* children, and not just those on the lowest rungs of the economic ladder. Accordingly, they argue that policymakers and youth advocates will be well served by changing their focus from the plight of the most marginalized or deviant children to the rights of *all* children, regardless of social background or disadvantaged status.

To ground their recommendations in concrete example, Rizzini, Barker, and Cassaniga describe several case studies of programs that have been successful with homeless children by using the strategy of "targeting within universalism" (Skocpol, 1991), that is, using public resources to implement inclusive programs for children from diverse socioeconomic groups. These programs aid all children in the Brazilian school system and have been especially successful in preventing low-income children from ending up on the streets and engaging in petty crimes to survive.

Persisting high rates of youth delinquency in both affluent and impoverished settings warrant better explanations than social scientists have been able to provide heretofore. Although social scientists appear to know a good deal about *who* commits certain crimes, a sound understanding of *why* the rate of youth delinquency remains high is still lacking. The answers, according to White, reside in the social ecology of poverty. Youth become delinquent not only because they are poor, but also because they live in communities that lack solidarity and social resources that cater to the needs of the disadvantaged. Poor urban youth are systematically more isolated from mainstream social institutions (such as schools and job opportunities) that inculcate social norms of responsibility. In turn, this not only leads to cultural and societal exclusion, but also encourages them to develop maladaptive strategies as they negotiate the developmental challenges of adolescence (see also Rhodes, Mihyar, and Abu El-Rous and Heitmeyer, this volume).

White discusses various approaches to youth deviance and social justice and argues that reduction in delinquent youth behavior requires a deep understanding of the broad situational and structural obstacles to normative youth development. After reviewing crime trends in several countries, White identifies striking similarities in the profiles of young offenders across all countries, who tend to be "men with low income, low educational achievement, no employment, a weak attachment to parents, and (who) move frequently."

He notes that minority and poor youth are overrepresented in the crime statistics in all social settings and that youth criminality attracts more attention than "adult crime" because it is committed more often in public space, making it relatively more visible, and because it is often sensationalized in the media. Youth are most visible and highly regulated in public spaces, and that is precisely where they most need to feel valued and welcomed. Accordingly, White poses a challenging policy issue: how to democratize the use of public space so that youth become primary stakeholders and have a voice in the use of that space.

White discusses three broad approaches to crime prevention – coercive, developmental, and accommodating. Deterrence involves lessening the opportunity to cause trouble by systematically limiting the presence or visibility of youth in the community; it is achieved by enforcing dress codes, limiting the number of youth who can gather together in public places, and imposing curfews. The developmental approach emphasizes the alleviation of social problems by including young people as part of the resolution process: that is, by harnessing the positive and transformative capacities of the young so that they connect to a wider process of community empowerment. This option requires that the government provide adequate services and facilitate multi-agency cooperation to intervene meaningfully in the lives of youth. Finally, an accommodating approach attempts to structure solutions that allow all sides to have their interests protected in a nonjudgmental fashion.

White concludes by highlighting several successful examples of accommodating approaches that deploy a holistic approach to intervening in the lives of youth and that include the youth themselves as valued partners in the development of crime prevention interventions. He argues that effective crime prevention depends not on harsh social control, but rather on enlightened social justice.

Prothrow-Stith documents rising rates of child violence throughout the world, but particularly in large urban centers with large pockets of concentrated poverty. For example, in the United States not only has the incidence of youth violence dramatically increased over the last decade, but the severity of these occurrences has escalated as well. Consequently, the federal government spends more than $8 billion annually to combat youth violence and support the health and development of children through education and crime prevention (National Economic Council, 2000). She argues that violence-induced youth injuries and deaths are preventable public health problems with readily identifiable social causes. To make her case, Prothrow-Stith reviews the effectiveness of public health intervention programs in the United States since 1986, noting that program developers concerned about increased youth homicides have actively sought to design interventions aimed at curbing the growing threat to youth health and well-being.

Public health officials have responded to these trends by proposing primary, secondary, and tertiary preventive measures. Primary strategies often involve public health messages that seek to reduce the level of societal violence in general, or attempts by the criminal justice systems to limit the number of guns in circulation. Secondary measures target specific at-risk subgroups and utilize educational interventions that emphasize behavior modification. More forceful attempts to decrease crime involve removing perpetrators from circulation entirely and constitute the most extreme or tertiary approach to violence prevention. Prothrow-Stith discusses specific programs that have had a significant impact on violent crime reduction by utilizing either primary or secondary strategies. Although incarceration is necessary in the most serious cases, the more proactive measures have been highly successful in preventing violent incidents.

Developmental psychologists also appreciate the importance of social environments for normative youth development, and they recognize five major constraints on the healthy development of youth – frustrated aspirations, changed family relations, neighborhood deterioration, truncated roles of children, and ineffective institutions. Creating prosocial, stable environments for children and youth requires elimination of these potential barriers. Rhodes, Mihyar, and Abu El-Rous describe the efforts of a program in Jordan to create "prosocial communities" in the midst of rapid local change by building on the existing institutional resource base of society and involving youth as well as parents in their neighborhood improvement. The program utilizes an action-oriented approach that involves an ongoing reorientation to meet the rapidly changing needs of the population being served – in this instance, poor urban youth from rural origins.

To illustrate the power of these principles, Rhodes and his colleagues selected two poor communities in Amman to develop and implement a program to create what they term "prosocial communities." Both communities are characterized by poverty, social alienation, frustrated aspirations, environmental deterioration, and ineffective institutions. And although youth shouldered adult responsibilities, such as income generation, in both communities, they were not given commensurate consideration in decision making. Consequently, they became alienated and rebellious.

The intervention program Rhodes and colleagues describe sought to design an environment that could replace maladaptive behaviors with constructive activities that would benefit the whole neighborhood. For example, a computer lab, a library, and a social center were created, and a summer camp for troubled boys included counseling and opportunities for prosocial activities (such as involvement with handicapped children in hospitals). These activities resulted in a marked positive change in both the attitudes and behaviors of the youth. Although youth were the focus of the intervention, improvements in their behavior also fostered changes in the adults, who became engaged with the children and increased their voluntary activity. The net gain for the neighborhood was the emergence of community consciousness.

Work, Life Skills, and Well-Being

Although reliable statistics over time and place are scarce, several international organizations estimate that up to 500 million children worldwide work – not only in developing countries, but in Europe and North America as well. In addition to clarifying tragic realities and common misconceptions about child labor around the world, McKechnie and Hobbs pose and address two important questions: To what extent is poverty the main causal predictor of child employment? And how is child employment related to life skills and education?

Estimates of child labor abound, but accurate assessments of the phenomenon are lacking. Addressing these questions is difficult for three main reasons: definitions of youth work vary cross-nationally; many countries do not keep (or want to keep) reliable statistics of child labor; and there is enormous conceptual ambiguity surrounding the term *child labor*. Also, scholars disagree about whether and how youth employment is beneficial or detrimental to their development.

Given the difficult methodological problems clouding the study of youth employment, McKechnie and Hobbs challenge researchers to address the conceptual and measurement problems surrounding the economic activity of school-aged children and to develop comparable cross-national definitions of who qualifies as a youth. Further, they argue that theoretical frameworks that adequately conceptualize the number of hours youth spent at work and the nature of activity performed are needed to assess properly the impact of work on the lives of children. This undertaking requires efforts to catalogue a broad range of economic tasks performed by youth, including those that defy easy description and fall outside the standard statistical reporting systems. As important, McKechnie and Hobbs recommend developing uniform standards that classify youth jobs in terms of whether they produce any developmental benefits for incumbents or whether they only have deleterious effects on youth development, such as undermining educational attainment. Potential benefits of work include sense of autonomy, self-esteem, responsibility, and ultimately, enhanced employability during young adulthood.

The rise of armed conflict throughout the world has exposed millions of children and youth to myriad life-threatening dangers, ranging from displacement, disease, and famine, to permanent psychological distress, to death. These problems are particularly acute in countries lacking a strong institutional framework upon which to build support services for youth, such as Uganda. After years of violence and terror at the hands of an unscrupulous dictator, Uganda has only recently started to realize some improvements in the physical well-being of its citizens. However, armed conflict continues to undermine these gains as warring factions destroy schools, hospitals, and homes, while also conscripting very young men into the armed conflict. According to Ogwal-Oyee, only 50% of Ugandan children are enrolled in elementary school, and the majority work to supplement meager family incomes. Large and growing numbers of children live in the streets because they have lost both parents to war or disease or because their parents are too poor to support them. All too often young girls become victims of rape and sexual abuse when warring factions displace entire communities.

After documenting how much Ugandan youth are rendered physically and emotionally vulnerable to war and epidemics, Ogwal-Oyee describes the Life Skills Intervention for Young People program, which the Ugandan government developed to help adolescents ages 12–20 recover from tragedies caused by the civil war and prolonged social unrest. The program targets out-of-school youth by providing them with essential skills to negotiate the challenges of orphanhood, physical risk, and the necessity to earn a living at a young age. The Life Skills program is designed to teach children and adolescents competencies ranging from coping with acquired immunodeficiency syndrome (AIDS)-related losses to making career choices, avoiding risky sexual behavior, developing negotiation skills, and fostering proactive health behaviors.

Baseline assessments, which showed that Ugandan children had very low life skills levels and adolescents only slightly better skills, were used to develop age-appropriate training modules. To implement the Life Skills program, schools were classified on the basis of the diagnosed life skills needs (which vary across communities) and their appropriate adaptation for rural and urban youth. Over 900 facilitators and educators, including the Scouts and members of school clubs, were trained in the life skills programs and provided instructional materials to conduct the classes. Through this network of nonformal educators, over 5,000 adolescents have benefited from the Life Skills program. The program's strategy is explicitly preventive and educational, rather than service providing, and it demonstrates that even a government with limited resources can have a positive impact on youth provided adequate commitment to such an agenda exists.

Conclusion

We began this chapter by pointing out that many of the hardships associated with rural poverty and underdevelopment can be alleviated in urban areas, but that rapid social transformation in cities can enhance the problems of normative youth development. The number of urban youth experiencing extreme poverty, inadequate nutrition, lack of access to education, premature entry into the labor market, and involvement in antisocial and illegal activities continues to grow. Despite significant variation in the social and cultural contexts of urban youth worldwide, those experiencing material disadvantage confront developmental challenges that are remarkably similar. The following chapters – representing interdisciplinary and cross-cultural perspectives, and featuring an unusual integration of practical and theoretical knowledge – illuminate many of these challenges and discuss a number of innovative programs to address them.

In the concluding chapter we identify several themes that undergird the array of programs and topics in this volume and try to illustrate how urban environments provide numerous venues to promote normative development for economically disadvantaged youth. Our focus on the special plight of urban youth does not minimize the formidable obstacles confronted by rural youth, which warrant a separate volume.

REFERENCES

Bradbury, B., and M. Jantti. (1999). *Child Poverty across Industrialized Nations.* Innocenti Occasional Papers, Economic and Social Policy Series, No. 71. UNICEF International Child Development Center.
Brockerhoff, M. P. (2000). An Urbanizing World. *Population Bulletin,* 55(3).
Massey, D., and Denton, N. (1993). *American Apartheid.* Cambridge, MA: Harvard University Press.
National Center for Children in Poverty. (2000). Child Poverty Rates Improve since 1993 but One in Six U.S. Children Is Poor. *News and Issues,* 10(3), 1.
National Economic Council (2000). "Background on Programs and Themes Announced in the Address: Fiscal Discipline and Nearing The Longest Economic Expansion in U.S. History." Supplement to President William Jefferson Clinton's State of the Union Address. 27 January 2000.
Preston, S. (1984). Children and the Elderly: Divergent Paths for America's Dependents (in Presidential Address). *Demography,* 21(4), 435–457.
Skocpol, T. (1991). Targeting within Universalism: Politically Viable Policies to Combat Poverty in the United States. In C. Jencks and P. E. Peterson (Eds.), *The Urban Underclass* (pp. 411–436). Washington, DC: The Brookings Institution.
United Nations. (1993). *The Global Situation of Youth in the 1990s: Trends and Prospects.* New York: Center for Social Development and Humanitarian Affairs, United Nations, ST/CSDHA/21.
United Nations Children's Fund. (2001). *State of the World's Children, 2001.* New York: UNICEF.
United Nations Children's Fund. (2000). Poverty Reduction Begins with Children. New York: UNICEF.
United Nations General Assembly. (1989). *Convention on the Rights of the Child.* Document ARES/44/25. New York: United Nations.
Wilson, W. J. (1987). *The Truly Disadvantaged: The Inner City, the Underclass, and Public Policy.* Chicago: University of Chicago Press.

II

YOUTH AS A FORCE FOR SOCIAL CHANGE

2 Steering by the Stars

Youth in Cities

Mamphela Ramphele

Introduction

The constancy of change and its varied impact on childhood, adolescence, and young people over time and space are striking universals. In the nineteenth century John Stuart Mill reflected on an analogous societal phenomenon of dynamic social and political change, denoting the Victorian epoch the "age of transition" (Mill, 1831). J. A. Froude, according to Houghton (1957), remembered the Victorian age of the 1840s as a time when

all around us, the intellectual lightships had broken from their moorings, and it was then a new and trying experience. The present generation which has grown up in a new open spiritual ocean, which it has got used to [*sic*] and has learned to swim for itself, will never know what it was to find the lights all drifting, the compasses all awry, and nothing left to steer by but the stars.

But Froude spoke too quickly. Researchers focusing on adolescence and youth across cultures are painfully aware of the many young people who have no access to reliable compasses and are left steering by the stars. Societies like that of South Africa, which have undergone major socioeconomic and political change, have young people who are bewildered by the vacuum created by the death of the old institutions as well as the slowness of the new to be born.

Why is it that human beings have difficulty making peace with the constancy of change? Why do we feel so vulnerable in the face of the changing reality around us? Why do we seem not to learn enough from past experiences to help us to nurture future generations with greater confidence? How much do we know of ourselves as members of a species that shows a rich diversity across cultures and yet stubbornly displays such strong common-alities? What does this species diversity amid strong commonalities teach us about how to approach the search for successful mediators for normative development for youth in our cities across the globe?

In exploring some of these questions I focus on several insights I have derived from the work of scholars who have explored these and other aspects of the human condition. The first starting point is David Hamburg's (1997) observation about the nature of the human infant as an ancient creature. The implications of this type of creature for managing change are significant. Second, the approach to managing change seems to depend on the attitude to risk and the manner in which risk is perceived and managed. Third, the tendency to focus on difference across multiple environments and in the possibilities presented by the challenges we face in both time and space denies us the opportunities to learn from others.

The Human Infant as an Ancient Creature

Hamburg identifies essential requirements for successful development of the ancient human creature shaped by millennia of biological evolution:

- An intact, coherent family dependable under stress
- A relationship with at least one parent who is consistently nurturing, loving, enjoying, teaching, and coping
- Easy access to supportive extended family members
- A supportive community
- Ongoing opportunities for learning about parenthood
- Perception of opportunities as a tangible basis for hope in the future
- Predictability in the adult environment, in preparation for the future

Hamburg's observations echo Erikson's words (1964: 113):

Defenseless as babies are, they have mothers at their command, families to protect the mothers, societies to support the structure of families and traditions to give cultural continuity to systems of child care and training. All this is necessary for the human infant to evolve humanly, for his environment must provide the continuity which permits the child to develop his capacities in distinct steps and to unify them.

How do these measure up in societies, such as South Africa's, where the legacy of race, class, and gender discrimination has eroded the very founda-tions of the vital institutions essential to child development? To complicate matters further, South Africa has yet to acknowledge and deal with the role reversal that came about in the 1970s and 1980s, when youth took on the role of liberating their frightened parents and communities. How successful has postapartheid South Africa been in reestablishing appropriate role differentiation to permit the emergence of supportive environments for normative developmental outcomes? The National Youth Commission must exercise caution in its efforts to empower youth, rather than again burden young people to take responsibility for problems framed as youth problems that are essentially problems of the society at large.

My own research findings in New Crossroads Township in Cape Town, South Africa, demonstrate just how ill prepared that community is to deal with this ancient creature. This community consists of 10,500 people of whom 54% are women and 36% children under 16 years. Nationally, 39% of the population is under 16 years. A third of the households are female-headed and household income averages $333 per month. Obviously, human infants growing up in this environment are vulnerable. Lacking protective supportive families to help them nurture their babies, mothers cannot successfully meet the requirements of the ancient creature. Society has failed the children in this community.

But what of adolescents and young people in general? Do they fare better in New Crossroads and similar communities? How well is postapartheid South Africa doing in supporting young people in realizing their potential? At best, the picture is mixed. At the heart of the dilemma of young South Africans is that adolescence is defined as a period of transition, the success of which is measured by whether and to what extent young people are able successfully to negotiate their engagement with social institutions. But how does anyone – young or old – negotiate with institutions that are themselves in transition?

In a longitudinal study spanning 7 years (1991–1998), a sample of 48 youth of ages 10 to 14 were followed, 16 of whom were intensely scrutinized. None of their families met any of Hamburg's criteria for normative develpment. All our young people experienced disruptions of family life, both nuclear and extended. Where extended family members were accessible, their support was varied and not dependable. In several instances, extended family members added to the burdens facing adolescents by increasing competition for scarce resources. For example, rural-based relatives would often visit without prior notification and stay for extended periods, significantly straining meager household resources, including physical space. Because the community has also experienced traumatic fractures under the divide and rule tactics of the apartheid era, its people live on the edge of survival, with little room for the development of trusting relationships.

The basis for social capital formation is undermined by both competition for scarce resources and mistrust, which in turn undermines social relationships.

There is also the uncertainty about the new South Africa. What tangible benefits will those who are poor and marginalized derive from the new democracy and its reconstruction and development focus? There are rays of hope, but given the enormity of the needs and the backlogs created by the past legacy, a tangible basis for hope eludes many youth. Signs thus far seem to indicate that the benefits of socioeconomic development will flow along the existing contours of absolute or relative privilege. The poorer one is, the less likely one is to benefit from the ongoing reconstruction unless local leadership is strongly committed to equity and resists widespread nepotism and corruption.

The very nature of a rapidly changing socioeconomic and political environment leaves little room for the sense of predictability young people require from the adult world. The stresses and strains of poverty have made some adults not only unpredictable, but also positively dangerous markers to the future. The Truth and Reconciliation Commission Report (1998) documents the deliberate mounting of misguided signposts by adults that misled and continue to mislead young people.

Does this mean that there is no hope for these young people? In spite of the abundant difficulties, there are young people emerging from this community and other similar environments in South Africa as success cases. What distinguishes the success cases from those who fall by the wayside? This question brings us to the next issue.

Risk Management

Adolescent research has correctly focused much attention on risk-taking behavior among young people as a negative predictor of successful development (Carnegie Council on Adolescent Development, 1995). Much has been written on exposure to risk factors such as smoking, drug abuse, sexual experimentation, and other negative behaviors. Intervention programs have been designed with greater or lesser success to reduce risk-taking behaviors in adolescents exposed to these risks. But for most inner city children, exposure to these risks is a fact of life. The challenge then becomes one of managing the risk.

Peter Bernstein (1996) writes: "Risk is a choice rather than a fate. The actions we dare to take, which depend on how free we are to make choices, are what the story of risk is all about. And that story helps define what it means to be a human being." Risk aversion does not protect against risk but may simply postpone the moment of truth when tough choices have to be made. Bernstein further argues that societies with cultures that incorporate the concept of risk have had to start by changing their attitudes not to the present, but to the future.

Risk management takes many forms and occurs at many levels: individual, family, community, institution, and society as a whole. South African youth in the 1970s managed the risk of growing up in a society that undervalued and humiliated them by challenging the powers that be. There is a tendency in current historiography to deny or underplay the role young people played in setting the agenda for change in South Africa. In recognizing the important roles of Nelson Mandela and Frederik Willem de Klerk in the negotiated settlement, most analysts of change ignore the fact that it was the youth population who injected a new purpose into liberation movements, which had almost given up on seeing the end of apartheid.

Young people also played a crucial role in breaking the cycle of fatalism that had enveloped Black South Africans in the aftermath of the brutal repression that led to banning liberation movements in the early 1960s. By launching the Black Consciousness Movement, young people were inspired, and in turn inspired their communities, to develop a positive self-image. Up to that point, Black people had begun to believe in the inferiority imposed on them by racism. Young people had come to terms with the fact that their own parents had failed to protect them from the viciousness of the racist system. Young people took on what was seen as an indestructible regime. It is therefore unfortunate that in his autobiography, *A Long Walk to Freedom*, Mandela is silent about the man who led the Black Consciousness Movement. Steve Biko's name does not even appear in the index of the book.

At the community, family, and personal levels, successful young people in our study were those who accepted the risks inherent in their environment and sought creative ways to manage them. For example, Bulelani, now a successful 20-year-old technikon (technical college) student, managed his gangster-infested environment with creativity and humor. He even joined a gang at the age of 14 in order to protect himself from abuse by a rival gang that had attacked him without warning one afternoon. Upon joining the gang, he made a conscious decision to set the boundaries of what his membership entailed. It entailed a kind of neighborhood watch role in which he did not succumb to attacking anyone but would fight instead, in defense of a safer neighborhood. He also refused to use a knife to stab anyone: "I only used a brick if attacked; I am very good with a brick," he said.

Bulelwa, a successful high school graduate and commercial college diplomat who is now 20 years old and married to another successful university graduate, used different risk management strategies. Faced with a divorced mother who was frequently depressed by the poverty resulting from being abandoned by her husband, Bulelwa sought other adults outside the family to give her the dependable support she needed. She also derived predictable markers of an alternative adult environment from outside sources to guide her future. Her marriage at the young age of 19 years can also be seen as a risk management strategy to secure for herself a dependable source of love and support as well as an escape from the harsh environment of New Crossroads. All these actions involved risk-taking. She dared to act to limit the deleterious impacts of her risky environment.

Both Bulelwa and Bulelani had to escape their neighborhood schools to receive a better education. Bulelani did so with the support of his mother, whose own courage and unconditional support enabled her to approach the headmaster of a previously White school and entrust her son to his care. For Bulelwa the escape path was through the Youth Center's intervention program, and her continued success was achieved at great cost to her and the relationship with her mother, whose support was erratic.

Both Bulelwa and Bulelani faced the additional obstacle of negotiating with peers in the township who perceived moves to schools outside the neighborhood as "selling out" or "playing White." People labeled as "sellouts" faced the risk of being killed via the dreaded "necklace" – an old car tire filled with petrol and set alight, thus condemning the victim to a gruesome death. Aware of the fatal consequences of being labeled a sellout, Bulelani managed to convince his peers that one benefit of getting a better education is that it enables him to run a weekend tutorial program. Fortunately his peers were too busy with survival in the township to hold him to his commitment, which would have been onerous. But his creativity in reframing the terms of discussion away from selling out to harnessing outside resources for the township may have both saved his life and given him the space to develop himself.

But what of managing the risks facing social institutions as South Africa goes through the transition to democracy? The proper positioning of key social institutions is central to enabling young people to negotiate their way successfully into a healthy engagement with society as adults. Institutional risk management strategies build on and require transformative leadership qualities. To lead effectively in such an environment demands clarity of vision, mission, goals, and values that have to be developed and shared by all the major role players within the institution. Nurturing new and potential ideas while preserving and enhancing traditional values poses a major challenge.

Higher education is a key area of engagement by young people; therefore, it is very important to secure support from existing institutions. Institutions that have been exclusive and elitist run the risk of being damaged by inappropriate interventions. For example, the transformation of the University of Cape Town entailed the management of the risks inherent in overwhelming a fragile resource base with demands for equity that could have easily compromised excellence. By reframing the debate to demonstrate that excellence is essential to equity, it was possible to convince activists that proceeding otherwise would amount to promoting equal access to mediocrity. For those resisting change, it was necessary to demonstrate that South Africa is internationally uncompetitive partly for failing to promote the equity that would have led to the development of a larger talent pool. Thus equity and excellence are complementary and not contradictory in postapartheid South Africa.

But why did Bulelani and Bulelwa choose to distinguish themselves from their peers? What was it in their approaches to risk management that made for success? This consideration leads to the third area of focus for this chapter.

Lessons from Commonalities and Differences

The idea of difference has occupied human beings for millennia. How significant are differences of skin color, hair texture, height, body shape, and so on? What role do nature and nurture play in shaping who we are? Anthropologists have made much of cultural differences and their significance. Some postmodernists went as far as stretching cultural relativity to moral relativity, prompting Gellner, a respected anthropologist, to ask why cultural relativists who had traveled and studied "alien" cultures had yet to find one that was totally unintelligible? Why is there an unwillingness to embrace some universal givens to the very essence of being human (Zechenter, 1997:327)?

Writings about child-rearing practices around the world are striking in revealing their strong commonalities across time, space, and cultures. The demands of the human infant, for instance, with its prolonged period of dependency, force adults to make certain choices. The fundamental need for nursing care is one that had to be met by adults both in Victorian England and in peasant Africa. Yet, it is the way these demands are met that differs from culture to culture and within cultures by social class. Peasant Ireland was probably much closer to peasant Africa than to Victorian England in its child-rearing practices. Yet it is the distinction between "Western" and non-Western that receives greatest emphasis in most cross-cultural comparisons. Is social class not more important in shaping cultural practices than simple geography?

John Gillis's (1997) study of the history of myth and ritual in family life raises some important issues in this regard. For example, the practice of dispersing children among kin and nonkin, which was common in late 18th- and 19th-century America and England, is still common in many poor Black communities. Yet this practice is depicted by many as a uniquely African *ubuntu* cultural practice of sharing. The multiplicity of caregivers to whom young people are exposed over a short period adds to their sense of insecurity and lack of anchorage. Failure to trace such practices historically across cultures denies us the opportunity to learn from them and to identify the myriad practices that unify rather than divide cultures and nations. Therefore, the exploration of successful mediators of normative development must encompass cross-cultural comparisons over time and space so that the similarities are understood and appreciated as are the differences.

For example, what is it about Asian immigrant families in the United States that makes their children succeed academically even if both parents are illiterate? Why is that pattern not repeated for other immigrant groups? What accounts for the economic success of Jews in spite of their having been, and in some cases still being, victimized? Bernstein suggests that up to the time of the Renaissance people in Europe and other parts of the globe perceived the future as little more than a matter of luck or the result of random variations. The demands of survival limit people to basic functions of existence that permit little scope for imagining a different future. It is when the conditions of life are seen as being amenable to human control and influence that risk management takes over from fatalism.

Cultures in which fatalism is deeply entrenched have greater difficulty in innovating and taking advantage of new knowledge. For example, even though the Hindus and Arabs were the front-runners in developing the use of numerals in mathematics, their fatalistic belief systems discouraged use of their new knowledge to maximum benefit. It took early Christians and Greeks to make the leap forward. Successful risk management arises from an acceptance of oneself as a free agent. This insight helps clarify what distinguishes Bulelwa and Bulelani from their peers – namely, their firm belief in their agency as human beings. Unlike one of our young people, who said, "I do not have dreams; I do not want to be disappointed. I only have hopes," Bulelwa and Bulelani dared to dream and to dream aloud.

A cross-cultural study by Scott and Scott (1998) in seven countries found that the most reliable marker of successful developmental outcomes among youth was self-esteem, which in turn derives from having a supportive family environment or dependable support from an adult who is readily accessible to the young person. Self-esteem is critical to the notion of human agency. It is when human beings dare to conceive of a future different from their present circumstances that their creative energies are unleashed. Bulelwa and Bulelani's self-esteem survived all the hazards of their environment in part because of their own innate tenacity, but also because of the support they received from adults both within and outside their environment.

Experience shows that where social and human capital is limited, as in the case of New Crossroads or among street children and their families, successful interventions are expensive and have to be long-term. The building of a critical mass of social and human capital is fraught with difficulties. Interventions need to engage inside players to take root. But the lack of trust in poor communities often makes a start in this direction slow and painful. The most effective intervention strategy in the lives of young people, and the best investment any society can make to secure future generations, is to create conditions that enable all families to invest in nurturing the ancient creature – the human infant. The eradication of poverty and inequity lies at the heart of the matter.

Successful interventions to enhance youth development need to incorporate strategies that enhance self-esteem in young people. Children on the street, abused young people, and marginalized groups in all cultures suffer from poor self-esteem. It becomes doubly difficult for them if their own parents, teachers, and other caregivers face the same problem, as in many postapartheid poor communities.

Leaving youngsters to steer by the stars is costly for any society. South Africa is paying the price. The high crime rate and the self-destructive behavior in evidence in many areas of our national life are indicators of the frustration young people feel. Young Black people put their lives at risk for the freedom we now enjoy. They lack the capacity to enjoy the fruits of their labor. We need to help unlock their potential by boosting their self-confidence to dare to take risks in the 21st century.

REFERENCES

Bernstein, P. L. (1996). *Against the Gods: The Remarkable Story of Risk.* New York: Wiley & Sons.

Carnegie Council on Adolescent Development. (1995). *Great Transitions: Preparing Adolescents for a New Century.* New York: Carnegie Corporation of New York.

Erickson, E. (1964). *Insight and Responsibility.* New York: W. W. Norton.

Gellner, E. (1985). *Relativism and the Social Sciences.* Cambridge: Cambridge University Press.

Gillis, R. (1997). *A World of Their Own Making: A History of Myth and Ritual in Family Life*. Oxford: Oxford University Press.

Hamburg, D. (1997). Preparing Adolescents for the 21st Century. In R. Takanishi and D. Hamburg (Eds.), *Meeting the Essential Requirements for Healthy Adolescent Development in a Transforming World* (pp. 1–12). Cambridge: Cambridge University Press.

Houghton, W. (1957). *The Victorian Frame of Mind*. New Haven, CT: Yale University Press.

Mill, J. S. (1831). *The Spirit of the Age*. Chicago: University of Chicago Press.

Scott, R., and Scott, W. A. (1998). *Adjustment of Adolescents – Cross-Cultural Similarities and Differences*. London: Routledge.

Truth and Reconciliation Commission. (1998). *The Truth and Reconciliation Commission Report*. Cape Town: CTP Printers.

Zechenter, E. (1997). "In the Name of Culture: Cultural Relativism and the Abuse of the Individual," *Journal of Anthropological Research*, 53(3), 319–342.

3   Children Show the Way

Participatory Programs for Children of South African Streets and Squatter Camps

Jill Swart-Kruger and Louise Chawla

Children in a World of Disparities

When South Africans went to the polls in April 1994 in the first national election of universal and equal suffrage in their country's history, they chose an assembly dominated by the African National Congress (ANC). As its first order of business, the ANC elected Nelson Mandela as president to lead the country into a new postapartheid society. When power passed peacefully into the hands of Mandela's successor, Thabo Mbeki, in 1999, South Africa's stature as a democratic society with open elections was cemented. It has only begun to embark, however, on the long road to healing the divisions of apartheid by creating a just society for all. This challenge will require the most astute balancing of political interests: a fair and wise weighing of the concerns of African, Colored, White, and Asian;[1] of young and old; of urban and rural; of wealthy, middle-class, and abjectly poor; of tribe and state; and of Western ideas and indigenous traditions. The challenges are daunting, and the stakes are high, not only for South Africa but for the world. If South Africa succeeds in its endeavor, it will become a model for the reconciliation of

[1] These are the racial labels that underpinned apartheid policies and are still used in official South African documents today.

Financial assistance for research in Canaansland was provided by the MOST Programme of UNESCO, UNICEF, and the Human Needs, Resources and the Environment Programme (funded by the South African Department of Environmental Affairs) of the Human Sciences Research Council. The views expressed in this document are those of the authors and are not to be attributed to any of the above-mentioned organizations. The authors also wish to thank Dr. Elbie Van den Berg and Dr. Chris Williams for reading and commenting on sections of this chapter.

pluralistic interests – which characterize most interdependent postmodern global societies.

Global society is characterized by a widening rift between rich and poor. In a global economy of 25 trillion dollars, an estimated 1.3 billion people have incomes of less than $1 a day (UNDP, 1997). The richest 20% of the world's people earn 86% of global income, compared to 1% for the poorest 20%, and the ratio of the income of the richest 20% to the poorest 20% had risen from 30:1 in 1960 to 86:1 by the end of the 20th century (UNDP, 1999). The advantaged are concentrated in Europe and nations of European descent, although they include the elite in nations of all colors. In South Africa, these disparities of color and privilege are mirrored in the starkest outlines.

National statistics demonstrate the formidable challenges. Over three quarters (76.3%) of the population in South Africa is African, 8.5% Colored, 12.7% White, and 2.5% of Asian descent (CSS, 1997). Nine indigenous languages, in addition to English and Afrikaans, have been accorded official status, and the social and cultural diversity this implies is constantly being increased by in-migration from neighboring African countries. There is also steady migration of rural people into the cities – more than half of South Africa's population (55.4%) currently resides in urban areas (May, 1998:209). In a country of splendidly diverse geography and natural resources as well as cultural diversity, 7% of the population earns 40% of national income (May, 1998:24). Almost half (45%) of the population is under the age of 18, and three in every five children live in appalling poverty, with many at risk of physical and sexual abuse and personal neglect (May, 1998:30).

Faced with so many diverse constituencies and their contending interests, President Mandela declared that a major standard of the nation's functioning would be the well-being of its children. In 1996, he led parliament to ratification of the United Nation's Convention on the Rights of the Child (CRC), which includes the principle of the "first call for children": that the essential needs of children should be given high priority in the allocation of resources at every level. As further demonstration of his conviction that children are the necessary bridge to a more just postapartheid society, he dedicated part of his annual salary to create the Nelson Mandela Children's Fund, an organization that has channeled 36 million dollars of private donations into projects for South Africa's children.

This chapter examines the lives of some of the beneficiaries of this fund and other national and international philanthropies: street boys under 18 years of age enrolled in a program of comprehensive services named *Street-Wise* and 10- to 14-year-old squatter camp children who participate in a program of child-based community development named *Growing Up in Cities*. We describe the goals for human development that these programs seek to foster, and ways they seek to provide participants with the skills needed to achieve self-sustaining, socially constructive lives. The programs are complementary. Street-Wise focuses on supporting street boys in crisis and on improving their position within their families and communities, whereas Growing Up in Cities seeks to improve conditions for precariously housed children within a squatter community.

"Goals for human development" and "effective life skills" are not neutral expressions. They presume a social and cultural context that makes certain goals desirable and specific skills effective. In the case of a pluralistic society like South Africa's, these goals and skills are in the process of redefinition as people seek new forms of citizenship for a viable new society. The elections of 1994 showed that for the majority of South Africans, the most inspiring models of citizenship were Nelson Mandela and other African National Congress freedom fighters who maintained their courage and commitment to an open society throughout the long years of antiapartheid struggle. Within the opening years of the new government, both sides of the struggle were involved in violence, resistance to the rule of law, and secrecies that need to be relinquished in time of peace (Krog, 1998). The programs described here represent two of many experiments that are under way to demonstrate how people can work together in more peaceful forms of struggle to eradicate poverty and build a just society.

Children's Rights in the Scheme of Human Rights

The underlying principles of Street-Wise and Growing Up in Cities are based on the Convention on the Rights of the Child (1989) and the African Charter on the Rights and Welfare of the Child (1990). The African Charter is especially valuable in recognizing that there are no rights without responsibilities, and that this is true for children as well as adults. In South Africa, the Convention has special resonance. When the new parliament moved quickly to ratify the Convention in 1996, its action stood in contrast to the apartheid government's abstention from the adoption of the Universal Declaration of Human Rights by the United Nations in 1948. Nevertheless, the Declaration's principles of human rights were beacons to the African majority and liberal White, Colored, and Asian minorities across the succeeding years.

The Convention on the Rights of the Child affirms the Declaration's basic principles of human dignity, fair treatment under the law, and entitlement to an adequate standard of living and education. As general principles, the Convention requires that governments promote conditions that ensure "to the maximum extent possible the survival and development of the child" (Article 6), and that in all actions concerning children "the best interests of the child shall be a primary consideration" (Article 3). Although the Convention stopped short of guaranteeing children suffrage, it did recognize their potential to be active citizens by advancing them rights to freedom of thought, association, and peaceful assembly; to express their views in all matters that affect them; and to seek and impart information and ideas of all kinds (Articles 12–15). This recognition was particularly merited in a country where children had given their lives in antiapartheid protests in Soweto and other townships (see Ramphele, this volume).

Williams (1991) has argued that every time rights are extended to a new group, the fundamental conception of rights has to be redefined. This is certainly true in the extension of rights to children. The liberal tradition of human rights is based upon two philosophies of human nature and human needs that have maintained an uneasy truce in contemporary politics and law.

On one side of the liberal tradition is Thomas Hobbes (1968), a material-ist, who conceived of human beings as intricate machines who are driven to amass power and wealth in order to ensure the recurrent satisfaction of their physical desires and to protect themselves against threats of war or uprisings of the masses. He emphasizes the importance of "negative liberties" in the form of citizens' rights to be free from interference by the state as they pursue the accumulation and enjoyment of their property. On the other side is John Locke (1983), a partisan of civil religion. Like Hobbes, Locke considers the acquisition of property central to the pursuit of happiness. However, in his Protestant conception of the larger scheme of things, people are God's prop-erty and must all face an individual accounting with their maker. Therefore, in addition to negative liberties, Locke advocates the right to freedom to act according to one's conscience. In this sense, Locke's philosophy is also profoundly individualistic.

Shapiro (1986) claims that the Hobbesian conception of the isolated in-dividual has triumphed over the civil religion of Locke as the basis of most legal contracts. Hobbes provided an entirely secular justification for rights in an increasingly secular age, and his asocial individualism suited his period of mercantile capitalism, when great private wealth was being amassed. Certainly it is the philosophy of Hobbes that underlies the current global movement of capital, in which South Africa is an important site for invest-ment. In South Africa, these tensions are reflected in the conflict between the government Growth, Employment and Redistribution (GEAR) policy, which promotes privatization and high returns on capital investments, in contrast to the demands of labor for social investments and full employment.

Children's rights are part of a gathering body of late 20th-century ideas that can be interpreted as a new secular basis for Locke's moral justification for rights and the balancing of rights and obligations. Like the movements for women's rights and equal rights regardless of race or ethnicity, the Convention on the Rights of the Child assumes that people do not enter the world with equal access to the exercise of rights. Therefore, some groups require social and government assistance to overcome historical disadvantages or special vulnerabilities. In line with the principle that extreme poverty is a violation of rights, the Convention obligates governments and citizens to seek a degree of social equity that will guarantee universal provision for basic needs. Like the environmental movement, the Convention seeks to speak for those who are often voiceless and unable to speak for themselves. There is a particularly close association between children and the environmental movement because action for sustainable development is predicated on the need to conserve the Earth's resources to ensure the well-being of future generations. Therefore in Agenda 21 of the United Nations' Conference on Environment and Development (United Nations, 1992) and the Habitat Agenda of the Second United Nations Conference on Human Settlements (UNCHS, 1996), children are identified as a major group who need to be involved in the management of their cities, towns, and natural environment. These movements indicate gathering international agreement that individuals need to recognize themselves as part of human and ecological communities, and to realize themselves not just through actions for private interest, but also through a commitment to shared social and environmental goods.

The Convention on the Rights of the Child makes it particularly apparent that rights must be understood within networks of social and environmental responsibility. Most of the articles concern the obligations of governments to provide for children's physical and social needs, which not only limit actions that might harm children, but also require the active promotion of healthy and nurturing environments. Children's rights require not just negative liberties, but also many positive forms of support. The Convention also implies that children need opportunities to grow into caring adults who will respect the rights of succeeding generations in turn. For its part, the African Charter stresses the responsibilities of children as social actors who need to uphold and strengthen the social fabric within which their personal rights are embedded.

Consonant with this liberal tradition of rights and evolving ideas about social and environmental obligations, Street-Wise and Growing Up in Cities simultaneously seek to foster children's individual identities and their identities and skills as members of their peer groups, families, and communities. Both programs seek to help participating children achieve autonomy, and to know and speak their minds as they develop economic independence. The programs work to provide children with access to education, communication skills, and a sense of self-efficacy, or a belief in their capacities to achieve desired goals through their own actions. Major goals of Street-Wise and Growing Up in Cities include providing each child with opportunities to express personal perspectives with growing skill and self-confidence, encouraging reasonable goals, and helping each child enjoy mastery experiences. Because the children with whom they work live in especially difficult circumstances, the programs also seek to promote resilience by providing role models of coping constructively, enlarging social networks of support, creating emotionally positive and open climates for learning, and seeking to strengthen or restore stable relationships with parents or caregivers (Losel and Bliesener, 1990; Luthar and Zigler, 1991; Werner and Smith, 1992).

These programs cannot stop with individual strengths, however. In a society that has only recently emerged from a violent police state and that remains torn by lawlessness and violence, hope for lasting peace requires that future generations learn democratic skills and values, and cultivate habits of mutual help. Living as they do on the streets and in a squatter camp, the children served by Street-Wise and Growing Up in Cities have to contend with discrimination and rejection by the larger society, which tends to perceive them as outsiders and a threat to the social order (see Sibley, 1981; Swart-Kruger, in press). Therefore, the chances that street children and those living in squatter settlements can improve their lives will be increased by learning to work together and to gain support and influence through numbers. As a precondition for a sense of self-worth, self-efficacy, and self-expression, both programs seek to create a safe space, physically and socially, in which the children can feel a positive identity as members of their group. In this space, the programs encourage the children to speak, to listen, to show tolerance for multiple perspectives, to care for each other, and to provide mutual support. Both programs also strive to provide participants with opportunities to combine a sense of self-efficacy with a sense of collective efficacy, or a belief in their ability to achieve shared goals (Bandura, 1997).

Some of these goals for human development and concepts of rights might differ from an African outlook. An emphasis on autonomy, self-expression, self-efficacy, and children's participation in planning their communities and settlements may appear to conflict with an African deemphasis of individuality among children, which has been recorded by certain anthropologists (see Weisner, 1984). Early ethnographies of indigenous childhoods in South Africa presume this deindividualization (see Van der Vliet, 1980), which appears to be reinforced by an emphasis on obedience to elders. African idioms seem to embody it as well, for instance, the Sesotho saying *Fura la ngwana ke ho rongwa* – "A child's most important work is to do duties assigned by its elders." The presumed dichotomy is not as clear-cut as often alleged (see Morton, 1996), but the programs' efforts to foster mutual help and community consensus are, nevertheless, in harmony with indigenous African values, such as community and solidarity, as expressed in the writings of African philosophers such as Gyekye (1992), Gbadegesin (1991), and Okolo (1995).

The following sections of this chapter describe the goals and methods of each program in turn. We begin with Street-Wise, a comprehensive program for street boys in four South African cities, which takes children who have often been traumatically "individualized" by the loss of their homes and families and seeks to build on their independence and resourcefulness while restoring social support. Subsequently, we discuss Growing Up in Cities, a process for community development that works with children as a group, in a well-defined locality, and through their successes seeks to catalyze inclusive processes of democratic development for all ages. In conclusion, we relate lessons from these two case studies to other research that tries to understand the most effective strategies to eradicate poverty and improve life chances for children.

Street-Wise: A Comprehensive Program for Street Boys

In South Africa, an estimated 15,000 children ranging in age from 3 to 18 years of age live on city streets – their peripatetic life-style makes it impossible to establish exact numbers. Reasons for their leaving home are complex and hinge on social and structural problems in South African society as well as personal factors (Swart-Kruger and Donald, 1994). In common with runaway youth in North America, South African street children describe their home environments as rejecting, deficient, and disorganized; their parents as punitive and unsupportive; and their scholastic lives as full of difficulties and failures. South African street children commonly say that they are unwanted by their families or that their families would be economically better off without them (Richter and Van der Walt, 1996). Presumably, very young children found on the streets have been abandoned by their caretakers or accidentally separated.

Street children in South Africa have much in common with street children elsewhere in the world: notably a valued sense of personal autonomy, a flight response to perceived personal threat, a generally strong peer group solidarity, and finely honed street survival skills. Although there has been considerable debate in the literature on how street children are labeled (Glauser, 1990), there is general agreement about the distinction between "working street children" and "street children." All street children work, but the description "working street children" is used widely to refer to children who do not live permanently on the streets and who have fairly regular contact with their families, whom they frequently also assist economically. The term *street children* generally indicates youth who actually live on the streets and have infrequent contact with their families or have abandoned their families altogether. South Africa has a high number of children who live on the streets and do not return home on a regular basis. This is largely attributable to former apartheid policies that relegated people of color to townships on the periphery of White cities, such as Johannesburg and Cape Town. The commercial areas that street children frequent are found in such cities, and once children have established themselves on the streets there, they find it both inconvenient and expensive to return regularly to their homes in townships or squatter camps. Although children were and still are found living rough on the streets of African and Colored townships, their pickings there are mostly meager. In South Africa, therefore, street children constitute a category of children who, on the whole, are reliant solely on themselves and their peers for their daily survival. Nevertheless, many retain strong emotional affiliations with their families and do periodically take them money or material goods (Swart-Kruger and Donald, 1994).

In the mid-1980s, most street children (95%) in nongovernmental organizations (NGO) shelters in Johannesburg and elsewhere in the country had some degree of schooling, albeit below level for their ages at the national average (Schärf, Powell, and Thomas, 1986; Swart, 1988; Williams, 1993). The appalling condition of the state education system, including victimization and humiliation of pupils by teachers, was partly, if not largely, to blame for the presence of many children on the streets (Schärf, Powell, and Thomas, 1986; Swart, 1988; Williams, 1993). Williams (1993:836) has questioned the use of terms such as *absenteeism* and *school dropouts*, proposing instead the term *school exclusion*, which "more accurately takes the blame away from those who are the victims of circumstances beyond their control."

In the province of Gauteng alone, which has the highest literacy rate in the country (69%), an estimated 70,000 children below the age of 14 years have either left school or never attended. In the country as a whole, an estimated 5 million young people of school-going age are not in school (CSS, 1997). Getting the country's educational system on track should prove important in reducing the numbers of new children on the streets.

Street-Wise began as a program of "pavement schooling" in 1986. Johannesburg was then an apartheid city, and African children living on its streets were there illegally. Therefore, police dispersed Street-Wise pavement classes. The children said they would prefer a building to house "their" school and to serve as a symbol of normality and permanence in their lives (Swart, 1988; MacCurtain, 1990). After many relocations from loaned premises, Street-Wise secured its own center. Street outreach, educational and residential programs, replaced pavement schooling. As branches were opened in various parts of the country, Street-Wise became the only program for street children in South Africa to be run on a national scale.

More recently, emphasis has been placed on family counseling, with a view to reassociate children with family members, and preventive work has begun. Possibly because these initiatives are time-consuming and expensive, little work of this nature has been undertaken in South Africa. The name Street-Wise – chosen in consultation with the children – builds on their positive attributes, which require extension.

Since its inception, Street-Wise has aimed to provide a therapeutic milieu for children based on the Rogerian notion of unconditional positive regard and empathetic understanding (Rogers, 1980; Swart, 1988). A low staff turnover so that children would have consistency in their interactions with caring adults was considered vital, because the children described their former family relationships as full of pain, anger, hurt, aggression, and rejection. In contrast, the constancy of a nurturing relationship with one or more adults has been confirmed as a positive factor in engendering resilience in children (Losel and Bliesener, 1990; Richter and Van der Walt, 1996; see Ramphele, this volume). Apart from difficult relationships in their homes, the children had experienced problems in relationships with adults on the streets, where they were sexually exploited, harassed by officials and members of the local community who saw them as a nuisance, and referred by social workers to places of confinement from which they regularly escaped (Swart, 1990a). Father Bill MacCurtain (1990:127), an early chairman of Street-Wise, felt that NGOs could play a special role in the lives of children by attracting staff members and volunteers capable of unconditional love.

Intervention programs require a well-defined purpose. In Street-Wise this is broadly articulated as the provision of opportunities for children to choose a personally enabling route back into mainstream society. With every new intake of children through its street outreach programs and drop-in centers, the range of possibilities for them in Street-Wise is discussed. We found it important to stipulate clearly that Street-Wise would not assume responsibility for the children's lives, and that involvement in Street-Wise requires a mutually agreed upon time for graduation from the organization. Exit from the program is negotiated individually and hinges on each child's personal growth, which is based on individual choices from the available options. This agreement helps to prevent children from sacrificing their hard won autonomy on the streets for a powerless dependency on the organization. Street children in South Africa appear to have a strong internal locus of control (Richter and Van der Walt, 1996; Donald, Wallis, and Cockburn, 1997), which can be usefully channeled in their personal transition from the streets back into the community.

In 1988 an impact assessment revealed that encouraging a high degree of participatory involvement in decision making by pupils in Street-Wise increased their personal commitment to completing programs. Educational programs that were supplemented by supportive residential programs also enhanced personal esteem among Street-Wise pupils more than educational programs alone. Sheltering facilities were subsequently opened at all branches of Street-Wise. In Johannesburg this move was especially urgent because of increased police harassment of street children (Swart, 1990a).

Although considerable infighting and competition for resources occur among street youth, they band together in the face of adversity and threat, in order to facilitate street survival (Donald and Swart-Kruger, 1994; Donald, Wallis, and Cockburn 1997). Strong peer group solidarity is generated on the streets through reliance on members for esteem, information, companionship, and instrumental support. Because this peer group solidarity becomes a substitute for adult sources of support, it often leads to problems of rebelliousness and hostility when staff try to enforce organizational rules and regulations. Until caring staff members develop the necessary relationship of trust, they feel rejected by the children, a perception that puts them at risk of resigning. Therefore, Street-Wise tries to lay a strong foundation of mutual cooperation right from the start by establishing basic rules for working together in participatory planning with the children. The key feature that emerges from initial discussions about rules is the imperative of respect for self and others.

The education program in Street-Wise was originally three-pronged and included basic literacy and numeracy training for those who were unschooled, bridging education for those who had not dropped too far behind in their schooling and who wished to return to school, and social and job skills training. Graduates of Street-Wise and other NGOs have reported that training in letter writing, job applications, interview responses, and etiquette has been valuable in enhancing personal confidence and self-esteem. They provide a means to bridge the gap between street and community life and facilitate an entry into a formal work environment (Jacobson, 1990:133).

Problems that emerged early in the program included low attention and concentration spans, which were due partly to prolonged glue sniffing (Jansen et al., 1990), partly to a street life-style driven by instant gratification, and partly to other distractions, such as hunger and outside social and emotional conflicts (MacCurtain, 1990). Glue sniffing increases with length of stay on the streets because street children sniff glue to shut out their fears of loneliness and the dark, which they associate with supernatural forces and interpersonal violence (Richter and Van der Walt, 1996; Swart, 1990b).

When designing its educational programs, Street-Wise quickly became aware that children living on the streets had immensely deprived home environments and were inexperienced in daily routines, which those who worked with them took for granted. Many could not use a telephone, flush a toilet, or use hammers or screwdrivers (see Kramer, 1986). Teachers accustomed to classroom passivity and respect for authority were taken aback by the assertive attitude of boys who refused to do anything they considered irrelevant. They responded positively to the challenge from the children to design appropriate and stimulating classes by engaging in a process of situated learning, in which basic literacy and numeracy skills emerged from discussions of daily routines and activities as well as the children's personal interests (see Lave and Wenger, 1991). The gambling game *tiekie-dice* was particularly successful in helping children to move from concrete to abstract mathematical skills (Swart-Kruger, 1997). Of special value was the input of a volunteer assistant who had had experience in African American ghettos in the United States. She had the children write and collate their own stories while instructing them in grammar and spelling in the process. The introduction of this personal dimension to their work greatly enhanced the children's desire to learn, and their growing folders of work in which peers and adults alike took interest became a source of improved self-esteem (Hirsch, 1993). The introduction of an empty "do-nothing" room, where children who said they did not want to do anything could go if they wished, played a useful role in channeling their motivations. A general view that street youth are deficient in cognitive skills such as recollection, logical reasoning, and concept formulation has been offset by findings that South African street children are able to solve complex context-embedded problems in innovative ways (Donald and Swart-Kruger, 1994; Richter and Van der Walt, 1996).

Williams (1992) has provocatively questioned the notion of universal literacy and the link proposed by Freire between mass literacy and liberation, noting that no clear causal relation exists between basic literacy and socioeconomic progress, nor between literacy and lessening of crime, poverty, and ignorance. He suggests that there might be little point in teaching street children to read and write because this process takes at least four years in primary school, whereas modern media provide a "skills bypass" through visual and aural information. These contentions are open to debate. He also neglects to address the mastery experience intrinsic in achieving literacy and numeracy skills that spur on formerly illiterate South African street children to fresh endeavors.

Street-Wise does not assist its students in income-generating street activities, because these are of little benefit in the long-term. In cities such as Bombay, India, many street children do not envisage rejoining mainstream society but rather move from begging to newspaper selling to shoe shining in an upwardly mobile spiral of street occupations. South Africa's street children, by contrast, usually wish to rejoin mainstream society, to live in conventional ways, and to have families and children who do not have to live on the streets (Swart, 1988, 1990a; Richter and van der Walt, 1996). Woodworking and tailoring programs were once run at the request of the children but were discontinued when expensive equipment was damaged through rough use and it became clear that there was a lack of real interest in using these skills to generate income.

Street-Wise staff also encountered initial problems in trying to prepare children for economic independence. Bandura's (1995:21–22) contention that people "simply eliminate from consideration vocations they believe to be beyond their capabilities" does not hold for youth who have spent some years of their lives on the streets and in shelters, even if they have been given information on a wide variety of job situations and enrolled in skills training programs. It is widely believed that boys who have lived on the streets will not hold down jobs successfully. This is partly due to job placement programs that set unrealistically low expectations for what former street boys can accomplish and therefore assign them to washing up in hotel kitchens, crating vegetables, or waiting on tables. When youth abandon these positions through personal frustration and boredom, they reinforce the public stereotype that former street children cannot be helped or trusted. Youth also have difficulty in keeping jobs as a result of a lack of social and behavioral skills and inexperience in knowing how to select appropriate positions from the outset (Jacobson, 1990:129).

Initially Street-Wise staff believed that these problems stemmed from a lack of training opportunities; hence they assisted students with registration for courses run by the Department of Manpower. Upon graduation, most showed no interest in working in the fields for which they had qualified. The longer they remained in Street-Wise, the more certain they became that the organization would provide paid employment in the form of personal offices, secretaries, and company transport, and the greater their fear became of joining the ranks of the unemployed once they left Street-Wise. These experiences impressed on Street-Wise staff the importance of helping students identify jobs commensurate with their aptitudes and real interests. Enlisting specific organizations to train youth in, for instance, clerical work, hairdressing, and computer skills proved more successful in convincing youth of their employment prospects and demonstrated the importance of acknowledging the heterogeneity of street children.

An incident in which a boy's uncle took him home and enrolled him in a traditional initiation school, after which he was considered an adult and joined his uncle's hawking business, alerted personnel to the likelihood of boys' having more supportive extended family networks than they had at first realized. Recognizing that city shelters could not hope to replicate these networks led Street-Wise staff to introduce a program of reconciliation with family members, subsequent to family counseling. Counseling is a lengthy process that entails a commitment to assist parents with personal problems that impact on their relationship with their children (McLoyd and Williams, 1990). Financial assistance is sometimes required to enable children to return home. Boys whose homes cannot be located or whose families are extremely abusive are referred to children's homes that specialize in long-term residence.

The problem of assessing the psychosocial growth of children who have been involved in Street-Wise has been difficult to solve. It is not clear at what stage and to what extent Street-Wise skills translate into long-term integrated development. Subjective observations by those who work most closely with the children convey to some degree whether or not an intervention is effective. A year after the implementation of the Street-Wise program, the chairman noted, "What is most heartening is the remarkable leap in concentration span . . . a growing self-confidence and the relaxed and happy atmosphere which now prevails" (MacCurtain quoted in Swart, 1988:37).

A formal psychological assessment (Richter and Van der Walt, 1996) undertaken with 99 street children attending Street-Wise yielded valuable findings that have underpinned subsequent program initiatives. It showed that many of the children would cope well in intervention programs, as a third of the sample had unimpaired intellectual and problem-solving abilities and no signs of psychological damage. The assessment also revealed that reaching the children shortly after they arrived on the streets would facilitate effective action. The younger boys were when they left home, the less schooling they were likely to have had, the longer they were likely to wait before entering a shelter; the longer boys were on the street, the more likely they were to show signs of psychopathology and an externalized locus of control and to score poorly on intellectual scales. Analysts hypothesize that this pattern could reflect "loss of motivation, the acquisition of values, behaviors and habits antithetical to sustained effort and concentration, and cognitive damage owing to drugs and injuries" (Richter and Van der Walt, 1996:216). Using a battery of tests in pre- and postassessments could conceivably provide more concrete evidence about the effectiveness of Street-Wise. Such procedures would, however, be very expensive for programs that rely on charity funding. In addition, South African children fresh from the streets are possibly too restless, their concentration span too limited, and their mistrust of adults too great, to allow for formal testing.

Growing Up in Cities: A Program for Child-Based Community Development

The experience of Street-Wise showed that it is possible for many street children's fragile support networks to be strengthened sufficiently to allow them to return to living with family members. This observation brought home the importance of undertaking prevention work by improving children's daily living environments. Street children typically are from poverty stricken environments. In South Africa almost half of the adult population has a monthly expenditure of no more than U.S.$60 (May, 1998). Currently the rate of children in Street-Wise who are from squatter camps ranges from 45% in the Johannesburg center to 80% in Soweto, which falls within the jurisdiction of Greater Johannesburg.

Indigent people commonly experience high levels of stress and dissatisfaction with life, and some of the most demoralized of all are shack dwellers (Møller, Schlemmer, and Strijdom, 1984). About 13% of South African homes are shacks (Van Tonder, 1997), where constant stress engenders feelings of hopelessness, helplessness, and resignation, which in turn lead to pervasive low-level depression and declining self-esteem (Richter, 1994). When poverty and prejudice permeate the environments of children, adversities become chronic and connected in complex ways (Nunes, 1994). Both poverty and prejudice are socially constructed, however, and therefore can be ameliorated.

The international Growing Up in Cities (GUIC) project aims to ascertain the views of 10- to 15-year-olds about what constitutes a sound environment for personal growth as a foundation for interventions to improve low- and mixed-income urban environments (Chawla, 2000). Originally conceived in 1970 by the urban planner Kevin Lynch in cooperation with UNESCO (Lynch, 1977), the GUIC project was revived in 1994 by the Norwegian Centre for Child Research in partnership with the Management of Social Transformations (MOST) Program of UNESCO and several other international agencies. The project returned to Lynch's study sites in Australia and Poland to record how urban change had affected children's lives. South Africa joined the GUIC program in 1995, to be followed by other new locations in Argentina, India, Norway, the United Kingdom, and the United States (Chawla, 2000). The new initiative stresses the importance of drawing children into participatory urban evaluation and planning so that their perspectives can be taken into account in policy-making and in practices that affect their lives. When children are given a voice in this way, urban development planning can incorporate the interlinked concepts of gender and generation (see Dodd, 1995).

In late 1996, Canaansland, a squatter camp in the suburb of Burghersdorp bordering on Fordsburg in inner city Johannesburg, was selected as the first GUIC study site in South Africa. The Greater Johannesburg Metropolitan Council (GJMC) identified it as the largest of 61 squatter sites in the inner city (GJMC, 1996). As is common in squatter settlements in and around Johannesburg, the site comprised a mix of indigenous African cultures, including some from other areas of the African continent.

Two studies were undertaken with children at squatter sites in South Africa prior to the work of GUIC. Both were completed before 1994, when South Africa's apartheid system was abolished and a new democratic government came to power. The first was an anthropological study with 7-year-old children in the Crossroads squatter settlement in the Western Cape, which concluded, "South African society seems neither to care about the surroundings and atmosphere that it offers children nor to attempt to minimize their trauma" (Reynolds, 1989:204). The second study (du Toit, 1992) examined the relationship between informal housing conditions and the psychological well-being of 7- to 8-year-old children in Bophutatswana (now the

North-West Province). This study concluded that each child's response was a unique synthesis "of internal and external determinants." Du Toit also noted that the proximity of supportive adults who could buffer potentially negative features of the environment was crucial for this age group. The continued presence on South African city streets of children 10 years and older who have run away from shack settlements clearly indicates that they do not find such settings personally fulfilling.

For the adults of Canaansland, the notion that children should be asked to evaluate their environments was foreign, but they agreed that the children should work with the GUIC team. Since research was conducted on Saturday mornings, they and the children coined the term *Saturday school* to give credence to what they interpreted as an extracurricular learning program. Through their interactions with the GUIC research team, first the children and eventually the adults (through exposure to the research findings) began to appreciate that the perspectives of the 10- to 15-year-olds could inform officials about shortcomings in the neighborhood.

There was neither space nor privacy to work on site, but parents wanted their children to be near at hand to ensure their personal safety, to run errands if necessary, and to receive messages. Applications for permission to work in buildings nearby were all politely refused until an Islamic NGO allowed work to proceed in unused upstairs rooms. Despite occasional instances of generosity toward the people of Canaansland, neighboring traders and residents made it clear that they objected to the presence of the squatters. Their presence allegedly lowered land values and increased crime and dirt, and residents feared that children who were in poor health might spread illness and disease. Fees at schools and preschools were too high for parents in Canaansland. This meant that preschool children were confined to the camp's cramped 1.48 Ha, which housed over 1,000 people, with their only play space a side street and a piece of land used as both a rubbish dump and a toilet. Racial and cultural elements also came into play. Local residents and traders were mostly Asian, many of whom had been forcibly relocated from the nearby suburb of Pageview in the 1970s when Pageview was purged of non-White people and redesigned for occupation by low-income White citizens (Carrim, 1990). The squatters, with alien customs and religion, were seen as culturally disharmonious in the area.

GUIC has a standardized set of research procedures: children's drawings of their area, group discussions, tours of the area, individual interviews, and schedules of daily activities. The research agenda was predetermined, and common questions required answers about the positive and negative features of the children's daily environment. However, within these boundaries a high degree of participation by the children in the research process it-self was encouraged (Chawla, 2000). The children themselves supplied the rules for each day as guidelines for group process. Data collection took place individually, as well as in groups, and was interspersed with games, songs, dances, and meals. A sequence of Saturday workshops gave the children time to discuss the research process between data collection sessions (Swart-Kruger, 2000).

Initially, the children showed low self-esteem when they refused to exhibit their drawings and other products because they were afraid they would be ridiculed. They were also unwilling to be photographed so that outsiders would not discover that they lived in a squatter camp and felt that they had little to contribute. When they realized there were no "right" or "wrong" answers and that all input was appreciated and valued, they relaxed, and the whole exercise took on the nature of a mastery experience for them (see Bandura, 1995).

When the research was completed, Mayor Isaac Mogase hosted a workshop at the Greater Johannesburg Metropolitan Council so that the children and researchers could share the work with him and the four local mayors, as well as urban planning officials. This, and the presence of donor agencies, nongovernmental organizations, community-based organizations, the Junior and Mini Youth Councils, and the Human Rights Commission, impressed upon the children and their caretakers that their insights were intended to inform urban policy and planning. In preparation for the workshop, the children elected two girls and two boys from their numbers to present their views and recommendations, focusing on four problem areas.

First, the children had no place for homework or extracurricular studies. Since adults expected them to complete household chores before they engaged in other activities, homework was relegated to the early evening when light was failing. Social cognitive theory (Bandura, 1995) has stressed the importance of self-regulatory skills for academic achievement in the face of adversity and distraction. A number of children in Canaansland showed great initiative in this regard, carrying tables out of doors between the shacks to work late in the afternoon or working inside by candlelight, despite distractions of persistent noise and drunken brawls. The children asked that a structure be erected on the adjacent vacant lot for use as a crèche (in South Africa *crèche* refers to a facility that has features similar to those of a U.S. preschool and day care nursery) in the mornings and for use by students in the afternoons.

Second, the children felt demeaned by the lack of sanitation and piped water on site. Girls, and some boys, who had the chore of replenishing water supplies within their shacks asked that toilets and potable water be provided on site as a matter of urgency. Third, because of poor-quality materials many shacks leaked in rainy weather, leaving children who slept on the floor in pools of water or relegating them to spend nights sitting upright on chairs. They requested donations of better-quality materials to reinforce and waterproof shacks.

Finally, the children found their self-esteem constantly undermined by verbal and physical abuse and other humiliations from passersby and the local community. Those who had to stay on the site most of the time because of their age or sex, and who played on pavements and side streets, suffered most. When children away from home were recognized as being from Canaansland, they were unjustly blamed for various misdeeds. For instance, shopkeepers would shadow children they presumed had entered to steal. The first three recommendations of the children had focused on short-term improvements in their environment. To solve this last problem, they suggested a long-term solution – that city officials provide more appropriate accommodations for them, possibly in the neighboring suburb of Mayfair.

At the conclusion of the workshops, participants gave GUIC the task of finding donor funding for a crèche and study facilities, and the local council the task of attending to matters of sanitation, potable water, schooling, health services, refuse removal, crime prevention, and traffic control. The provision of these facilities and services is important to the well-being of children who otherwise suffer from their material deprivation and from exclusion from "their society's circle of care" (Nunes, 1994; Chawla, 2000). Canaansland adults who attended the workshop had an opportunity to express their needs for adult literacy and job skills training.

Overall, the task of enabling the children to contribute in a meaningful way to consideration of urban issues was successful. A follow-up meeting also revealed that four features of the workshop had stimulated a sense of collective self-efficacy among the children (see Bandura, 1995). The children judged the value of their input in terms of the mayor's speech, which had stressed the importance of the voice of children in urban planning; the display of their drawings on the walls and on overhead projector transparencies; the positive response from the audience when they made their presentations; and the commitment to action at the end of the workshop.

Six months later, before any of the agreed upon workshop resolutions had been implemented, the entire Canaansland community was forcibly relocated to vacant land 40 km outside Johannesburg, in a manner reminiscent of forced relocations during the apartheid era and in gross violation of human rights enshrined in South Africa's new constitution. This action was taken jointly by local government officials and members of the regional department of housing and land affairs in order to free land for the erection of low-cost housing (Swart-Kruger, 2000). Neither Mayor Mogase's office nor GUIC representatives were informed of this relocation, which had, apparently, been orchestrated at the same time that GUIC researchers began working with the children. Researchers later discovered that some officials present at the workshop knew about the planned relocation yet remained silent. The relocation was publicized in the local press and on television (Abrader, 1997; Ndlela, 1997).

Children suffer greatly in forced relocations. Their nutrition and schooling are seriously undermined, and their psychological well-being is damaged by witnessing their adult caretakers' helplessness to prevent the destruction of their personal possessions (Dizon and Quijano, 1997). Eviction can also harm a child's sense of belonging when established social networks are destroyed (Ekblad, 1993). Forced relocation is in every respect a violation of the rights of children as embodied in the Convention on the Rights of the Child (Dizon and Quijano, 1997). When GUIC posted news of the relocation on the Internet, protest letters addressed to the mayor, to other public officials, and to President Mandela streamed into South Africa from all over the world. In May 1998, when reaction to the relocation of Canaansland had died down, a similar relocation took place (Victor, 1998), and in June 1998, a third squatter site in inner-city Johannesburg was demolished (West, 1998). It was difficult not to be cynical when the press reported that a senior official in local government, who had previously called for information on poverty reduction for policy formulation, justified forced relocations on the grounds that squatting in the inner city was "devastating to the city's economy as it tends to drive business away" (West, 1998).

When Mayor Mogase visited Canaansland residents at the new site with foodstuffs and toys 6 weeks after the relocation, he lessened their feelings of worthlessness and rejection by society. GUIC did not have the resources to assess the impact of the eviction on the children but made a conscious effort to counterbalance any possible negative effects by retaining close ties with children from the research group. The play and study center planned for them in the inner city was constructed at the new site instead, through the generosity of several donors.

Poverty hearings in South Africa in April 1998 exposed nationwide human rights abuses, ineffectual local government, and lack of support for those willing to help themselves (Stucky, 1998). At their new site, the Canaansland community again experienced these problems in daily life and asked GUIC for guidance in accessing development resources. The Adult Basic Education and Training (ABET) Institute at the University of South Africa (Unisa) then trained them to keep accounts and to write reports and funding proposals, and the Unisa Law Department helped them formulate their constitution. In a series of meetings arranged by GUIC with a representative of the Nelson Mandela Children's Fund, provincial and local government officials and representatives of Canaansland and the wider community helped to resolve differences and jealousies resulting from a perceived preference for the Canaansland community to other needy people in the area.

Nunes (1994) reminds us that long-term effectiveness in intervention programs requires short-term help to reduce individual suffering. The solidarity that is currently being established among adults in Canaansland, and the reformulation of their identity as residents of a wider area, Thulamntwana, are important to prevent a spiral of downward mobility in the community as a whole. Despite adversities in their current setting, the children of Canaansland appear to have developed a greater degree of self-confidence than was evident on their first involvement with GUIC. Now as a rule, the residents' committee accepts the validity of children's viewpoints in matters of concern to them.

Through the GUIC and Street-Wise programs, children with wavering self-esteem are consciously encouraged to mobilize their capabilities to achieve desired objectives and are reassured that they can make positive contributions in defining and finding solutions to their own problems. According to Bandura (1995:4), positive reinforcement of this kind is likely to drive people who might otherwise dwell on perceived personal deficiencies to greater effort to solve problems. If, in addition, problem-solving situations are structured to bring about success, as happens in Street-Wise and GUIC, individuals are encouraged to strive for further successes.

Lessons for Street-Wise and GUIC

Street-Wise represents a model of crisis intervention; Growing Up in Cities, a long-term process of community development. Together, they seek to strengthen children, their families, and their communities to withstand the assaults of especially difficult circumstances and to gain the means to basic livelihoods and dignity. In some respects, the difficulties that these children and families face reflect the special hardships of a postapartheid society. The basic outline of the stories told here, however, is all too common in a world where 1.3 billion people are estimated to live in severe poverty (UNDP, 1997). There are countless others like these children and their families, struggling with malnutrition and homelessness in societies of great disparities, and under governments that invest more in serving the interests of the well-to-do than in providing basic services for the poor. Given these commonalities in the circumstances of the very poor, it is possible to relate GUIC and Street-Wise to international analyses of effective models of intervention to promote children's and families' health, resilience, and acquisition of essential life skills.

In their research-based approach to program design, Street-Wise and GUIC are similar to the Urban Child Project carried out by UNICEF in Brazil, the Philippines, India, Kenya, and Italy in the early 1990s, with particular attention to the needs of street and working children. One conclusion of the Urban Child Project is that the forces that place urban children at risk need to be understood and addressed at multiple levels of international and national pressures, state and city policies and practices, and community and family stresses (Blanc et al., 1994). These multilevel causes of children's distress require that the most effective programs on children's behalf need to adopt multilevel approaches to intervention, although the level of emphasis may shift over time. This framework may be applied to the work of Street-Wise and GUIC.

Both South African projects have invested a major amount of their resources in organizing microlevel support that draws on and strengthens children's relationships with their families and their communities. Thus Street-Wise provides street boys with immediate access to drop-in shelters and nutrition, while it begins the slower process of counseling, health care, education, job training, and reconciling them with their families whenever possible. The primary focus of GUIC is to demonstrate processes of child-focused community evaluation and project design that will lead to visible physical and social improvements in their local environment.

At the mesolevel of the province and city, both projects seek to bring about a change in the way that government officials and the public perceive children from the streets and squatter camps, by increasing understanding of the children's circumstances and showcasing their resourcefulness and aspirations. They demonstrate that provision for basic needs is in fact a recognition of basic rights, and, conversely, that the type of opportunities for reflection and action that Street-Wise and GUIC offer should not be seen as adaptations for "special" children, but as basic requirements for all children to grow into self-confident and self-sufficient citizens (see also

Rizzini, Barker, and Cassaniga, this volume). To this end, both projects use the media of public events, newspapers, television, and the Internet and produce publications that bring the children's conditions to life for a general educated public. They also pressure city and provincial government to provide more responsive and coordinated services. And by their example, the two projects present more effective alternatives to existing government policies. In the process, they create networks of well-intentioned government officials and nongovernmental organization staff who are willing to work across sectors on children's behalf.

On the macrolevel of national and international awareness, both projects spread their messages through publications and presentations and attempt to influence South Africa's National Plan of Action for Children and specific policies related to street children and squatter settlements. GUIC-South Africa has benefited by being part of an international action-research network that involves a continuous sharing of experience and ideas. As a result, it has been able to introduce South African officials to the concepts of appointing a representative for children within each municipality, as well as including child impact assessments in preliminary planning for any major development decision. These ideas are now under consideration.

To list these accomplishments is not to suggest that any of them has been easy or complete. Members of Street-Wise and GUIC and their allies among donors and government officials continue to face severe obstacles in the form of public and government indifference or even hostility to the poor, inappropriate policies, uncoordinated services, and inadequate resources. The examples of these programs point to the need for nongovernmental organizations and government to work together to facilitate self-help efforts by children and families alike to meet basic needs such as nutrition, water, shelter, sanitation, education, and income generation. However, these approaches conflict with entrenched habits of "resolving" the problems of the poor by putting them out of sight and out of mind. At its worst, this reaction leads to abuses like the violent removal of the Canaansland community, which replicates the policies of the apartheid era.

The approaches of Street-Wise and GUIC conform to the principles of broader efforts derived from a generation of work to eradicate poverty (Anzorena et al., 1998) and provide "primary environmental care" for low-income communities and their children (Hart, 1994; Satterthwaite et al., 1996). Both begin with "learning not doing for the first phase in order to understand how to work best with communities" (Anzorena et al., 1998:183). In the cases of both Street-Wise and GUIC, this first phase has consisted of systematic, multimethod research to enhance understanding of children's perspectives and their own priorities for improving their life conditions.

From this base, GUIC-South Africa has moved into the role of providing organizational and advisory support to the community through an extended process of open meetings by a community committee that endorses the priorities of its 10- to 14-year-olds. GUIC also helps community leaders identify other means for improving the settlement environment. In this role, one of the most important functions of GUIC members is to negotiate with municipal and provincial government and donor agencies with and on behalf of the community. GUIC also uses the example of Canaansland to pressure government for permanent changes in the direction of more humane, coordinated responses to the needs of squatters. What distinguishes GUIC from most community-based initiatives is that young people have participated in all phases of this work. A basic principle of successful models of poverty eradication is that the poor need to be involved in planning, implementing, and managing projects on their behalf (UNDP, 1997; Anzorena et al., 1998). But GUIC represents a new model that also responds to the participation clauses of the Convention on the Rights of the Child, Agenda 21, and the Habitat Agenda by making children and youth integral to these processes. According to the philosophy of GUIC, children and youth learn how to become active citizens of democratic societies by contributing to community decision making.

Finally, Street-Wise and GUIC represent another stage of successful intervention by "moving from 'doing' to training and technical support" (Anzorena et al., 1998:183). Staff at Street-Wise run workshops and serve as technical resources for the design of multifaceted systems of support and educational curricula for street children. Members of GUIC-South Africa facilitated a workshop on community organizing for the leaders of Canaansland and nearby squatter settlements and are helping to create workshops on participatory research and planning with children for people at national, regional, and international levels.

The conditions of the children in Street-Wise and GUIC and the millions of children like them around the world ultimately need to be addressed in the larger context of the rift between north and south, rich and poor, along with countervailing efforts to extend the meaning of rights to include basic equity in food, shelter, education, employment, and social inclusion for all. As Fuller (1986:61) noted, "The peoples of South Africa, black and white, have an opportunity to instruct the world in how to mend this rift. If they manage to create a society in which the distinctions of North and South are transcended, they will at once become . . . a case history and role model for a more equitable development of the world economy." Growing Up in Cities and Street-Wise provide examples of some of the directions that this reconciliation must take.

REFERENCES

Abarder, G. (1997). Fordsburg Squatter Camp Goes Up in Smoke as Residents Are Moved. *The Star*, November 17, p. 3.

Anzorena, J., Bolnick, J., Boonyabancha, S., Cabannes, Y., Hardoy, A., Hasan, A., Levy, C., Mitlin, D., Murphy, D., Patel, S., Saborido, M., Satterthwaite, D., and Stein, A. (1998). Reducing Urban Poverty: Some Lessons from Experience. *Environment and Urbanization*, 10, 167–186.

Bandura, A. (1995). Exercise of Personal and Collective Efficacy in Changing Societies. In A. Bandura (Ed.), *Self-Efficacy in Changing Societies* (pp. 1–45). Cambridge: Cambridge University Press.

Bandura, A. (1997). *Self-Efficacy*. New York: W. H. Freeman.

Blanc, C. (1994). *Urban Children in Distress. Global Predicaments and Innovative Strategies*. Langhorne, PA: Gordon and Breach.

Carrim, N. (1990). *FIETAS: A Social History of Pageview*. Johannesburg: Save Pageview Association.

Chawla, L. (Ed). (2000). *Growing Up in an Urbanizing World*. London: Earthscan.

CSS (Central Statistics Service) (1997). *Statistics in Brief: RSA*. Pretoria: Central Statistics Service.

Dizon, A. M., and Quijano, S. (1997). *Impact of Eviction on Children*. (Report). The Urban Poor Associates (UPA), the Asian Coalition for Housing Rights (ACHR), and the United Nations Economic and Social Commission for Asia and the Pacific (UN-ESCAP).

Dodd, R. (1995). Foreword. In V. Johnson and E. Ivan-Smith (Eds.), *Listening to Smaller Voices* (p. 4). Somerset: ACTIONAID.

Donald, D., and Swart-Kruger, J. (1994). South African Street Children: Developmental Implications. *South African Journal of Psychology*, 24, 169–174.

Donald, D., Wallis, J., and Cockburn, A. (1997). An Exploration of Meanings: Tendencies towards Developmental Risk and Resilience in a Group of South African Ex–Street Children. *School Psychology International*, 18, 137–154.

Du Toit, M. (1992). *Huis, Paleis, Pondok... Kinders in Informele Woonomstandighede*. Pretoria: Unisa, Institute for Behavioural Sciences.

Ekblad, S. (1993). Stressful Environments and Their Effects on Quality of Life in Third World Cities. *Environment and Urbanization*, 5, 125–134.

Fuller, R. (1986). We Are All Afrikaners. *In Context*, Autumn, 60–62.

Gbadegesin, S. (1991). *African Philosophy*. New York: Peter Lang.

GJMC (Greater Johannesburg Transitional Metropolitan Council). Joint Political Committee. Metropolitan Planning, Urbanisation and Environmental Management. (1996). *Homelessness in the Johannesburg Inner City* (Report 1996–11–29). Johannesburg: Greater Johannesburg Transitional Metropolitan Council.

Glauser, B. (1990). Street Children: Deconstructing a Construct. In A. James and A. Prout (Eds.), *Constructing and Reconstructing Childhood* (pp. 138–156). Brighton: Falmer Press.

Gyekye, K. (1992). Person and Community in African Thought. In K. Wiredu and
    K. Gyekye (Eds.), *Person and Community* (pp. 101–122). Washington, D.C.: Council
    for Research in Values and Philosophy.
Hardoy, J. E., Mitlin, D., and Satterthwaite, D. 1992. *Environmental Problems in Third
    World Cities.* London: Earthscan Publications.
Hart, R. (1994). Children's Role in Primary Environmental Care. *Childhood,* 2,
    92–102.
Hirsch, R. V. (1993). *A Day like Any Other: Stories, Poetry and Art by Street Children in
    South Africa.* Johannesburg: COSAW
Hobbes, T. (1968). *Leviathan.* C. B. Macpherson (Ed.). London: Pelican Books. First
    published in 1651.
Jacobson, G. (1990). From Care to Community. In M. Biderman-Pam and B. Gannon
    (Eds.), *Competent Care, Competent Kids* (pp. 129–149). Cape Town: NACCW.
Jansen, P., Richter, L., Griessel, R., and Joubert, J. (1990). Glue Sniffing: A Description
    of Social, Psychological and Neurological Factors in a Group of South African Street
    Children. *South African Journal of Psychology,* 20, 150–158.
Kramer, S. (1986). Street Children and Education. In ISMA (Eds.), *Street Children—Four
    Perspectives* (pp. 1–4). (ISMA paper no. 40). Johannesburg: Institute for the Study of
    Man in Africa.
Krog, A. (1998). *Culture of My Skull.* Johannesburg: Random House.
Lave, J., and Wenger, E. (1991). *Situated Learning.* Cambridge: Cambridge University
    Press.
Locke, J. (1983). *A Letter Concerning Toleration.* Indianapolis: Hackett Publishing. First
    published in 1689.
Losel, F., and Bliesener, T. (1990). Resilience in Adolescence. In K. Hurrelmann and
    F. Losel (Eds.), *Health Hazards in Adolescence* (pp. 299–320). Berlin: De Gruyter.
Luthar, S., and Zigler, E. (1991). Vulnerability and Competence: A Review of Research
    on Resilience in Childhood. *American Journal of Orthopsychiatry,* 61, 6–22.
Lynch, K. (1977). *Growing Up in Cities.* Cambridge, MA: MIT Press.
MacCurtain, B. (1990). An Education Programme for Street Children. In M. Biderman-
    Pam and B. Gannon (Eds.), *Competent Care, Competent Kids* (pp. 122–128). Cape
    Town: NACCW.
May, J. (1998). *Poverty and Inequality in South Africa.* Durban: Praxis.
McLoyd, V. C., and Wilson, P. (1990). Maternal Behaviour, Social Support, and Economic
    Conditions as Predictors of Distress in Children. *New Directions in Child Development,*
    46, 49–69.
Møller, V., Schlemmer, L., and Strijdom, H. (1984). *Poverty and Quality of Life among
    Blacks in South Africa.* Cape Town: Second Carnegie Inquiry into Poverty and
    Development.
Morton, H. (1996) *Becoming Tongan: An Ethnography of Childhood.* Honolulu: University
    of Hawaii Press.
Ndlela, S. (1997). Squatters Are to Be Forcibly Removed. *City Vision,* November
    21, 6.
Nunes, T. (1994). *The Environment of the Child.* The Hague: Bernard van Leer Foundation.
Okolo, C. B. (1995). The African Person. In P. H. Coetzee and M. E. S. Van den
    Berg (Eds.), *An Introduction to African Philosophy* (pp. 393–401). Pretoria: Unisa
    Press.
Reynolds, P. (1989). *Childhood in Crossroads.* Cape Town: David Philip.

Richter, L. (1994). Economic Stress and Its Influence on the Family and Caretaking Patterns. In A. Dawes and D. Donald (Eds.), *Childhood and Adversity: Psychological Perspectives from South African Research* (pp. 28–50). Cape Town: David Philip.

Richter, L., and Van der Walt, M. (1996). The Psychological Assessment of South African Street Children. *Africa Insight*, 26, 211–220.

Rogers, C. (1980). *A Way of Being*. Boston: Houghton & Mifflin.

Satterthwaite, D., Hart, R., Levy, C., Mitlin, D., Ross, D., Smit, J., and Stephens, C. (1996). *The Environment for Children*. London: Earthscan.

Schärf, W., Powell, M., and Thomas, E. (1986). Strollers—Street Children of Cape Town. In A. Burman & P. Reynolds (Eds.), *Growing Up in a Divided Society* (pp. 262–287). Johannesburg: Ravan Press.

Shapiro, I. (1986). *The Evolution of Rights in Liberal Theory*. Cambridge: Cambridge University Press.

Sibley, D. (1981). *Outsiders in Urban Societies*. Oxford: Blackwell.

Stucky, C. (1998). Iniquities Rife, Poverty Hearings Find. *The Sunday Independent*, April 5, p. 1.

Swart, J. (1988). "*Street-Wise*": Opening the Way to Self-Actualization for the Street Child. *Africa Insight*, 18, 33–41.

Swart, J. (1990a). Of the Streets: A Study of Black Street Children in South Africa. In P. Hugo (Ed.), *Truth Be in the Field* (pp. 259–273). Pretoria: Unisa Press.

Swart, J. (1990b). *Malunde: The Street Children of Hillbrow*. Johannesburg: Wits University Press.

Swart-Kruger, J. (1997). Situated Learning: "Tiekie-dice" amongst Street Children in South Africa. *Journal of Psychology in Africa*, 1, 1–11.

Swart-Kruger, J. (2000). *Growing up in Canaansland: Children's Recommendations on Improving a Squatter Camp Environment*. Pretoria: HSRC and UNESCO-MOST.

Swart-Kruger, J. (in press). "Gaining and Losing a Voice: Children in a South African Squatter Camp." In L. Chawla (Ed.), *Growing Up in an Urbanizing World*. London: Earthscan.

Swart-Kruger, J. M., and Donald, D. (1994). Children of the South African Streets. In A. Dawes & D. Donald (Eds.), *Childhood and Adversity: Psychological Perspectives* (pp. 107–121). Cape Town: David Philip.

UNCHS (United Nations Centre for Human Settlements). (1996). *The Istanbul Declaration and the Habitat Agenda*. Nairobi: UNCHS.

UNDP (1997). *Human Development Report 1997*. Oxford: Oxford University Press.

UNDP. (United Nations Development Program). (1999). *Human Development Report 1999*. Oxford: Oxford University Press.

UNICEF. (1990). *First Call for Children*. New York: UNICEF.

United Nations. (1992). *Agenda 21*. New York: United Nations.

Van der Vliet, V. (1980). Growing Up in a Traditional Society. In W. D. Hammond-Tooke (Ed.), *The Bantu-Speaking Peoples of South Africa* (pp. 211–233). London: Routledge & K. Paul.

Van Tonder, D. (1997). The Road to Egoli. *MUNIVIRO*, 13, 6–7.

Victor, R. (1998). Angry Diepsloot Squatters Block Road after Their Shacks Are Demolished. *The Star*, May 14, p. 3.

Weisner, T. S. (1984). Ecocultural Niches of Middle Childhood. In W. A. Collins (Ed.), *Development during Middle Childhood* (pp. 335–365). Washington, DC: National Academy Press.

Werner, E., and Smith, R. (1992). *Overcoming the Odds*. Ithaca, NY: Cornell University Press.

West, B. (1998). Inner-City Squatter Settlement Set Alight. *The Star* June 26, 1–2.

Williams, C. (1992). Curriculum Relevance for Street Children. *The Curriculum Journal*, 3, 277–290.

Williams, C. (1993). Who Are "Street Children"? A Hierarchy of Street Use and Appropriate Responses. *Child Abuse and Neglect*, 17, 831–841.

Williams, P. (1991). *The Alchemy of Race and Rights*. Cambridge, MA: Harvard University Press.

4 Adolescents as Collaborators

In Search of Well-Being

Felton Earls and Mary Carlson

We aim to accomplish two goals in this chapter: The first is to introduce an evolving intellectual context that sets forth our ideas about youth well-being; the second is to introduce an approach that involves working directly with young people and integrates their perspectives and knowledge as research collaborators. This orientation, which emphasizes the child as citizen–participant, has not only dramatically altered our view of childhood, but has challenged our views of social science and changed our approach from one of working *for children* to one whose purpose is to work *with children*.

For the past few years, we have been making a concerted effort to establish a theoretical foundation for adolescent well-being and at the same time develop scientific strategies to explore the theory. The exercise has taken us on a far-flung journey, largely inspired by the United Nations Convention on the Rights of the Child (CRC), which was adopted by the General Assembly in 1990 and ratified. We have used the CRC as part of an ethical framework for research activities and policy initiatives in our international work with the assistance of the United Nations Children's Fund (UNICEF) in these countries and in our domestic work.

The work with adolescents presented in this chapter constitutes two endeavors in a formative stage. The first is the Project on Human Development in Chicago Neighborhoods (PHDCN). The Young Citizen Program, as a component of the PHDCN, is concerned with how young people characterize their quality of life and well-being. We are also interested in youth's capacity as research collaborators to provide a perspective that will enlarge the issues we are investigating.

The chapter is developed in five sections. The first section articulates a position on the nature of social science research, using the PHDCN as an exemplar. This provides a background for the four sections that follow, which cover, respectively, the themes of (1) the definition and measurement of youth well-being, (2) the conceptual ideas related to child citizenship and participatory rights as core to the notion of well-being, (3) a progress report on the research about well-being and citizenship that involves youth as collaborators, and (4) reflections about the immediate and long-term implications of this work.

The Project on Human Development in Chicago Neighborhoods (PHDCN): From Normative to Critical

At the beginning of the 1990s, the PHDCN was planned and designed by an interdisciplinary group of social scientists who sought the broadest possible consultation from researchers concerned with youth well-being. The underlying concepts, measures, sampling methods, and analytical challenges were vigorously debated and carefully crafted. This collected wisdom resulted in several choices that produced a multilevel, multicohort longitudinal design (Tonry et al., 1991; Earls and Reiss, 1994). Chicago was selected as the single urban site because it offers a highly diverse array of neighborhoods, thereby permitting a sample representing a range of urban contexts stratified by race/ethnicity and social class.

Throughout the early period of project development the study focused on negative outcomes. Young people were viewed as carrying a propensity for problem behavior. A comprehensive assortment of contextual, familial, and individual risk factors were included in the measurement protocol (Buka and Earls, 1993), presuming that knowledge about these factors would eventually form the base of a rational program of prevention (Earls, 1991). Throughout this entire period, there was no record that any serious consideration was ever given to consulting youth about the observations and assumptions adults were making about their lives. This we consider normative, in that no one questioned the absence of any youth participation.

Before reconstructing an approach to studying the lives of children and youth, it was necessary to carefully identify the specific assumptions that proved useful in launching the study. Three themes were delineated: The first is reflected in a strong bias to attribute cause to the *individual*. This proclivity has a strong and implicit rationale. It is, after all, individuals who commit crime, take drugs, or behave violently. Even in high-risk contexts, not all youth behave badly. This perspective runs deep and to a degree seems reasonable. But it leaves open a broader question on how deeply embedded in social context human behavior really is. In order to make space to test this hypothesis rigorously, the bias toward individual level determinants had to be challenged.

A direct consequence of balancing individual and societal levels of explanations in a design was to create the capacity to show how institutions and policies may seriously constrain, and even undermine, children's capacity to achieve well-being. We witnessed extreme examples of this among abandoned children being raised in state-run institutions in Romania and children living and working on the streets of megacities in Brazil. These extreme conditions generated by poverty are rivaled in Chicago by the poor quality of child care and public education.

A second theme regards the concept of *prevention*. We reasoned that we could measure risk factors in a longitudinal design that would eventually be translated into age-graded prevention trials. But in an operational sense, this kind of reasoning can be deceptive. Multiple risk factors operating in a complex system may provide a better framework, making it unlikely that we would find a specific set of risk factors to identify children at high risk and assign these same children to an experiment that would prevent the onset of antisocial behavior or substance abuse.

The third theme concerned the idea of what constitutes the *serious youthful offender*. The perspective was narrow. Dangerous behavior was directly translated into malign motivation, and the context in which the child had grown up and in which the behavior took place was seldom systematically considered. Knowing the age of onset and the frequency of specific behaviors was sufficient to judge an underlying abnormality and to predict the offending career of the perpetrator. But this portrayal also is incomplete. Adolescents experiment; their peers recruit and seduce others to take risks; boredom and lack of opportunity invite risk-taking with little regard for consequences.

These three themes became implicit assumptions for the design of the PHDCN. We selected and developed measures to capture "objective" behavior that could be counted and classified precisely enough to label and to treat (i.e., to prevent, to intervene upon, and so on). The rationale was simple: The ideas were easily recognized and supported by our professional peers and potential funders, and it facilitated the operationalization of the design we had adopted. Applying for grants subjected us to intense cross-examinations about our ideas and methods. The benefit of this process was to ensure rigorousness, sometimes at the expense of creativity. But working with an interdisciplinary team required a degree of flexibility that encouraged novel ways of approaching a concept or measure. Our decision to operate in a "fishbowl" meant that criticism from anyone – professional or nonprofessional – was invited and taken seriously. In the process we were repeatedly confronted with two divergent points of view: one that questioned the need for social science (e.g., Don't we already know the answer?) and one that reflected a high level of skepticism that such an ambitious project could justify itself. The opposing point of view was optimistic, believing that the comprehensive scope and large scale were needed to understand development of transgressive behavior. Responding to such divergent opinions forces continued introspection and reconciliation.

In the process of operating in this open way, several transitions resulted in a reconstruction of the research agenda regarding how children were to be approached. The first came about while interviewing children about their exposure to violence. In a way, this issue represents the opposite of our initial interest in uncovering the causes of violent behavior. If some children behave violently, others must be victims. Are there similarities between perpetrators and victims? Is exposure to violence a possible cause of becoming a perpetrator? Is witnessing a violent event as consequential of ongoing exposure as direct exposure to single, catastrophic events? These questions illustrate the revolution of our thinking about the children who were the focus of our interests. We shifted our thinking to consider them not as dangerous persons, but as insecure, apprehensive, anxious, or desensitized persons. The realization that witnessing violence can be both real and fictional (or virtual) introduced a further complication. We proceeded to think critically about posttraumatic stress disorder, and about strategies to measure reliably and accurately both victimization and the witnessing of violent events (Selner-O'Hagan et al., 1998).

Simultaneously, we began to consider how to implement the principles of the CRC as a progressive approach to research in child development. In some ways the CRC constitutes a revolution in thinking that could not have been readily anticipated. Unlike in the civil rights and women's suffrage campaigns, there is not a long history of conflict and confrontation that compels a process of change to improve the welfare of youth. The UN committed itself to advance principles of the survival and protection of children. And over the next decade, they worked quietly to draft a remarkable document and establish nearly universal consensus that these principles should become part of an international covenant.

In short, the deep consideration we placed on the insecurity of children was consonant with the principles outlined in the CRC. Why should children be exposed to violence? What were adults doing to prevent such events or to minimize their impact? These questions mapped directly onto concepts of the right to protection from harm, to feel wanted and secure, and to be afforded a degree of respect that reinforced society's duty to provide the conditions for safety.

Thinking about rights in the abstract is a far cry from being able to apply these abstractions in work with youth, and practical applications are yet another step removed from integrating a rights approach into measurement and interpretation of data. The act of reconstruction requires a strategy to implement these steps. Aside from the vagueness of such an enterprise, we had to acknowledge the political character of human rights generally, and child rights specifically. The departure from normal science was provocative and risky, but in our minds, it was anything but tentative. The revision of childhood brought about by the near-universal ratification of the CRC represents an irreversible process that requires a readaptation toward most human endeavors concerning children. Inventing the CRC and learning how to think from its radical framework are to recognize that the notion of rights is incomplete.

The idea of rights has to be translated into action and measures, and new policies, perhaps new institutions, have to be established as a consequence of the actions shaped by the rights framework. Working within the domestic confines of the United States has been difficult, in large part because of the perception of child rights in the context of litigious and adversarial issues of juvenile justice and child custody. As we describe, the concept of child rights presented in the CRC goes considerably beyond spotlighted legal cases that apply to situations of crime and custody.

To begin conceptualizing the broad child rights perspective, we sought advice from UNICEF and visited its research center in Florence. Through our UNICEF contacts we visited programs and communities in Barbados, Brazil, Costa Rica, Mexico, and Romania to witness how the articles on the rights of the child are being implemented through entirely new institutional structures and policies. As a result, we reconstructed the foundations on which the PHDCN is designed.

Over the past few decades, social science in the United States has struggled to acquire a strong academic presence at the risk of becoming elitist and isolated from the way lives are actually lived. By discouraging nonscientists from participating in the formative stages of research, researchers fail to acknowledge the democratic values and institutions that have social and political science agendas. Our concern rests with the reality that children and youth are systematically and nearly universally excluded from the planning, design, and execution of research about their own lives. Including child citizens in research approximates the goal of representing the "common individual" in the modern history of the human rights movement.

The more integral democratic values are in the design and execution of social science projects, the more valid and useful their products will be to the objectives of achieving freedom and equality. In the process, social science achieves a closer approximation to reality. We claim that youth participation in research adds significantly to substantive validity and adds another dimension to the research (and policy implications), namely, democratic legitimacy. We maintain that democratic legitimacy should be added to the conventional reliability and validity standards to which social science research must aspire and be considered in peer-review and funding decisions of social science research on adolescent well-being. The following sections describe how this democratic legitimacy might be achieved. First, however, we consider the meaning of the term *well-being*, especially since this concept represents the guiding principles of the CRC.

Definition and Measurement of Well-Being

The construct of well-being, though widely used by social scientists, is conceptually and empirically weak (WHOQOL Group, 1995; Pal, 1996). One challenge to the definition and measurement of well-being is the wide assortment of terms used to characterize the phenomenon. Therefore, we first discuss their origins and applications, as they contribute to the theoretical concerns we raise in the next section. The terms can be organized into four sets. The first set consists of terms that apply to *individual* characteristics, which include personal well-being, self-efficacy, agency, and satisfaction. The second set refers to the *context* of development and includes quality of life, standard of living, opportunity structures and commodities, resources, and goods. The third set relates to the *absence* of well-being and includes symptoms, impairments, deficits, and suffering. The fourth set refers to matters of a *collective* nature and includes trust, shared understanding, collective efficacy, rights, and social responsibilities.

Our assessment of the current state of the field leads us to conclude that within and between these various domains, concepts of well-being have not been well established, and consequently few measures have been satisfactorily developed and tested. To underscore the types of efforts that characterize where real advances are being made, we provide three case examples. Collectively, they provide a broad view of how researchers, practitioners, and policymakers are making a concerted effort to establish a more positive and constructive account of youth development. The first describes an initiative undertaken by the U.S. government to derive a set of indicators of well-being. The second documents an effort to derive a psychometrically sound instrument to measure well-being in terms of quality of life. The third is a comprehensive endeavor developed at the Search Institute to provide a diagnostic kit for communities to gauge their capacity to foster well-being of youth (Scales and Leffert, 1994).

A National Picture of Youth Well-Being

The U.S. Federal Interagency Forum on Child and Family Statistics was created to produce a report providing a comprehensive and integrated picture of children's well-being. The Forum's first report, *America's Children: Key National Indicators of Well-Being* (U.S. Federal Interagency Forum on Child and Family Statistics, 1997), includes 25 indicators categorized under five broad domains: Population and Family Characteristics, Economic Security, Health, Behavior, and Social Environment and Education. Criteria for the selection of indicators include established validity for large segments of the population, capacity to monitor trends on a regular basis, and ease of understanding. In addition, an effort was made to balance the indicators across the various domains and to include those that captured relevant developmental aspects of children's lives. This report recognizes that many important aspects of children's lives are missed in available statistics.

One of the more novel indicators in the report, detached youth, refers to youth ages 16–19 who are neither attending school nor working. The data show a modest decline in proportions that fit this description, from 11% in 1985 to 9% in 1996. Not surprisingly, females have somewhat higher rates than males, and African Americans and Hispanics have nearly double the rates of Whites. This indicator isolates an extremely disadvantaged group, one marginalized both from the job market and from citizenship. But, of course, like other indicators in the Forum report, the category of detached youth does not reflect well-being. Rather, well-being is portrayed on the basis of those characteristics and circumstances that threaten or even undermine it. In fact, the tenor of the report portrays youth as persons whose well-being is primarily determined by their readiness for labor force participation. Although the significance of this marker of adulthood should not be diminished, individual well-being is also determined by a sense of engagement and empowerment in matters of a civic and political nature. The absence of any markers of these dimensions in a national study represents its most serious drawback.

Development of a Measure of Well-Being

Scientists at the Department of Health Services at the University of Washington have been developing a new measure of well-being, called the

Youth Quality of Life Scale (YQOL) (Edwards, T. C., Huebner, C. E. M., Connell, F. A., Patrick, D. L., personal communication). Several steps, guided by an oversight committee of experts in the field of youth development, were undertaken to develop the YQOL, including in-depth, open-ended interviews with adolescents and focus groups with parents of adolescents. Descriptive categories of well-being, based on this information, were derived, and a conceptual model to guide their research was formulated. Overall, 19 domains of well-being were extracted from the interviews and a series of questions were developed for each.

Without minimizing the scientific importance of this undertaking, it is reasonable to question an approach that relies on children exclusively as subjects, and not as citizens. In our survey work, we no longer use the term *subjects* but refer to them as *participants*. This conceptual shift involves a dramatic change in the orientation of research. Persons providing information to researchers automatically become actors with a stake in the way the information is to be used, which involves rights of access and interpretation. Human subject review of procedures, which require the protection of persons involved in research, only partly addresses the implications of this orientation.

Questions included in questionnaires, such as the YQOL, are designed to portray the status of individuals. Consequently, little can be gleaned about the intensity of youth's involvement in the world around them, about how they make decisions and set priorities, about what opportunities exist for them to express opinions, and about what use is made of such occasions when they are available. The view of youth derived from such approaches is static and one-dimensional, not dynamic, complex, and contradictory, as persons really are. We accept the idea that much research is not intended to achieve such a penetrating view of persons and that it is not even necessary to understand all relationships between persons and their circumstances. Yet we find that unidimensional portrayals represent a constraint imposed by conventional social science methods (especially those with a strong positivist orientation) that threaten the integrity of the research endeavor. To advance research in the area of adolescent well-being, we make the claim that a new orientation to measurement is needed – one that can capture fairly subtle ways in which young people are able to gain control over their lives.

Toward a Comprehensive Assessment of Well-Being

Since 1989, the Search Institute of Minneapolis, Minnesota, has worked on developing and applying a conceptual framework of youth well-being to communities across the United States. In defining the community contexts necessary for the growth of well-being, the framework combines concepts of health promotion and human development as well as the particular attitudes, values, and skills that represent well-being over the life course. These features, dubbed *developmental assets*, are divided into 20 external assets and 20 internal assets. The external assets include four domains – adult support, empowerment, boundaries and expectations, and constructive use of time – and the internal assets include four domains – commitment to learning, positive values, social competencies, and positive identity. The external assets are opportunities, resources, and positive experiences available to youth in their families, schools, and communities. The framework takes on a developmental orientation by recognizing that the attitudes, motivations, and skills representing internal assets develop and mature in relation to the external assets. The conceptual framework and definitions provided by this group foster a more coherent system than that offered by many other researchers in the field. Importantly, it includes an array of assets that reflect our primary concern with the meaning of youth citizenship (though the word *citizenship* does not actually appear in the Institute's documents).

Using a classroom-administered questionnaire, the Institute's researchers have collected data on nearly 100,000 youths in Grades 6 to 12, sampled across approximately 200 communities throughout the United States. They find that the number of both external and internal assets declines as children advance in age and grade level; that girls have a slightly higher number of assets than boys; and that youth with behavior problems have fewer assets than those who evince high levels of prosocial behavior.

The two domains of empowerment and participation are relevant to our focus on the pivotal role of citizenship in defining well-being. Empowerment is defined by three subdomains of community values: youth, youth as resources, and services to others. Participation is defined by the attributes of equality and justice, planning and decision making, and sense of purpose. Despite some important limitations to this body of work, the findings are useful in demonstrating that a majority of children are not engaged, not prepared, and perhaps not even motivated to become active and committed citizens in a democracy. To quote the authors (Benson et al., 1988: 141):

We found in a large aggregate sample that certain developmental experiences which predict civic engagement are relatively uncommon among public school students in grades six through twelve. These include sustained intergenerational relationships outside the family, the experience of neighborhood support, and the perception that adults in my community value youth.

The Search Institute's survey of developmental assets is a first step in drawing attention to the conditions required to promote youth well-being. Identifying community resource deficiencies is necessary to design appropriate intervention strategies. Their current work is largely devoted to locating communities interested in achieving this goal. To this end, they have identified various obstacles that need to be addressed as a precondition for asset enhancement, among them the professionalization of care and services for youth and the absence of high levels of civic engagement. The deficit-reduction paradigm so widely adopted by professionals may well undermine local activism and high levels of commitment to youth. Many of the principles undergirding their approach seek ways to bring about collaboration and coordination between professionals and local groups acting in the best interest of children. This view of local communities as being embedded in larger contexts of professions, political pressures, and economic development is compatible with our own evolving view in understanding collective efficacy for children at the neighborhood level (Sampson, Morenoff, and Earls, 1999).

We now turn to a discussion of the meaning of citizenship as it relates to the well-being of young people and to the production of societal conditions that can sustain well-being. This serves as a background to understanding the direction that our own research with adolescents is taking.

Child Citizenship and Participation in a Deliberative Democracy

Children are the last major group to be included in the remarkable progress toward full citizenship and democratic participation that has occurred worldwide over the last three centuries (Marshall, 1963). By the 18th century, civil and legal dimensions of citizenship and the idea of human (or natural) rights became universally accepted in the West. In the 19th century, the idea of political citizenship was introduced and the movement toward universal suffrage was launched. In the 20th century, the struggles were around welfare (or social and economic) rights, as opposed to legal/civil and political rights. At the same time that citizenship was emerging as a political concept in the West, children were becoming increasingly differentiated from adults (Aries, 1962).

As families developed a heightened concern about matters of health and moral education for children, practices that isolated them within schools and families were championed. Over the last few decades, both extended and nuclear family structures have weakened and the quality of schools has declined. As these crucial social supports for children have been undermined, must we not reconsider the role of these traditional institutions? Should we not be open to the status of all children as *citizens* with genuine participation in societal activities designed to promote and protect their development and well-being?

The provision and protection rights in the CRC contain articles that address rights to survival and development, but the participation rights are among the more controversial sections of the Convention. Our purpose here is not to discuss the merits of involving children in electoral democracy, but rather to highlight the rights of children to participate in those aspects of deliberative democracy for which no minimal age limits are established. How can we begin to envisage what child–citizen involvement in deliberation looks like in real practice?

Deliberative democracy is a recent elaboration of the principle that democratic legitimacy emerges from the public deliberation of citizens. Some scholars of the 20th century strongly supported a democracy in which only elites would participate, which was based on the premise that the average citizens (and particularly the poor and less educated) are apathetic and unable to contribute to rational public discourse (Schumpeter, 1943; Dahl, 1966). The model of a broad-based citizenship actively engaged in rational discussions contrasts with one that reviews the average citizen as lacking the intellectual and social capacities required for rational democratic participation (Pateman, 1970). Given such reservations about the capacities of many adult citizens, the idea of involving children in public discourse appears even more preposterous.

With a strong conviction that both ordinary children and adults are capable and deserve to participate in the democratic process, we have examined the contemporary debates over the cognitive and social requirements (and implications) of authentic deliberative democracy. The last two decades have seen exciting developments in political theory around deliberative democracy – the idea that legitimate lawmaking emanates from the public deliberation of citizens. This news requires public debate and persuasion (rather than force and coercion) to resolve the deepest moral, political, and social controversies in modern societies. A normative account of democratic legitimacy evokes the ideals of rational legislation, participatory politics, and civic self-government, all based on the philosophical principle of respect for persons. The prominence of respect as a basis for deliberative democracy is grounded in a Kantian view of people as ends, not means (Chambers, 1996). Furthermore, the legitimacy of laws and public institutions is not merely based on consent; rather it assumes a form of autonomous consent that is both reasoned and deliberative.

Discourse Procedures and Democratic Legitimacy

In his detailed and exhaustive critique of modern social philosophy and the social sciences, Jurgen Habermas (1984, 1987, 1990, 1996) develops a complex set of ideas that include rational, communicative, universal, and empirical mechanisms that serve as foundations for the ideal speech situation, communicative action, and discourse ethics (see White, 1995). Habermas's writings on the public sphere and communicative action are similar to the renewed interest in the United States on civil society and democratic participation (Putnam, 1993; Gutmann and Thompson, 1996). In addition to Habermas, several contemporary philosophers and social scientists have taken up an interest in participation and deliberation since the 1980s (see Bohm and Rehg, 1997). The controversies that exist in the area of deliberative democracy are not so much about how democratic participation provides for a legitimate expression of the will of the people in comparison to simple aggregative voting, as about the procedural constraints and goals that are required to direct the deliberative process.

The concept of children and youth as either capable of deliberative practices or entitled to participate in a process of democratic discourse may not appear reasonable on first hearing. Indeed, the CRC articles specifying the participation rights of the child are among the most controversial aspects of the Convention. Articles 12–15 on the rights to express opinions, to access information, and to enjoy freedom of thought and association have been slow to gain acceptance from parents, teachers, and other adult citizens. The idea of political rights for children requires a concept of the child as capable and competent, rather than needy and helpless; it also requires adults to accept children as active and valuable members of society. The principles and articles of the CRC do not relate exclusively to needs, but rather give appropriate recognition to the existing and emerging capacities of children and youth to express themselves and to contribute actively to their own well-being. They further hold that children are not to be diminished in their civil status because of their inherent physical and psychological vulnerabilities, their relative lack of experience, their social and economic dependency, and their need for support and guidance from family and other adults. Nor are they to be given the same liberties or obligations as adults. Rather, the participation rights recognize the importance of consistent and reliable support and guidance from adults in the exercise of children's emerging capacity for participation (Hart, 1992). The social and developmental significance of participation rights in the CRC is that it provides the foundation for integrating children and youth into the family, community, and nation by placing emphasis on their evolving capacities rather than their special needs.

Hence the concept of children as citizens – exercising the right to participate with adults in the deliberative activities of the democratic process – is the catalyst for achieving personal and socially sustainable well-being.

Procedural Equality and Deliberative Capability

Regardless of the specific rules or goals that theorists may require to assess the intrinsic or extrinsic value of a deliberative process, the standard of equality remains crucial. The issue of procedural equality can be stated simply as that of equal opportunity to speak and be heard. But that is not sufficient. For reasons similar to those that led us to incorporate the capability approach of Amartya Sen into our theoretical and empirical approaches to child development (Earls and Carlson, 1995), other social theorists concerned with adult deliberative process also have turned to Sen. The application of Sen's capability approach to the substantive evaluation of procedural equality in discourse exposes the weakness of equal opportunity as a concept. Bohman (1997) and Knight and Johnson (1997) contend that theories of deliberation must have more demanding requirements of political equality, to avoid favoring "the virtuous, the well educated or the better off." Bohman (1997) argues for a minimal threshold (as well as a ceiling) for a citizen to be capable of adequate political functioning. Knight and Johnson (1997) stress the importance of equal opportunity to influence one another, as well as the difficulty of measuring politically relevant capacities in actual political equality. Our interest in children of different ages engaged in deliberative activities requires a substantive evaluation of their level of verbal, cognitive, and social capacities to claim true equality. Our interest in incorporating Sen's capability approach into issues of child development precedes our application of Habermas's discourse procedures to children, and we take seriously the caution of measuring genuine equality. The power of capability theory to address adult capacities and rights illustrates the application of these same concepts to deliberative competencies of children.

Amartya Sen (1982, 1984, 1987, 1992, 1993, 1997) has written extensively on the ethical and instrumental shortcomings of modern utilitarianism and neoclassical economics as approaches to distribution of opportunities and resources in societies. He asks: Do people have access to resources or options that allow them to pursue their objectives, given the capacities they possess (and value), to function in many different domains? Thus, capability theory adds an important new dimension to the discussion of well-being and distributive justice beyond that of satisfaction/utility or of primary goods on which classical and modern utilitarian and liberal theories are founded.

Sen's capability approach begins with the concept of functionings, recognizing that needs and capacities of individuals vary considerably within a population and that the distribution of resources must be made accordingly rather than merely proposing equal distribution. *Functionings* are defined as the various things an individual may value doing or being and provides for an important new dimension for evaluating the physical and psychological capacities of individuals, which may vary as a function of age, experience, state of health, and so forth. For our purposes, the concept of functionings provides a basis for considering children and youth's developmental status, which in the CRC means "evolving capacities." A second important concept is that of capability sets, which are represented by the collections of different material and social resources (or options) that allow the expression of specific functionings. Important in this conception is the understanding that functionings and resources must correspond to valued functionings to be recognized as significant within the capability framework. For example, the lack of books in the capability set of a literate person represents a deprivation in that the functioning of reading cannot be expressed or practiced without written materials. Given the overwhelming evidence for cortical and/or sensitive periods early in neural and behavioral development, the distribution of family, community, national, and global resources with respect to the age distribution of a population attains major significance (Carlson, Earls, and Todd, 1988; Earls and Carlson, 1993). The synthetic framework of the CRC, communicative action, and the capability approach that we use to guide our theory and practice permit consideration of emergent functionings that permit children of different ages to engage effectively in deliberative activities that impact their development and well-being.

Table 4.1 illustrates several types of capacities that contribute important functionings for which there should be appropriate sets of resources and opportunities from which children can select to support and elaborate these deliberative functionings. These include expressive and receptive language skills, social and emotional skills to build trust, to have confidence to express, to criticize and persist, to accept criticism, to express feelings and wishes, to command, to resist, to allow, to forbid, and to explain. These skills can be cultivated through rearing practices and social activities of families, in the curricula of schools, and in the engagement of communities in the lives of children. Finally, the importance of recognizing children's right to engage in deliberative activities with adults concerning issues that impact on their lives is based on both (1) the *extrinsic* (and instrumental) value due to the greater insight available to adults into the child's well-being that can be obtained through their participation and (2) the *intrinsic* value that

Table 4.1 Development of Deliberative Capability – Sen[a]

Deliberative Well-Being	Deliberative Freedoms	Well-Being Achievements
Deliberative functionings (DF)	**Deliberative capability sets (DCS)**	**Deliberative capabilities**
DF 1 Linguistic	DCS 1 Linguistic	Linguistic
a. Expressive	a. Time for discourse	a. Ability to communicate
b. Receptive	b. Space for discourse	b. Ability to convince
DF 2 Cognitive	c. Responsive speakers	c. Ability to argue
a. Critical	d. Attentive listeners	Cognitive
b. Perceptual	DCS 2 Cognitive	a. Ability to understand
c. Decision-making	a. Exposure to information	(facts, norms, feelings)
d. Comprehension	b. Exposure to varied viewpoints	b. Ability to agree
DF 3 Emotional/motivational	DCS 3 Emotional/motivational	c. Ability to doubt
a. Initiative	a. Adult guidance	d. Perspective-taking ability
b. Confidence	b. Adult encouragement	e. Decision-making capability
c. Expressive		Emotional/motivational
d. Curiosity		a. Capacity to evoke trust
e. Trust		b. Capacity to evoke respect
f. Security		c. Capacity for trust
g. Intentional		d. Capacity for respect
		e. Capacity for action
		f. Capacity for restraint

(Centre divider, read vertically: AGENCY CHOICE)

[a] A synthesis of Sen's (1993) capability approach (in which he specifies that valuable human functionings, in relation to capability sets, permit and support the expression of these latent functions into achieved functionings) with Habermas's (1984, 1987) requirements for ideal discourse among adults. We have proposed a grouping of potential deliberative capacities for children (based on Habermas, 1984, 1987; Bohman, 1997) necessary for effective deliberation.

deliberative experiences can have for the development of competence and confidence of children.

Adolescents as Collaborators: A Case Study

Against this paradigm shift in how children and youth are treated in research, the challenge is to enlist youth in the research context as citizens. As adults, we could lay claim to their rights to participate as citizens, but the goal is to transform these young people from children to child–citizens. The process requires tolerance, patience, and above all comfort with ourselves as authority figures. Until the youth adopted the concept in their definition of well-being, "authority figure" was not a salient feature of our self-perception. That is, as we focused on them as children, they were fixed on us as authority figures. Achieving a citizen-to-citizen relationship with our subjects was a precondition for all subsequent research activities. There were no directions, no formulae, no literature to guide us in this process. For the most part, the goal had to be pursued intuitively with an understanding of the need for informal modes of interaction. Whereas one of us leaned toward being more formal, structured, and goal-driven, the other was less reserved in manner, relating personal anecdotes about our lives as parents and formerly as children. We both understood that trust and respect were necessary before shared understanding could be achieved. Over time, we called and met their parents, dropped them off at home after meetings, called them long distance about important matters, established e-mail exchanges, and occasionally took them to dinner and invited them to visit our home. These activities were approached in the context of a job, for which both we and the children were paid. The young citizens were no less (and no more) focused and persistent than the average adult working with us. For all of the preparatory time in getting to know each other, we achieved a great deal in a short period.

As a result of this process (and in a matter of weeks) we witnessed changes in the posture, attitude, and assertiveness of these young people – changes that mark their crossing the threshold of citizenship. There is the risk that citizenship can be a bland concept, an abstraction sufficiently remote from day-to-day reality as to render it virtually useless to teenagers, whom most adults perceive as bored and uninterested. This awareness led us to establish the moment of citizenship as the beginning of engagement in the research process.

Within a period of 6 weeks the young citizens established themselves as researchers. Their introduction to social science research occurred in two ways: First, they were situated in our research offices in Chicago, where they witnessed a cadre of 50 people engaged in the day-to-day running of a social science project. Second, they were given formal presentations about the study and participated in numerous discussions about the mechanics of social science research. We emphasized that theory preceded method and procedure. Several dialogue sessions were devoted to understanding why children felt insecure, why so many children lived in disadvantaged circumstances, and why the opinions and voices of children were generally considered unimportant. The 8 to 10 hours of discourse devoted to these themes yielded a positive result.

Once consensus was reached on the focus and content of a theory from the children's perspective, the group sought to develop a method to test their ideas. The effort to derive a theory was well worth the time and may have been a key event sustaining the group in pursuing its goal of producing a research product. In the process the group moved from mutual trust to shared understanding. We consider the methods, analysis, and interpretation of data generated from this child-initiated theory as reaching a new level of validity, and it is this aspect of the work that we denote *democratic legitimacy*. In an experiment approaching the child as citizen, we report a satisfactory measure of success. Even before the internship ended, we began considering replication and strategies to take the process to a systems level.

Because there was no blueprint to create the space and tolerance required for a child-initiated process, achieving this capacity relies heavily on the adult's skill to step back without disengaging. As indicated by our very close monitoring of the day-to-day organization and activities of the Young Citizens' Program, the requirement to remain engaged is by far the most demanding. Two essential features are important to understand what child initiation means. First, adults must provide some structure to kindle the motivation and provide incentives for children to initiate. In the context of our research study the purposes and design of the work provided sufficient structure. Second, we discovered the importance of having an adult present. Good guidance, like good nutrition, had to be a regular and engaging affair. Somewhat surprisingly, we learned that it was all too easy to overestimate the children's readiness to keep activities moving forward when an adult partner was temporarily absent. Another surprising aspect of this experience was the frequency of absenteeism, despite the children's loss of salary. Apparently, the need for free time was more important to them.

Our objectives are guided by a set of four specific questions: First, given our intent to engage adolescents as collaborators, how could we gauge their levels of participation? Hart's ladder of participation (Figure 4.1, introduced later) represents a convenient conceptual device, but putting it into practice is another matter. Second, how genuine is youth participation? That is, how interested and committed are the youth to the project and its purposes? Are they working toward increasing their understanding of the problems under consideration? Are the adults really allowing sufficient space for child initiation? Is there mutual respect? Has trust developed? Third, in what ways do young citizens and adult researchers benefit from engaging adolescents as collaborators, and how does one best measure these benefits? Finally, what will it take to bring this kind of activity to scale?

The Application of Capability and the Practice of Discourse Ethics

During the past few years we have become engaged in several long-term discourse sessions deliberating various themes of child well-being by following the communicative ethics procedures of Habermas. In the first effort, we engaged the staff and parents of a child and family service organization (based in a Mexican American community in Chicago) in a series of sessions on the roles of academics, service providers, and parents in detecting, evaluating, and responding to stress in the lives of young children. Encouraged by the successful application of these dialogue principles with adults, we recruited four high school students, ranging in age from 13 to 17, from different neighborhoods and schools across the city. At the end of the first year, we added a new group of six high school students to the original group of four. These 10 students, along with one adult facilitator (and our occasional visits, conference calls, and constant contact with the facilitator), sustained a summer program for 8 weeks. These young citizens (YCs), three of whom had reached their 18th birthday, along with the adult facilitator engaged in dialogues as the primary approach to developing a sense of citizenship and becoming familiar with the specific articles of the CRC. They convened at the PHDCN office for 20 hours a week with the goal of learning about child rights and using a deliberative approach in designing a social science project to figure out how to measure the well-being of other YCs in Chicago. The rules established for deliberation, derived from Habermas's precepts, included mutual respect, perspective taking, mutual understanding, and social action. The youth began their dialogues with a comprehensive study of the CRC, but with the shared goal of developing their own theory of well-being, a set of companion research questions, and a measure of well-being to collect data from other YCs around the city. Once data were collected, they agreed to analyze, interpret, and summarize their findings in collaboration with the facilitator and us.

During the 2–3 hours of open-ended dialogue they had each day over the first week, they became acquainted with each other and each others'

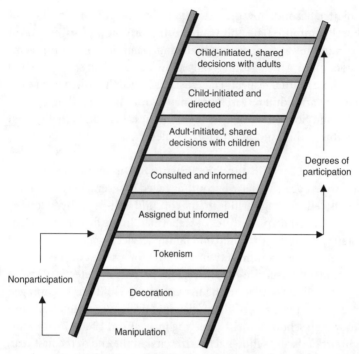

Figure 4.1. The ladder metaphor is based on the adaptation by Hart (1992) of Arristein's levels of adult participation. The first three rungs represent levels of nonparticipation, followed by increasing levels of child–adult engagement. Note that the highest level of participation is child-initiated but decisions are shared with adults.

families, schools, and neighborhoods; at the same time, they debated what the individual articles of the CRC meant to them. They frequently used Roger Hart's Ladder of Participation (Figure 4.1) to evaluate the deliberative process over the 8-week period and referred to whether they were at a low level, "informed but not consulted," or working toward the highest level, "child initiated, adult-supported." In addition to using the ladder in reference to the adults' respect for their equality in the group, they often referred to disrespect or coercion from other YCs or the 18-year-olds (Young Adult Citizens) in the group. Overall, in their self-evaluations at the end of the Program, they reported that mutual respect and equality guided the group process.

Given the major concern of deliberation theorists about the hazards of cultural diversity for successful deliberation, it is notable that age, sex, ethnic, and educational differences did not create problems. Instead, differences in outgoing versus reserved personalities became the greatest obstacle to group exchanges. Discourse involves working out differences through a noncoercive exchange of reasons. Facilitating this process requires time and effort. Some issues required several weeks of discussion before they were resolved, such as whether the Standard of Living (Article 27) was more important than issues of Juvenile Justice (Article 40). Lively exchanges of ideas notwithstanding, all the YCs argued that rationality would be decisive in setting differences.

A second important aspect of the YC deliberations was perspective taking. This was established as they came to appreciate the value of understanding their diverse backgrounds and sharing common concerns about the lives of adolescents in Chicago. Unanimously, they felt oppressed by the threats of drugs and violence that plagued their neighborhoods and schools. As part of the formal structure of the Program, we began the first week by showing a UNICEF film, *Raised Voices,* in which young people in the United States, Brazil, the United Kingdom, and South Africa engaged in activities that demonstrate the application of participation rights. This appeared to have a lasting impression on the group as they worked within the CRC framework, reflecting frequently on the fact that only U.S. and Somalian youth were unprotected by CRC ratification. With appreciation for the group's diversity, we exposed them to the life experiences of groups different from them through videos. The film documentary version of Nicholas Lehman's *Promised Land* tells the story of African American migration from Mississippi to Chicago, followed by segregation into public housing projects. This account provided an important new perspective to the YCs, including those living in the Robert Taylor Homes (a large public housing complex of high-rise buildings), who had not known about the coercive political actions behind their construction (and now their demolition).

We also showed the fictionalized film *El Norte,* which described the migration of adolescents from Guatemala and Mexico, and Irving Stone's *Heaven and Earth,* a story of a Vietnamese girl who experienced war in her village and later immigrated to the United States. These videos encouraged them to think about contemporary Chicago from a historical perspective and to appreciate the diversity of perspectives that exist in a major U.S. city. These films gave them an expanded perspective to evaluate the significance of the 40 articles of the CRC and provided a context for them to work toward a consensus about how they would choose to measure the well-being of other YCs in Chicago.

Their exercise in using deliberative procedures to reach mutual understanding (ranging from compromise to consensus across different issues) focused on ranking the 40 articles of the CRC in order of importance. This was at times an exercise in *judging* what was important to them personally versus what might be important to the group as a whole, or to other YCs across the city. Rather than trying to find a unanimous ranking through dialogue, they decided to vote on the 40 articles. Because their initial voting plan did not restrict the number of votes an individual could cast, some voted for 4 articles and others voted for as many 16 of the 40 articles. On applying the votes, they observed that three or four of the articles had noticeably more votes than others. When we questioned the legitimacy of some YCs' having more votes, they agreed to revote, restricting the number of votes to no more than six per person. Using this aggregative approach, they narrowed the choice to the top 20 articles, then resumed the deliberative process to decide whether and how they might use the CRC to develop their theory about the important dimensions of well-being for all Chicago YCs. This interchange of deliberative and aggregative exercises in an effort to arrive at mutual understanding is itself an important lesson in the greater authority and rationality of the deliberative approach. Although the YCs below the age of 18 are denied the right to vote, they experienced the power of deliberation as a political mechanism that is available to children of all ages.

Finally, in the last few weeks they arrived at a strategy to satisfy the special interests of different group members (and their corresponding views of how other YCs would see it) to capture the depth and the range of dimensions of well-being reflected in the CRC. They reached a consensus that the most significant aspect of their lives concerned their relationships with adults, whom they preferred to describe as "authority figures." The three most important authority figures for their well-being are parents, teachers, and police officers.

In continuing sessions, the group decided to develop a questionnaire asking other YCs to rank the role of these authority figures in the articles of the CRC that they deemed most important as a group (e.g., protection from violence, protection from drugs, respect for opinions, respect for privacy, amount of time spent in conversation with them). They worked with the research staff of PHDCN to format and carefully word the questions and printed copies to prepare for their fieldwork. With cooperation from the Chicago Park District, they were able to interview about 70 YCs in the summer recreation programs in different areas of the city. Preliminary analyses of these data show that the support available from parents, teachers, and police officers declines significantly from 13 to 17 years of age and for both sexes. Given the established legitimacy of this questionnaire, it will be formally tested for its reliability and validity as we plan for its broader use.

An important conclusion from this work on child rights is that these YCs did not view lack of involvement with authority figures as the basis for their insecurity and feelings of marginalization. This appreciation for the importance of adult engagement, support, and protection as children grow up in a threatening urban environment is consistent with the provisions of the CRC. The extension of rights to children is not intended to produce liberated youth; rather, the goal of this social movement is to elevate the fundamental importance of children's and youth's participating with adults in a common search for well-being.

Next Steps and Future Implications

Sen's capability theory provides the foundation for the Human Development Index (HDI), which is reported on an annual basis by the United Nations Development Programme (1993). The HDI is formulated to reflect two interrelated components: the formation of capabilities in the form of good health, literacy, knowledge and skills, and satisfactory standard of living; and the level of achievement people can acquire (within available resources) through these capabilities in economic productivity, creativity, and political and social activity. The first component is indexed by years of life expectancy, the second by educational achievement; the third component is indexed by a measure of purchasing power. The HDI combines these indicators into a compound index that is used to rank nations. It can also be adapted to compare levels of development within a given society by disaggregating the overall index by sex, region, urban–rural locale, and so on. The HDI is a crude indicator of quality of life or standard of living, yet it represents a highly significant departure from economic indicators that are based solely on income and economic productivity.

As far as we are aware, the HDI has not been disaggregated according to the period of the life span. Our point of departure is to recognize the confluence of capability theory and communicative action as stepping stones into the worlds of young people. By describing research in Chicago, we aim to adapt and refine the theoretical underpinnings of HDI and apply these to the lives of adolescents. If our developmental assumptions are correct, at both the individual and collective levels, then an Adolescent Development Index (ADI) should be a sensitive indicator of the quality of life, well-being, and standard of living. It might also serve as an indicator of the future social and economic vitality of a population.

We agree with the conclusion of the 1993 HDI report that "people's participation is the central issue of our time." This phenomenon is reflected

in increasingly decentralized governance, the empowerment of local community organizations, and expanding markets. This recognition means that
the impulse for participation must be thoroughly understood and *nurtured*.
The research programs described here are responsive to this goal. Through
a focus on adolescents, we underscore the importance of civic education as
an essential ingredient in the successful transition from childhood to adulthood. If our assumption that participation increases a sense of control and
predictability of one's environment is correct, then it should be recognized
as a fundamental part of personal fulfillment. Preparation for this kind of
civic engagement represents the highest form of well-being.

The utility of the human capability perspective is that it encompasses
how people decide to use their abilities as well as their usefulness to society.
The higher individuals' capability, the more valuable they are to the collective capabilities of their society. Thus, the objectives of a democratic system
are to expand the range of people's choices to make societal development
simultaneously more participatory and more equitable. It is in this sense
that the deliberative approach is distinct from liberal and utilitarian (and
communitarian) theories, for it does not support the unrestricted satisfaction of individual choices but requires respect for everybody's potential,
needs, and interests. It is in this aspect of theory that we find the interface
with dialogic and other nonaggregative processes most compelling. Again,
we emphasize the critical nature of the adolescent period of the life cycle
for building and consolidating the skills required for personal fulfillment
and democratic participation. Now, in the widest sense of the concept of
health promotion, we are prepared to advance an agenda requiring multiple
sectors of society to join forces to secure the lives of the future generations.

There have been many special moments spent with these young citizens,
and the only reason to hesitate in describing these in detail is that it would
make us less rigorous, more subjective, and thus less convincing than we
might be otherwise. Yet these types of data are so compelling that their
inclusion illustrates how profound can be the total experience of being a
social scientist. We choose one snapshot from many experiences to indicate
its especially enduring place in our intellectual memory.

The event was an intimate walk through an urban park on a Saturday
midday. We had breakfast at the local restaurant with two of the Young
Citizens. On our way to drop them off at home we passed by a large park. It
was July. The green of the park and the warmth of that day evoked an impulse
to stop the car and take a stroll in the park. This spontaneous decision made
immediate sense to all four of us. We walked rather aimlessly for the next

hour. Nothing of any great magnitude happened on this walk, yet it was an event of importance for each of us. For the adults, it confirmed that we were positive authority figures. In fact, it made us more than "figures": It made us simply older people enjoying and showing deep respect for younger people. One youth pointed to a ball field where he had played some intense games; the other talked about a family crisis that had seriously undermined her schoolwork. We thought simultaneously about once being teenagers, being the parents of teenagers, and now being social scientists–authority figures to these teenagers.

This incident represents as good an example as we can imagine of what it means for adults and children to experience citizenship. It was a fine moment, one that we think exemplifies the highest state of well-being. It was no meager achievement; indeed, a great deal of effort had gone into creating the possibility for such a shared experience. It is the type of experience that any social scientist should have. As important as acquiring the skills of sampling, protocol construction and testing, securing of informed consent, conducting of statistical analyses, and publishing of papers, we would argue, is walking in the park.

REFERENCES

Aries, P. (1962). *Centuries of Childhood.* New York: Vintage.

Benson, P. L., Leffert, N., Scales, P. C., and Blyth, D. A. (1998). Beyond the 'village' rhetoric: Creating healthy communities for children and adolescents. *Applied Developmental Science,* 2(3), 138–159.

Bohman, J. (1997). Deliberative Democracy and Effective Social Freedoms: Freedom, Capacities, Resources and Opportunities, In J. Bohman and W. Rehg (Eds.), *Deliberative Democracy: Essays on Reason and Politics* (pp. 243–277). Cambridge, MA: MIT Press.

Bohman, J., and Rehg, W. (1997). *Deliberative Democracy: Essays on Reason and Politics.* Cambridge, MA: MIT Press.

Buka, S., and Earls, F. (1993). Early Determinants of Delinquency and Violence. *Health Affairs,* 12, 46–64.

Carlson, M., Earls, F., and Todd, R. D. (1988). The Importance of Regressive Changes in the Development of the Nervous System: Towards a Neurobiological Theory of Child Development. *Psychiatric Developments,* 6, 1–22.

Chambers, S. (1995). Discourse and Democratic Practices. In S. K. White (Ed.), *The Cambridge Companion to Habermas* (pp. 233–259). Cambridge: Cambridge University Press.

Chambers, S. (1996). *Reasonable Democracy: Jürgen Habermas and the Politics of Discourse.* Ithaca, NY: Cornell University Press.

Dahl, R. A. (1966). Further Reflections on the "Elitist Theory of Democracy." *American Political Science Review,* 9, 296–306.

Earls, F. (1991). Not Fear, nor Quarantine, but Science: Preparation for a Decade of Research to Advance Knowledge about the Control of Violence in Youth. *Journal of Adolescent Health*, 12, 619–629.

Earls, F. (1994). Violence and Today's Youth. *The Future of Children*, 4(3), 4–23.

Earls, F., and Carlson, M. (1993). Towards Sustainable Development for American Families. *Daedalus*, 122, 93–121.

Earls, F., and Carlson, M. (1995). Promoting Human Capability as an Alternative to Early Crime Prevention. In P.-O. Wiktrom, R. V. Clarke, and J. McCord (Eds.), *Integrating Crime Prevention Strategies* (pp. 141–168). Stockholm: National Council for Crime Prevention.

Earls, F., and Reiss, A. (1994). *Breaking the Cycle*. Washington, DC: National Institute of Justice.

Federal Interagency Committee on Child and Family Statistics. (1997). *America's Children: Key National Indicators of Their Well-Being*. Washington, DC: U.S. Government Printing Office.

Gutmann, A., and Thompson, D. (1996). *Democracy and Disagreement*. Cambridge, MA: Belknap/Harvard University Press.

Habermas, J. (1979). *Communication and the Evolution of Society*. Boston: Beacon Press.

Habermas, J. (1984). *The Theory of Communicative Action*. Vol. 1. *Reason and the Rationalization of Society*. Boston: Beacon Press.

Habermas, J. (1987). *The Theory of Communicative Action*. Vol. 2. *Lifeworld and System: A Critique of Functionalist Reason*. Boston: Beacon Press.

Habermas, J. (1990). *Moral Consciousness and Communicative Action*. Cambridge, MA: MIT Press.

Habermas, J. (1996). *Between Fact and Norms: Contributions to a Discourse Theory of Law and Democracy*. Cambridge, MA: MIT Press.

Hart, R. A. (1992). *Children's Participation: From Tokenism to Citizenship*. Florence: Innocenti Essays, UNICEF.

Knight, J., and Johnson, J. (1997). What Sort of Equality Does Deliberative Democracy Require? In J. Bohman and W. Rehg (Eds.), *Deliberative Democracy: Essays on Reason and Politics* (pp. 279–319). Cambridge, MA: MIT Press.

Marshall, T. H. (1963). *Sociology at the Cross Roads*. London: Heinemann.

Pal, D. (1996). Quality of Life in Children: A Review of Conceptual and Methodological Issues in Multidimensional Health Status Measures. *Journal of Epidemiology & Community Health*, 50, 391–396.

Pateman, C. (1970). *Participation and Democratic Theory*. Cambridge: Cambridge University Press.

Putnam, R. D. (1993). *Making Democracy Work: Civic Traditions in Modern Italy*. Princeton, NJ: Princeton University Press.

Sampson, R., Morenoff, J., and Earls, F. (1999). Beyond Social Capital: Spatial Dynamics of Collective Efficacy for Children. *American Sociological Review*, 64, 633–660.

Scales, P. C., and Leffert, N. (1994). *Developmental Assets: A Synthesis of the Scientific Research on Adolescent Development*. Minneapolis, MN: Search Institute.

Schumpeter, J. A. (1943). *Capitalism, Socialism and Democracy*. London: Allen & Unwin.

Selner-O'Hagan, MB, Kindlon, D. J., Buka, S. L., Raudenbush, S. W., and Earls, F. (1998). Assessing Exposure to Violence in Urban Youth. *Journal of Child Psychology & Psychiatry*, 39, 215–224.

Sen, A. K. (1982). Rational Fools: A Critique of the Behavioral Foundations of Economic Theory. In A. K. Sen (Ed.), *Choice, Welfare and Measurement* (pp. 84–106). Cambridge, MA: MIT Press.

Sen, A. K. (1984). Rights and Capabilities. In A. K. Sen (Ed.), *Resources, Values and Development.* Cambridge, MA: Harvard University Press.

Sen, A. K. (1987). *On Ethics and Economics.* Cambridge: Basil Blackwell.

Sen, A. K. (1992). *Inequality Reexamined.* Cambridge, MA Cambridge, UK: Harvard University Press.

Sen, A. K. (1993). Capability and Well-Being. In M. Nussbaum & A. K. Sen (Eds.), *The Quality of Life* (pp. 30–53). Oxford: Clarendon Press.

Sen, A. K. (1997). *Economic Inequality.* Oxford: Clarendon Press.

Tonry, M., Ohlin, L. E., Adams, K., Earls, F., Rowe, D. C., Sampson, R. J., and Tremblay, R. J. (1991). *Human Development and Criminal Behavior: New Ways of Advancing Knowledge.* New York: Springer-Verlag.

United Nations Development Programme. (1993). *Human Development Report.* New York: Oxford University Press.

U.S. Federal Interagency Forum on Child and Family Statistics. (1997). *America's Children: Key National Indicators of Well-Being.* Federal Interagency Forum on Child and Family Statistics. Washington, DC: U.S. Government Printing Office.

White, S. K. (1995). *The Cambridge Companion to Habermas.* Cambridge: Cambridge University Press.

WHOQOL Group. (1995). *World Health Organization Quality of Life Scale – 100.* Geneva: World Health Organization.

III

URBAN YOUTH EXPERIENCES IN
CROSS-CULTURAL PERSPECTIVE

5 Have Cities Ceased to Function as "Integration Machines" for Young People?

Wilhelm Heitmeyer

Freedom from physical and psychological harm is not only a primary requirement for the well-being of young people, but an essential precondition to prevent violent behavior (see Ramphele, this volume). Whether this central aspect of youth well-being can be developed and maintained depends on complex socialization and integration processes. Individual socialization must involve emotional security and acceptance, and social integration must guarantee unconstrained access to the education system and labor market. Together, these institutions are essential to ensure a sense of belonging and equal participation in public life. Especially important, youth must perceive themselves as members of groups, milieus, or ethnic communities with equal rights.

For young people living in the Federal Republic of Germany, social advancement through education, access to good jobs, and social security could once be taken for granted. Yet in contemporary German society, growing numbers of youth are resorting to criminality and violence because their exposure to urban social, occupational, and political disintegration involves various forms of social exclusion, destabilization of life contexts, and emotional rejection. Growing numbers of young people respond to these developments by resorting to violence as a way of establishing their membership, recognition, and status. That this trend is particularly strong in cities creates great doubts about the city's ability to fulfill its former function as a robust integration machine, while also ensuring peaceful coexistence among groups of differing social status or ethnic origin.

Translated from the German by Jonathan Harrow at the University of Bielefeld, Germany.

In this chapter I consider whether the city, long heralded as an "integration machine," can continue to produce social cohesion in the face of population diversification through immigration coupled with poor economic performance and strained systems of social support. After reviewing recent trends in social exclusion and violence among youth in German cities, I propose strategies for dealing with the spatial concentration of disadvantaged youth.

Have Integration Problems Increased?

With the current pressure of chronic high unemployment, almost 50% of the working population now expect that their own children will not attain the same social status or material prosperity as their parents (see the opinion survey reported in Die Zeit, 1998). Anticipated social decline and the fear of uncertain social integration are accompanied by negative expectations regarding the ability of the social, economic, and political system to protect citizens from the myriad hazards of life (Figure 5.1). Expectations about the future are even more negative among those who have frail protection against risks such as illness or unemployment (Bulmahn, 1997:8).

Young people also have similar expectations regarding their future as mature adults. Repeated surveys on how individuals view their future prospects over recent decades revealed a different picture at the end of the 1990s that departed from the secular trend (Jugendwerk der Deutschen Shell, 1981, 1985, 1992). For many years, youth viewed the future of society rather pessimistically (because of changing threats such as war and environmental catastrophes), but individual prospects optimistically. This changed during the late 1990s, as the majority of youth were pessimistic about both social and individual prospects for the future. Even 12- to 14-year-olds, who are too young to worry about starting working life, fear unemployment (Jugendwerk der Deutschen Shell, 1997:13). This trend is particularly strong among youth living in eastern Germany as well as among Turkish migrant youth. Although disparities in education between German youth and those of other nationality groups, particularly Turkish youth, have always existed, these have grown since the mid-1990s (Beauftragte der Bundesregierung, 1997). Growing educational inequality reduces youth's chances of integration and possibilities for social advancement. At the same time, problems of self-ethnification, of a return to dependence on the group of ethnic origins, have increased. Assuming that a modern society must be able to integrate all of its members, these trends bode ill for German youth.

Several mechanisms determine the capacity of modern societies to achieve full social integration. One is *access to functional systems*, particularly

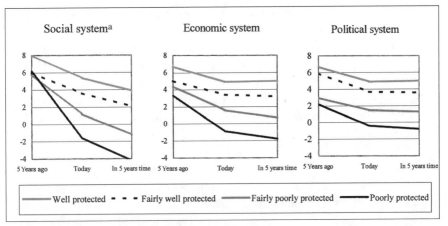

Figure 5.1. Perceptions of the risk protection provided by German social, economic, and political systems, past, present, and future. Means on a scale from −10 to +10. [a]Rated according to responses to the item "How well do you think you will be protected in the future against illness, old age, and unemployment?" *Source: Allgemeine Bevölkernungsumfrage der Sozialwissenschaften (ALLBUS). 1996. Mannheim.*

the labor system. Recent trends reveal that large groups are less able to attain any stable integration in the market and that that lack generates problems of recognition and economy security. The youth unemployment rate has also increased continuously in recent years. In western Germany the unemployment rate of 15- to 19-year-olds rose from 5.5% to 9.4% between 1992 and 1998, and for 20- to 24-year-olds, it increased from 6.2% to 10.8%. Youth unemployment in the eastern part of the country was higher still, rising from 9.6% to 15.0% for 15- to 19-year-olds and from 16.4% to 21.7% for 20- to 24-year-olds over this period (Amtliche Nachrichten der Bundesanstalt für Arbeit, 1996–1999). Joblessness is particularly high among foreign-born youth, as one-third of non-German youth have no vocational training, and 83% of these youth lack formal school qualifications and do not complete vocational training (BMBF, 1999). Youth from the former Soviet Union as well as all young persons with little or no academic qualifications experience similar problems.

Integration in modern societies also requires *compensatory social policies.* However, there are clear indications that the economically generated social polarization into poor and rich is no longer balanced out as the welfare state breaks down. For social integration prospects, this means that major cracks are appearing in the foundations of legitimization as social injustices become pervasive. Approximately 15% and 22% of youth in western and eastern Germany, respectively, are poor, and currently one in five children and adolescents is growing up in poverty (Bundeszentral für politische Bildung, 1997:523).

A basis of *shared values and norms* is also of great importance for social consensus. Although increasing pluralization has many advantages and leads to increases in freedom, it also reduces certainty about which norms are binding and which are open to discussion. This uncertainty becomes apparent in the enormous increase in crime rates among 14- to 18-year-olds and 18- to 21-year-olds, particularly in eastern Germany (Pfeiffer et al., 1998:11).

Safeguarding stable social memberships is a crucial part of the integration process. Recent trends reveal disintegration in many social institutions, such as the family, even as "new" memberships as functional substitutes remain vague. Such institutional disintegration processes lead to problems of acceptance and emotional insecurity. Divorce rates have risen continuously, and during the 1980s one in three marriages ended in divorce, with attendant strains on children and adolescents (Schäfers, 1998:144).

Participation in social life is a fifth requirement for social integration. However, recent trends reveal declining trust of and indifference toward central institutions. Polls reveal that the general public no longer feels able to change or influence societal ills or feels excluded altogether. This perceived helplessness is especially visible in migrant communities. That many political institutions are losing credibility is evident in both the rising number of youth who do not vote and the increases in the numbers who support antidemocratic, extreme right-wing organizations, particularly in eastern Germany. These recent trends reveal that society is confronted with significant barriers to social integration.

Two structural considerations are also important to an appreciation of the current social context and the new integration challenges confronting youth. The first concerns the modernization processes that, from an economic perspective, are determined increasingly by the logic of new maxims of deregulation and flexibility that can be denoted *disintegrative capitalism*. Concurrently, the two-sided nature of individualization processes needs to be understood. Increasing freedom to shape one's path through life is also accompanied by rising obligations to do so. Although today's youth have greater autonomy when compared with earlier youth generations, they often find themselves making decisions without a clear understanding of the consequences of their choices. The breakdown of traditional norms means that youth confront new opportunities to forge better lives, but also increases their accountability for choices and their attendant consequences. Individualization means that it is no longer possible to plan one's life within the context of large-sized groups; rather, life has to be mastered against a background of crumbling social milieus that are no longer able to ensure feelings of membership or belonging. These two circumstances pose a structural dilemma: On the one hand, youth confront dynamic social trends that expand cultural opportunities to shape their lives; on the other hand, they are simultaneously faced with decreased opportunities to realize these options.

There are many signs that *ambivalence* is becoming the central life paradigm of contemporary German youth. The bright and dark sides of this development can be summarized as follows:

- Opportunities to plan one's life and the variety of options increase, but the predictability of paths through life declines.
- Opportunities to make decisions expand, but the need to make decisions also increases.
- Equality increases in some domains, augmenting individual pressure to compete for social placement and status.
- To the extent that old structures and ways of dealing with change break down and new options multiply, the need for discrimination grows.
- Emancipation from a biographical straitjacket increases the risk of losing one's social roots.
- Opportunities for greater individualistic self-expression are accompanied by a destabilization of social contexts.
- Predictability lessens even as its importance for integration remains or increases.
- The breakdown of tradition opens up new opportunities for self-expression and self-actualization, but self-evident ways of regulating conflicts are lost.

Against this background, youth socialization is characterized by complicated developmental exploration aimed at (1) developing and securing memberships and social relations, (2) acquiring status positions, (3) gaining identity-relevant competencies for action and emotional security, and (4) building concepts for planning one's life. The wide-ranging ambivalence involved in this process means that youth must anticipate completely different ways of processing problems when they arise. These may range from waiting to see what happens, to seeking help to navigate new social settings, to behaving autoaggressively and violently.

The second structural consideration that affects the integration prospects of youth stems from the political decisions and historical processes that determine options for various groups of young persons. Until 1999, this included a prevailing policy of refusing to view Germany as an immigration country and awarding citizenship according to *jus sanguinis*, or only after long waiting periods. This policy denied legal and political integration to young persons of non-German origins, who were effectively told that they did not belong, even if they had been born in Germany. Moreover, it encouraged not only offensive discrimination, but also enmity toward various sectors of the German population.

In addition, the historically unique collapse of the former German Democratic Republic (GDR) means that there are now two German societies, the eastern society exhibiting a modernization lag that continues to generate enormous integration problems for large numbers of eastern youth. The historical changes in Eastern Europe have also precipitated an influx of young migrants of German origin from the former Soviet Union, who experience growing integration problems as full members of German society.

In all, extremely complex problem states are emerging. They can be summarized as revealing that German society fails to provide sufficient access to education, work for large segments of youth, and (for migrant youth) political participation and access to legal recourse. Not only are terms of *membership* violated, but even more decisive, social *recognition* is withheld. Lacking those two critical ingredients, social membership produces destructive consequences that are either self-directed or directed at others.

Growth in violence, particularly in cities, can be viewed as a particular indicator for this situation (see Figure 5.2).[1] Although these longitudinal trends cannot be assessed reliably for eastern German society, comparisons for 1996 reveal a much higher level in violent crime compared with the western part of the country – approximately 58% higher for adolescents and 93% higher for young adults. Although such indicators must be interpreted with caution because they refer to a small segment of the young generation, the differentials indicate that violence seems to be an attractive way of attaining superiority, prestige, recognition, and membership in powerful groups (see Ransford, 1968). This is particularly so for groups that exhibit cumulative or specific experiences of exclusion or who try to process their anticipated fears through violence (see Heitmeyer et al., 1995/1998). For these youth, violence offers an attractive and tragic alternative pathway.

Of course, structural trends in society cannot be used to derive individual behavior; the numerous "moderating" factors that must be taken into account cannot be presented in detail here. Therefore, I shall limit myself to

---

[1] These increases in police statistics on suspects parallel statistics on convictions, so that findings cannot be traced back to changed control practices alone.

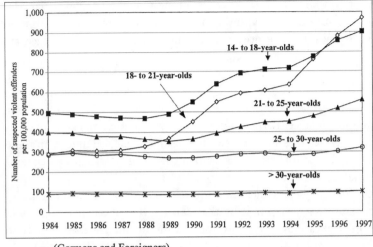

(Germans and Foreigners)

Figure 5.2. Suspected violent offenders in West Germany, 1984–1997. *Source*: Pfeiffer, Chr., Delzer, J., Enzmann, D., and Wetzels, P. 1998. *Ausgrenzung, Gewalt und Kriminalität junger Menschen.* DVJJ- Sonderdruck. Hannover: Dt. Vereinigung für Jugendgerichte und Jugendgerichtshilfen e. V.

the urban context and investigate whether and how far specific urban developments have had a major impact on the living conditions and behavior of German youth.

Contours of Urban Development: Disintegration, Misuse, Fall of Civilization

Discussions of the ability of a society to integrate all constituents and the necessary modes and structural conditions for this to occur have always assigned a major positive role to the city. Particularly for the integration of foreigners and for the peaceful coexistence of different social milieus, the city has been viewed as a robust "integration machine" based on plurality and anonymity (Häußermann, 1995:96). This concept was considered to be especially true of European cities because of their "social" characteristics. Whether it will be possible to maintain either the quality of this integration or its positive features is highly questionable in terms of general social trends in German cities.

The lure of cities has resulted in an ethnocultural heterogeneity that, in conjunction with demographic trends, will soon lead to greater shifts in the relative composition of Germany's urban population. According to Eisner (1997), this trend, coupled with its attendant consequences, began

in the 1960s, when the negative effects of individualization on social relations emerged in tandem with the onset of the economic marginalization
of more social groups. Processes of disintegration that have emerged are
largely responsible for the growth in violence throughout Europe since then,
and for increased concerns about the "end of the civilized city" (Eisner,
1997). A major reason for these growing tensions is that cohabiting with
foreigners in urban settings has also been identified as a serious problem.
Xenophobic violence, perpetrated mostly by young members of the majority society, testifies to great ethnic tensions, which Häußermann and
Oswald (1997) characterize as a sign of the "fall of urban civilization"
(9, translated).

Accordingly, there are increasing apprehensions that the structural, regulatory, and cohesion problems that can be viewed as macrotrends in
modern societies may also cause the integration machine of the city to
fail – and not just in the "uncontrollable" global cities (Heitmeyer, 1997).
Because the city no longer provides its residents with adequate access to
the functional systems of work, education, and political institutions, it
can no longer ensure subjectively satisfying residential conditions for all
population segments. Moreover, cities are increasingly unable to shape a
public forum in ways that provide opportunities for various social groups
and newcomers to become familiar with and tolerant of diverse ideas on
values and norms as a way of developing cohesion. Feldtkeller (1994) asks
whether we are facing a trend toward a "misuse of the city," whose real
social purpose has been lost (Feldtkeller, 1994:13). Is the European city of
the 21st century on a path toward the 19th century (Häußermann, 1998)?
Currently several authors are pessimistic about the prospects for cities to
function as effective integration systems. Keim (1997) discusses the decline
of urban life, a conclusion reached earlier by other authors, as in Sennett's
(1991) emphasis on cultural destruction from an American perspective.
From a French perspective, Touraine (1996:94, translated) maintains that

on the one hand, this decline of urban society favors the elites. On the other hand, it is the
reason why complete social classes are withdrawing from social life. Studies on young
beurs, French citizens of Algerian origins, have shown that they frequently no longer
identify either with France or with Algeria, but, at best, with their city, their quarter,
or the district in which they live. In extreme cases, they only continue to feel that they
are members of a group, a gang, that defines itself through rivalry or by distinguishing
of itself from another gang. In the United States and Great Britain, this phenomenon
is even more marked. Between the two opposing classes of society, we find the lower
middle class, who live in single-family houses or apartments. Their lives are restricted to

mass consumption and they do not participate in urban life either through new cultural customs or through political activity.

Such a problem description questions whether processes of social disintegration also acquire sociospatial forms in German cities, what the ecology of disintegration looks like, and what consequences are to be anticipated for community life.

Segregation and the Living Conditions of Young Persons

As a spatial form of social inequality, residential segregation implies different opportunities to access places, property, and social resources, as well as the power of definition over the aesthetics and symbols of specific locations. To understand the social and economic situation of youth in German cities in context of opportunities for integration, it is necessary to acknowledge important differences between the east and the west. Eastern Germany has a great number of single-structure housing developments called *Plattenbauten* (prefabricated buildings). Since the unification, these monotonous environments have witnessed a breakdown in social institutions and a persistent lack of training opportunities and jobs. Conditions in the city of Magdeburg illustrate the problem. Although youth under age 17 constitute about one fifth of the population (18.8%), they represent over two fifths (44.2%) of welfare recipients (Ortlepp, 1998:95). The confluence of these factors is conducive to widespread anomie and massive violence. Such housing developments are largely responsible for the high levels of violent crime in eastern Germany. This violence carries political undertones in that it is directed against the small minority of foreigners (approximately 1.8% of the residents in eastern Germany). For example, the goal of establishing "nationally liberated zones" is promoted by extreme right-wing groups in the context of family breakdown (Hefler et al., 1998:199).

Western Germany reveals three different types of urban contexts that differ from the "social flashpoints" of eastern Germany, but have similarly deleterious consequences for youth. One type results from the migration of eastern Europeans of German origin into new housing developments, facilitated by generous financial support from the government during the 1980s. Support for these migrants, which included resettlement assistance and language courses, has been drastically cut. Consequently, migration into western German cities has been declining. However, homogeneous streets of entire districts continue to draw members of this immigrant group together, resulting in segregation and ethnic isolation not yet associated with the concentrated poverty evident in comparable circumstances in the United States. Nevertheless, enormous integration problems can be anticipated among the new migrant youth generation, which are indicated by persisting language barriers (most speak Russian). Social isolation and cultural isolation are manifest in exceptionally high crime rates and group violence, which presumably emanate from "normal" life in the former Soviet Union. Because anomic tendencies and social isolation shape the living conditions of second-generation youth from the former Eastern bloc, their chances of integration are reduced enormously. Their integration prospects dim even further as their skills become increasingly inadequate for German labor markets.

A more familiar type of urban development is the traditional problem neighborhood containing a mixture of unemployment, high shares of welfare recipients, and broken families that provide inadequate emotional care and resultant academic failure. These residential areas were built as new housing schemes on the edge of major cities during the 1960s and 1970s but currently are largely neglected by urban policymakers. Many of these "fringe" developments are completely isolated from the rest of the city. In these "forgotten" settlements, violence becomes a vehicle for young residents to attract the general public's attention.

With their articulated emphasis on regional development, urban planners are conspicuous in avoiding public discussion of the social problems confronting fringe communities. Presumably, the deliberate silence prevents stigmatizing of residents of these fringe settlements. In effect, benign neglect means that few young persons can transcend these constraining environments by themselves, and only at great personal effort. Currently there exist only a handful of urban intervention programs like that in North Rhine-Westphalia, where urban districts with a particularly strong need for renewal receive special grants to promote a more integrative urban development. Meanwhile, the fate of youth and adolescents is tied to the limitations of their social worlds.

A third type of urban community emerging in the cities of western Germany is defined by structural segregation of ethnic groups. The formation of ethnic neighborhoods and communities within western German cities has generated great political concern because public leaders assume that ethnic and cultural conflicts will follow and that the integration prospects of young migrants and their offspring will be compromised. The following sections pay particular attention to the matter of ethnic residential segregation as a way of considering whether Europe's multiethnic societies "are increasingly becoming a reflection of conditions in the modern USA"

(Wilson, 1992:235, translated). Consideration of this phenomenon will reveal whether the European city has ceased to function as an integration machine.

Effects of Residential Segregation on Multiethnic Urban Society

The debate on residential segregation takes place on several levels and is highly controversial; as a result, both positive and negative appraisals abound. On the positive view, segregation represents coalitions whose common feature, according to Feldtkeller (1998:6, translated), is the "principle of avoiding disturbances.... Our city quarters...are no longer places of exchange, of interaction, of civil dealings with strangers. They have been designed as cleanly segregated islands on which each separate interest is protected as completely as possible from disturbances and bother."

The better-off milieus avoid the disturbance of poverty and cultural difference in housing choices. German natives who are already tired of or disappointed with multicultural living (partly because their paternalism is no longer appreciated by young migrants) have the option of leaving such districts and are doing so in growing numbers. Berlin-Kreuzberg, in which almost 50% of the mostly Turkish non-Germans are now unemployed, is a prime example. If they do not strive for personal integration into mainstream German society, the new migrant elites prefer undisturbed activity in segregated, homogeneous districts because this condition facilitates their political goals. And the scientific-journal community now makes a virtue out of necessity by positively evaluating ethnic and income segregation produced by powerful market transactions. However, these assessments have shaky foundations. Arguments that allegedly protect minorities by stating that there is less pressure to conform in homogeneous urban communities are erroneous because these homogenous areas register the highest levels of urban deviance. The pressure that demands conformity is greatest when opportunities to live elsewhere are limited. Elias and Scotson (1993) make this clear in their analysis of the establishment and outsiders. Yet, heterogeneous urban districts show much higher levels of integration and tolerance toward foreigners and disruptive youth than do ethnically homogeneous districts. Nonetheless, the central preconditions for integration remain the same, namely, functioning networks, coupled with a public awareness that they have not been abandoned by urban politics.

Another argument supporting segregation is the claim that there is less pressure to be upwardly socially mobile in segregated residential areas. However, this claim leads to the *mobility trap*, which states that the existence of an ethnic segment protects opportunities for advancement for this segment (see Esser, 1998:10, referring to Wiley, 1970). "Although such opportunities are often limited, from the perspective of their beneficiaries, they have the advantage that success is relatively certain, in any case, more certain than success in an institute of further education in a society that continues to be alien" (Esser 1998:10, translated). This distorted view of the alleged benefits of segregation for young migrants is strengthened even further by the illusion of sufficient work, status, and recognition within an ethnic economy (see Beauftragte der Bundesregierung für Ausländer Fragen, 1997). The long-term risk is formation of new dependencies on religious or political organizations that are hostile to integration (see Heitmeyer et al., 1997).

The paradoxical tragedy of the Turkish community in Germany needs close monitoring for all those reasons. Its large size permits the construction of an insular infrastructure that may well strengthen within-group solidarity but can undermine the critical challenge of national integration. That approximately two thirds of Turkish youth no longer seek apprenticeships in the German dual vocational training system signals a retreat from the task of integrating future generations into German mainstream society. Declining language competency among elementary school children is another troubling indicator of resistance to integration. The motive of safeguarding cultural identity through the mother tongue becomes a problem when it precludes interaction with the native population, making later integration through the labor market and other institutions more difficult if not impossible. Not surprisingly, segments of the Turkish community who can afford to do so are moving to heterogeneous residential areas both to take advantage of better opportunities afforded by integrated districts and to avoid the deleterious consequences of high ethnic residential segregation. For all of these reasons, the negative consequences for youth of segregated urban districts should not be underestimated.

Although ethnic colonies also have positive functions, "there can be no doubt that their long-term negative consequences are more severe. This is because ecological segregation frequently forms the starting point for an ethnic stratification in which the disadvantages become cemented" (Hill, 1984:369, translated). Improving daily life in the community and thus increasing cultural security often are accompanied by a deterioration of individual labor market opportunities and declining social security. This problem has only become visible in urban contexts recently because vocational qualifications of second- and third-generation migrants are inadequate for handling new technologies. The city of Frankfurt provides a particularly good example (Stadt Frankfurt, 1997:39, translated):

Among young migrants, approximately one-third are integrated into the labor market, one-third are in noncommercial, state-run vocational training, and a further third has an unclear training or employment status. It is unlikely that either the labor market or the existing training possibilities will be able to offer them any economic participation.

Currently, it is unclear whether immigrant youth will find suitable employment that provides them satisfying social placement. This reality raises questions about whether it is in the interest of foreign born youth to be ethnically encapsulated through nonresidential segregation and to face restricted job options in the ethnic economy. On the basis of recent trends, we cannot rule out the formation of an urban underclass consisting of migrant youth (Wilson, 1987).

One additional aspect of ethnic residential segregation warrants comment. In the segregated residential areas of both the prosperous and the less prosperous, the degree of homogenization makes "every irregularity seem to be a threat" (Feldtkeller, 1994:36, translated). This is because ethnic ghettos become public spaces infected with fear as avoidance leads to misunderstanding and intolerance.

Overall, the purportedly positive effects of segregation stand on shaky foundations. What results are group-specific interests that advance disintegration and encourage inward-looking closure and conflicts along the borders of urban and ethnic and mainstream communities. Sampson and Wilson's (1995) analysis shows that ethnic segregation and economic structural change in the United States produce social isolation and barriers to structural mobility, which in turn precipitate violence (see also Eisner, 1997:228). For this reason, criticism of urban policies designed to prevent segregation should be viewed with skepticism. These critics frequently claim that preventing segregation to make foreigners invisible is a form of institutional discrimination designed to preclude the development of a collective identity. However, this argument neglects that face-to-face communication necessarily decreases through mass communication, and that social mobility can undermine ethnic identity over the long run. Consequently, the negative outcomes of residential segregation are far more severe than the lack of daily face-to-face communication with coethnics to reinforce identity. In the words of Häußermann and Oswald (1997:22, translated)

Where ethnic communities have been able to form, the pressure of unemployment and marginalization has often placed such a burden on the former solidarity and internal integration that the sociospatial separation from the "natives" no longer represents any useful aid to integration in society as a whole, but even increases the stigmatization and evokes the nightmare of the ghetto.

Viewed from a generational perspective, the second- and third-generation migrants emancipate themselves from their ethnic constraints; yet they face failure because segregation forecloses opportunities available to integrated youth. The dominant orientation of second- and third-generation migrant youth toward the values of their host society coupled with denial of social integration create tensions that are reinforced through segregation. Indeed, the repeatedly proclaimed ethnic social networks are already revealing cracks. In some circumstances, structural segregation imbues third-generation youth with fears that they will be unable to form the multicultural identities needed to straddle both their ethnic and the host communities. For example, in the Turkish community, ethnic ties take on an ethnic–religious direction when Islamic organizations and local mosque associations construct social infrastructure that includes ethnic sports associations and investments in companies with religious owners (see Klein and Kothy, 1998). This leads to subsocieties in which "interethnic interactions are dropped after the institutional completion of the ethnic colony" (Esser, 1986:110, translated).

Recent demands for internally integrative segregation in German cities now take on an ideological character in order to consolidate structural segregation (see Siebel, 1997).[2] This is the result of ignoring the interests of young migrants who have grown up in a modern society. Instead, youth are forced into ethnic sociospatial constraints. Also, migrant social networks are idealized as a strength, though their fragility is readily apparent. Furthermore, conflicts within migrant groups (e.g., within the Turkish community) and between them and other groups are denied. Finally, the victim roles generated through discrimination and violence are used to justify segregation on grounds that it is internally integrative, according to paternalistic groups in the majority society. This practice renders youth prisoners of purportedly well-intended role assignments that not only cripple their active powers, but also weaken their ability to evaluate their cultural background critically.

---

[2] This demand for "internally integrative" segregation has been exploited by the establishment, the new powerful elites among the migrants, and even extreme right-wing groups. The latter have advocated "ethnopluralism," which they hope to achieve through remigration. Extreme right-wing groups have also gained support in two separate domains by switching arbitrarily from complaints about visibly being a "foreigner in one's own country" to boasting about nationally liberated, foreigner-free zones.

Table 5.1 Changes in Non-German Population Shares, Ages 20–40, in North Rhine–Westphalia Cities

City	1992(%)	2010(Projected %)
Duisburg	17.4	45.9
Remscheid	18.1	44.7
Koeln	19.3	42.9
Gelsenkirchen	14.8	42.0
Duesseldorf	17.8	41.6
Wuppertal	17.2	40.9
Solingen	17.5	40.9
North Rhine–Westphalia	11.9	31.5

Source: Birg, H. (1994). Perspectiven der Bevölkerungs- und Wanderungsent wicklung mit ihren Chancen und Risiken für den Wirt schafts- und Wohn standart "Landlicher Raum." In *Ländliche Räume in Nordrhein–Westfalen: ILS-Schriften* 85, 17–30.

Segregation and Interethnic Conflicts

Structural segregation in German cities is not yet as advanced as in French suburbs (see Dubet and Lapeyronnie, 1992) or large American cities (see Wilson, 1987). However, there are reasons to assume that time processes of social disintegration (through unemployment, welfare cuts, etc.) become consolidated in sociospatial terms here in German cities as well. Not only minorities, but segments of the majority population who coreside in isolated urban districts are affected. In this context, the German scholarly literature, and especially the political debates, ignores one crucial element, namely, relations between the autochthonous and the migrant population. Table 5.1 illustrates this point with data from a few cities in the state of North Rhine-Westphalia.

The predictable increase in the population of persons from 20 to 40 years of age – ages when adults need to be active in the labor market, assume personal responsibility for housing, and begin families – is shifting the composition of the population in numerous cities and urban districts. This demographic growth is not a problem per se. Problems occur when demographic *increase* is accompanied by a *decrease* in job opportunities and the supply of affordable housing. Because trends differ greatly across urban areas, at least three scenarios are plausible.

The *cumulation scenario* assumes that the continuous growth in the non-German population segments will be accompanied by a continuous decrease in available jobs and housing. Consequently, the visible impoverishment of second- and third-generation migrants will lead to greater social inequality and residential segregation. Rapid growth of the migrant population will also be accompanied by a decrease in the autochthonous population, who would face job and housing shortages in shared social space. This will lead to the *expansion* of new urban constellations that have only been known in Germany in a few urban districts, for example, in the cities of Duisburg, Hamburg, Dortmund, or Berlin.

The *equalization scenario* presumes that demographic trends will be balanced by economic changes such that job and housing opportunities grow in pace with population. This variant assumes also that migrant skill acquisition will keep pace with demands of jobs created in the new economy and that the continued transformation of the labor market toward a service society will create more vacancies. A third requirement for the equalization variant is that the expansion of the ethnic economy generates new job vacancies, thereby limiting not only the consolidation of structural segregation, but also competition with the majority of society.

The *exchange scenario* is most optimistic and presumes that the rapid aging of the host society will offer sufficient new integration opportunities by vacancies in desirable positions for minority groups. Accordingly, competition for jobs will weaken and structural segregation with its complicated elements of unemployed, poor, welfare recipients, and persons of non-German origins will also dissipate. However, this assumption requires not only more highly skilled young migrants but also no further decline in the job availability.

Recent trends indicate that the pessimistic cumulation scenario seems most probable. Whereas the equalization variant is a hopeful possibility, the exchange variant is highly unlikely. Therefore, there are many indications of a stronger trend toward future segregation. This implies that the social disintegration of German urban society continues, and that conflicts over resources and social space, positions and recognition, and values and norms, will express themselves more forcefully in the future, even in the form of parallel societies. In circumstances where such conflicts arise, there is an increased threat of escalation, because conflicts are perpetrated by organizations with collective identities.

This scenario presumes that central problems will become more apparent because, as a productive way of processing ethnic and cultural difference, urbanism requires prior social integration (see Siebel, 1997:35). Yet, structural segregation increasingly precludes integration prospects. Therefore, a central future concern is whether and how possible conflicts can be contained or prevented in light of segregation trends. Here as well, at least two scenarios are conceivable. One initially denies the problems identified, viewing segregation as a solution rather than a problem because the urban districts involved are removed from public discourse. This conception can even be conceived as a form of peaceful coexistence in which the greatest possible distance is constructed and politicized ethnic communities become a stabilizing factor. Segments of the left-wing liberal and multicultural spectrum support this approach, although they do not concern themselves with political and religious arenas both within the segregated communities and within parts of the autochthonous population.

Clear hostilities are visible in the behavior of majority population segments. The intensification of foreignness in life-styles as well as visual and auditory symbols is used to justify xenophobia. This is particularly evident among groups who must deal with their own uncertainty (regardless of status) about occupational integration. When resources are scarce, insecure members of the dominant group insist on protecting their welfare even at the cost of others. Residential segregation then becomes an excuse for exclusion, by interpreting it as migrants' unwillingness to become integrated. As well, some migrants do not strive for the opportunities to achieve integration – and they do not see the causes as stemming from their avoidance behavior through the educational institutions; rather, they see exclusionary and discriminating behavior toward their own group.

The second proposition views the starting point for conflicts in the consolidation of segregation. Because social distance cannot be maintained either in public forums or in urban institutions, rejection can threaten identity. This applies to the younger generation insofar as they are concentrated in segregated residential districts. The potential for conflict increases as identity-deficiency usage of social space rises and differences in opportunities to access social systems and resources are restricted by the minority group size. In these circumstances, space symbolizes the lack of social status and recognition, and it becomes a collective battleground for resolving experiences of powerlessness. Young migrants as well as the majority youth demonstrate their rebellion daily on narrow sidewalks, on public street corners, in pedestrian precincts, and so forth. Violent clashes between Turkish migrants and youth from the former Soviet Union are commonplace, predominantly in the eastern German cities.

Preventing Structural Segregation: Implications for Urban Policymaking

Against the backdrop of ambivalence toward the costs and benefits of segregation, I direct attention to an ethnicity-blind integration policy. I maintain that urban policymaking should intervene even against voluntary segregation of both prosperous and ethnic communities because segregation "is a decisive motor for the reproduction of social inequality" (Dangschat, 1997a:643, translated). Remarkably, residential segregation is frequently ignored in public discourse, overshadowed by multicultural arguments that give importance to ethnic diversity. However, only ethnicity-blind integration can establish the preconditions to diminish rising urban conflicts. Reducing urban violence requires strategies to prevent conflicts from becoming identity politics, which are manifested as clashes over territories between the established residents and newcomers, or as struggles over religious symbols in public space.

Whether "ethnicity-blind" urban integration policies have any real chance of success is an open question given the arrangements of segregation that have emerged, coupled with perceptions that authorities have lost control of urban constituencies. As the ability of authorities to use housing schemes and social accommodation policies to appease demands of constituencies for access to basic necessities of urban life declines, these outcomes become the domain of market mechanisms. Because the market cannot ensure social integration without deliberate intervention, other mechanisms for reducing spatial segregation are required. Hence the role of the city as an integration machine hinges crucially on whether the ethnic and cultural conflicts and violence within urban social space can be subjected to regulation. This depends on numerous circumstances' impact on the urban context, such as the ability of the labor market to absorb growing numbers of unskilled migrants (see Friedrichs, 1998). The shift in financial burdens to cities, because labor market failure imposes welfare payments on city budgets, further strains the ability of German cities to reduce segregation via deliberate social integration policies. Identity movements based on demands for sociospatial separation by either prosperous majorities or disadvantaged minorities further undermine prospects for reducing segregation. Declining ability to control housing policy is crucial for the future segregation of German cities. Because cities once had up to 30% of urban housing at their disposal, they were able to impede widespread segregation. As these possibilities have declined, enforced segregation has become entrenched, accompanied by a refusal to recognize involvement in mainstream urban life. This tendency is especially pronounced in France (see Lapeyronnie, 1998; Loch, 1998). Given these circumstances, overt or covert ethnic approaches by city officials become default options unless urban authorities introduce a policy of police control in the absence of urban social housing policy (see Jaschke, 1998).

Häußermann and Oswald (1996) specify the dilemma of urban integration policy, namely, that whereas cities live from migration, they have no possibility of implementing a migration policy. Yet it remains unclear what form an urban migration policy could take. Its necessity is illustrated by the demographic trends reported previously for the cities in the state of North Rhine-Westphalia, which represent a population replacement of old natives by young foreigners. The conflict between natives and migrants manifests itself frequently as xenophobic violence, which is fueled by rising sociospatial inequality. The tendency for communities to seal themselves off grounds conflict in social space. The emotionally charged disputes over public space when the Muslim call to prayer is broadcast through amplifiers, the identity-relevant competition over restricted space for display and contacts between youth of varying ethnic origins, and the fear-filled spaces in selected city districts are all products of prior neglect. Demographic trends point to predictable changes that federal policymakers ignore but that require migration policy reforms that provide legal recourse and grant political participation. In numerous German cities, such enlightened policymaking has already capitulated in resignation.

Whether and which new qualitative features of change in urban development will emerge, and the consequences they will have for community life, are difficult to ascertain. Eisner (1997) marks the 1960s as a turning point in producing the individualization and economic marginalization that have advanced urban social disintegration and produced higher rates of violence. It remains to be seen whether the consequences of economic globalization and the new waves of legal or illegal migration that are likely will lead to increased conflict in new multiethnic "German" cities. The emerging challenges are already in view; ideally these emerging tensions and social pressures will not engender policies of control and repression. Touraine (1996:24, translated) is correct:

> The city is no longer the symbol of the triumphant modern age, but of the disunity of a society in which economies are increasingly less social. The city is no longer the spatial expression of the modern age. Its maintenance is nonetheless the goal of all those who oppose the increasing distance between a globalized economy and a disintegrating urban society.

Conclusion

Experiences of disintegration and violence affect youth in very different ways, depending on their origins and circumstances. Youth in eastern

Germany are profoundly affected by the rigorous social transformation that not only strains their socialization because of the pace of change, but also threatens their social integration. The high rates of violence, particularly toward foreigners, stem from their profound insecurities and lack of recognition. The widespread xenophobia appears related to a lack of orientation (Kleinert et al., 1998:23).

Violence is a particular problem in western Germany, where youth not only have to manage difficult socialization processes but also are unable to remain competitive in skill acquisition. For them mobility is blocked and social recognition withheld. Young immigrants of German origins from the former Soviet Union are in a particularly difficult situation. In addition to overcoming negative socialization stemming from prior experiences with violence, they experience limited opportunities for social integration. In response, many insulate themselves in extreme cultures of violence. A fourth group of youth – those of non-German origins – confront major threats of exclusion in the third generation. In addition to experiencing problems in socialization (e.g., through violence in highly authoritarian families, as Pfeiffer and associates [1998] report), growing numbers are failing to become integrated in the labor market. Most are also denied political participation and religious recognition.

The prevailing policies in Germany pay insufficient attention to the problems arising from processes of disintegration and segregation, despite their likely growth in the future. Rather than strengthening youth integration policy, particularly in urban domains, three policy approaches will likely predominate: First, market expansion is being encouraged to promote individual competitiveness and allegedly make German society more dynamic. This approach ignores that resulting inequities when mapped on persisting spatial segregation will further expand disadvantages of the weaker social groups, including large shares of youth. Campaigns for a new morality, as a second policy thrust, promote normative compliance regardless of the social conditions and the status pressures youth confront on a daily basis. Preference for new measures of repression accompanied by stronger control and surveillance in urban space constitutes a third policy approach to manage social change and growing uncertainty. Not surprisingly, when the traditional forms of social recognition through work and mainstream social institutions become increasingly inaccessible, new forms of recognition are sought. Ethnic encapsulation provides a problematic solution to social recognition because it frequently involves cultures of violence.

In these circumstances is a pressing need for new ideas about cultures of acceptance. This need does not just apply to migrant youth in segregated urban areas, but increasingly to the majority youth as well. Otherwise, and particularly in the cities, youth will resort to reciprocal hostility as a source of recognition. Although this source of recognition is based on destruction, young persons see matters differently – better such recognition than total rejection. As more and more young people receive unsatisfactory answers to Richard Sennett's (1998) question "Who needs me?" the perils of youth urban violence loom large.

The analysis of urban development and the ability of the city to integrate minorities and excluded segments of the majority population leads to rather pessimistic conclusions about both the life perspectives of growing numbers of marginalized youth and the degree of conflict in community life. This can be seen in the criteria that Siebel (1997:36) identifies as essential conditions for relative success: tolerance, universal human rights, economic growth, expanding labor markets, and a maintainable network of social support. Obviously, these conditions are not being satisfied in German cities. Rather, urban life as a "regulated social indifference between strangers on the basis of an ensured systemic integration" is increasingly under threat (Häußermann, 1995:95).

Despite the urgent need for urban structure policies to prevent functional segregation from becoming structural segregation, increasing constraints remain. In the economic domain, these constraints derive from limited opportunities as regional economies respond to the pressures of globalization. Yet, "the more strongly cities seek competition and the stronger global effects become, the more massive the socioeconomic and sociospatial divisions will be" (Dangschat, 1995). The potential for future economic polarization is documented in the "family atlas" of the Germany Youth Institute (Betram et al., 1993), which concludes that the greater the economic success of a region measured in terms of the usual economic indicators, that is, per capita income or gross national product, the worse its performance in human and social terms as far as the natural social networks and the life quality of the young, the old, and the family. It seems to be impossible to forge simple mechanical links between economic categories and genuine social integration that also provides emotional security. This lack of connection between the economic and the social has far-reaching consequences, as shown by our study that examines the relationship among disintegration, uncertainty, and violence, particularly xenophobic violence (Heitmeyer et al., 1995, 1998). We found strong associations between emotional disintegration (particularly behind the facades of intact families) and violence and between uncertainty and violence. This tendency indicates that simple economic solutions are unable to tackle what are essentially social problems.

Unfortunately, urban social policy currently involves the administration of shortages.

Against this background, new possibilities for dealing with the spatial concentration of socially disadvantaged and foreign-born youth are very limited. Nonetheless, four policy alternatives exist:

1. Complete exclusion through segregation, marginalization, and exclusion from the social welfare system
2. Partial integration in the context of segregation with minimal access to social supports from voluntary self-help organizations and personal networks
3. Partial integration in the context of state-supported social welfare programs targeted to pockets of poverty
4. Complete integration through the dismantling of segregation and extensive application of social welfare systems (see also, Rodenstein, 1987:113)

According to Dangschat (1998:72), the European solution will probably be a mixture of the second and third alternatives, with some tendency toward an "American solution," namely, a mixture of the first and second alternatives. In German cities, alternative one already applies to the growing number of illegal migrants and segments of third-generation Moroccan youth (e.g., in Frankfurt) or Turkish youth (e.g., in Berlin-Kreuzberg). These youth are no longer eligible for state welfare assistance because the law on foreigners would then make them liable to deportation. On balance, Germany appears to be embarking on a policy path that dismantles compensatory social policies linked successively with stronger social controls and repression, along the lines Wacquant (1997) depicts for the United States. It is therefore correct to fear that Wilson (1992) may well be right when he maintains that numerous European urban societies will mimic current urban conditions in American cities, a trend that bodes ill for future generations of youth.

REFERENCES

Allgemeine Bevölkerungsumfrage der Sozialwissenschaften (ALLBUS). (1996). Mannheim: Zuma.
Amtliche Nachrichten der Bundesanstalt für Arbeit: Arbeitsmarkt. Jahresbände. (1996–1999). Nürnberg.
Beauftragte der Bundesregierung für Ausländerfragen über die Lage der Ausländer in der Bundesrepublik Deutschland. (1997). Bonn.
Betram, H., Bayer, H., and Bauereiss, R. (1993): Familien-Atlas: Lebenslagen und Regionen in Deutschland. Karten und Zahlen. Opladen: Leske & Budrich.

Birg, H. (1994). Perspektiven der Bevölkerungs- und Wanderungsentwicklung mit ihren Chancen und Risiken für den Wirtschafts- und Wohnstandort "Ländlicher Raum." *Ländliche Räume in Nordrhein-Westfalen: ILS-Schriften* 85, 17–30.

BMBF (Bundesministerium für Bildung und Forschung). (1999). *Jugendliche ohne Berufsausbildung*. Bonn.

Breton, R. (1965). Institutional Completeness of Ethnic Communities and the Personal Relations of Immigrants. *American Journal of Sociology*, 70, 143–205.

Bulmahn, Th. (1997). Reformstau und Verunsicherung. In *Informationsdienst Soziale Indikatoren* (ISI), 18, pp. 6–9.

Bundeszentrale für politische Bildung. (Ed.) (1997). *Datenreport 1997*. Bonn.

Dangschat, J. S. (1995). *Klassentheorie und postfordistische Gesellschaft*. Vortragsmanuskript. Soziale Ungleichheit und Sozialstrukturanalyse. Hannover: DGS-Sektion.

Dangschat, J. S. (1997a). Sag' mir, wo Du wohnst, und ich sag' Dir, wer Du bist! Zum aktuellen Stand der deutschen Segregationsforschung. *Prokla: Zeitschrift für kritische Sozialwissenschaft*. H. 109, 619–647.

Dangschat, J. S. (1997b). Entwicklung von Problemlagen als Herausforderung für die soziale Stadt. In W. Hanesch (Ed.), *Überlebt die Soziale Stadt? Konzeption, Krise und Perspektiven kommunaler Sozialstaatlichkeit* (pp. 77–107). Opladen: Leske & Budrich.

Dangschat, J. S. (1997c). Residentielle Segregation – soziale Ungleichheit im Raum. In Forschungsverbund "Zukünfte in Stadtregionen": Tagung zu Indikatoren der Stadtforschung am 26./27, Juni in Dortmund. pp. 3–56. (Unpublished paper).

Dangschat, J. S. (1998). Warum ziehen sich Gegensätze nicht an? Zu einer Mehrebenen-Theorie ethnischer und rassistischer Konflikte um den städtischen Raum. In W. Heitmeyer, O. Backes, and R. Dollase (Eds.), *Die Krise der Städte* (pp. 21–96). Frankfurt a. M.: Suhrkamp.

Dubet, F., and Lapeyronnie, D. (1992). *Im Aus der Vorstädte: Der Zerfall der demokratischen Gesellschaft*. Stuttgart: Klett-Cotta. Reform macht Angst. (1998). *Die Zeit*, 30, Juli 9.

Eisner, M. (1997). *Das Ende der zivilisierten Stadt? Die Auswirkungen von Modernisierung und urbaner Krise auf Gewaltdelinquenz*. Frankfurt a. M./New York: Campus.

Elias, N., and Scotson, J. L. (1993). *Etablierte und Außenseiter*. Frankfurt a. M.: Campus.

Esser, H. (1986). Ethnische Kolonien: "Binnenintegration" oder gesellschaftliche Isolation? In J. H. P. Hoffmeyer-Zlotnik (Ed.), *Segregation und Integration* (pp. 106–117). Berlin: Quorum-Verlag.

Esser, H. (1998). Ist das Konzept der Integration gescheitert? Landeszentrum für Zuwanderung Nordrhein-Westfalen, Solingen, pp. 12–21.

Feldtkeller, A. (1994). *Die zweckentfremdete Stadt. Wider die Zerstörung des öffentlichen Raums*. Frankfurt a. M./New York: Campus.

Feldtkeller, A. (1998). In der Falle: Zur sozialen Verantwortung von Stadtplanung. *Frankfurter Rundschau* vom 1.30. p. 14.

Friedrichs, J. (1998). Vor neuen ethnisch-kulturellen Konflikten? Neuere Befunde der Stadtsoziologie zum Verhältnis von Einheimischen und Zugewanderten in Deutschland. In W. Heitmeyer, O. Backes, and R. Dollase (Eds.), *Krise der Städte. Analysen zu den Folgen desintegrativer Stadtentwicklung für das ethnisch-kulturelle Zusammenleben* (pp. 233–265). Frankfurt a. M.: Surkamp.

Häußermann, H. (1995). Die Stadt und die Stadt-Soziologie: Urbane Lebensweise und die Integration des Fremden. *Berliner Journal für Soziologie*, 1, 89–98.

Häußermann, H. (1998). Zuwanderung und die Zukunft der Stadt: Neue ethnisch-kulturelle Konflikte durch die Entstehung einer neuen sozialen "underclass"? In W. Heitmeyer, O. Backes, and R. Dollase (Eds.), *Krise der Städte: Analysen zu den Folgen desintegrativer Stadtentwicklung für das ethnisch-kulturelle Zusammenleben* (pp. 145–177). Frankfurt a. M.: Suhrkamp.

Häußermann, H., and Oswald, J. (1996). Stadtentwicklung und Zuwanderung. In B. Schäfers and G. Wewer (Eds.), *Die Stadt in Deutschland* (pp. 85–99). Opladen: Leske & Budrich.

Häußermann, H., and Oswald, J. (1997). Zuwanderung und Stadtentwicklung. In H. Häußermann and J. Oswald (Eds.), *Zuwanderung und Stadtentwicklung.* Leviathan (Sonderband 17), 9–29. Opladen: Westdeutscher Verlag.

Hefler, G., Rippl, S., and Boehnke, S. (1998). Zum Zusammenhang von Armut und Ausländerfeindlichkeit bei west- und ostdeutschen Jugendlichen. In A. Klocke and K. Hurrelmann (Eds.), *Kinder und Jugendliche in Armut* (pp. 205–224). Wiesbaden: Westdeutscher Verlag.

Heitmeyer, W. (Ed.). (1997). *Was treibt die Gesellschaft auseinander?* Frankfurt a. M.: Suhrkamp.

Heitmeyer, W., Collmann, B., Conrads, J., Matuschek, I., Kraul, D., Kuehnel, W., Moeller, R., and Ulbrich-Herrmann, M. (1995/1998). *Gewalt: Schattenseiten der Individualisierung bei Jugendlichen aus unterschiedlichen sozialen Milieus.* Weinheim/München: Juventa.

Heitmeyer, W., Schröder, H., and Müller, J. (1997). *Verlockender Fundamentalismus.* Frankfurt a. M.: Suhrkamp.

Hill, P. B. (1984). Räumliche Nähe und soziale Distanz zu ethnischen Minderheiten. *Zeitschrift für Soziologie,* 13(4), 363–370.

Hoffmann-Nowotny, H.-J. (1996). Soziologische Aspekte der Multikulturalität. In K. J. Bade (Ed.), *Migration–Ethnizität–Konflikt: Systemfragen und Fallstudien* (pp. 103–126). Osnabrück: Rasch.

Jaschke, H.-G. (1998). Polizei und Sozialarbeit im städtischen sozialen Brennpunkt. In W. Heitmeyer, O. Backes, and R. Dollase (Eds.), *Krise der Städte: Analysen zu den Folgen desintegrativer Stadtentwicklung für das ethnisch-kulturelle Zusammenleben* (pp. 398–415). Frankfurt a. M.: Suhrkamp.

Jugendwerk der Deutschen Shell. (Ed.). (1997). *Jugend '97: Zukunftsperspektiven: Gesellschaftliches Engagement, Politische Orientierungen.* Opladen: Leske & Budrich.

Jugendwerk der Deutschen Shell. (Ed.). (1992). *Jugend '92: Lebenslagen, Orientierungen und Entwicklungsperspektiven im vereinigten Deutschland.* Opladen: Leske & Budrich.

Jugendwerk der Deutschen Shell. (Ed.). (1985). *Jugendliche und Erwachsene '85: Jugend der 50er Jahre – Heute.* Opladen: Leske & Budrich

Jugendwerk der Deutschen Shell. (Ed.). (1981). *Jugend '81: Lebensentwürfe, Alltagskulturen, Zukunftsbilder.* Opladen: Leske & Budrich.

Keim, K. D. (1997). Vom Zerfall des Urbanen. In W. Heitmeyer (Ed.), *Was treibt die Gesellschaft auseinander?* (pp. 245–286). Frankfurt a. M.: Suhrkamp.

Klein, M. L. and Kothy, J. (1998). Entwicklung und Regulierung ethnisch-kultureller Konflikte im Sport: Migranten im Spannungsfeld von deutschem Vereinssport und ethnischer Kolonie. In W. Heitmeyer, O. Backes, and R. Dollase (Eds.), *Krise der Städte:*

Analysen zu den Folgen desintegrativer Stadtentwicklung für das ethnisch-kulturelle Zusammenleben (pp. 416–442). Frankfurt a. M.: Suhrkamp.

Kleinert, C., Krüger, W., and Willems, H. (1998). Einstellungen junger Deutscher gegenüber ausländischen Mitbürgern und ihre Bedeutung hinsichtlich politischer Orientierungen. *Aus Politik und Zeitgeschichte*, 31, 14–27.

Lapeyronnie, D. (1998). Jugendkrawalle und Ethnizität. In W. Heitmeyer, O. Backes, and R. Dollase (Eds.), *Krise der Städte: Analysen zu den Folgen desintegrativer Stadtentwicklung für das ethnisch-kulturelle Zusammenleben* (pp. 297–316). Frankfurt a. M.: Suhrkamp.

Loch, D. (1998). Soziale Ausgrenzung und Anerkennungskonflikte in Frankreich und Deutschland. In W. Heitmeyer, O. Backes, and R. Dollase (Eds.), *Krise der Städte: Analysen zu den Folgen desintegrativer Stadtentwicklung für das ethnisch-kulturelle Zusammenleben* (pp. 266–299). Frankfurt a. M.: Suhrkamp.

Malik, K. (1997). Gefährliche Pluralität: Das Konzept der multikulturellen Gesellschaft ist ambivalent. *taz*, 7.2. 15–17.

Ortlepp, W. (1998). Zur Sozialisation von Kindern und Jugendlichen der Stadt Magdeburg unter den Bedingungen sozialer und gesellschaftlicher Veränderungen. In J. Mansel and G. Neubauer (Eds.), *Armut und soziale Ungleichheit bei Kindern* (pp. 90–105). Opladen: Leske & Budrich.

Pfeiffer, Chr., Delzer, J., Enzmann, D., and Wetzels, P. (1998). *Ausgrenzung, Gewalt und Kriminalität junger Menschen*. DVJJ-Sonderdruck. Hannover: Dt. Vereinigung für Jugendgerichte und Jugendgerichtshilfen e.V.

Rada, U. (1997). Alle sind gleich, aber nur unter sich? Segregation statt Integration? Plädoyer gegen einen angedachten Paradigmenwechsel in der Migrationspolitik. *taz dossier*, 11.26. 15–17.

Ransford, H. E. (1968). Isolation, Powerlessness, and Violence: A Study of Attitudes and Participation in the Watts Riot. *American Journal of Sociology*, 73, 581–591.

Rodenstein, M. (1987). Durchstaatlichung der Städte? Krisenregulierung durch die kommunale Selbstverwaltung. In W. Prigge (Ed.), *Die Materialität des Städtischen, Stadtentwicklung und Urbanität im gesellschaftlichen Umbruch*. Stadtforschung aktuell, 17 (pp. 107–123). Basel: Birkhäuser.

Sampson, R. J., and Wilson, W. J. (1995). Toward a Theory of Race, Crime, and Urban Inequality. In J. Hagan and R. D. Peterson (Eds.), *Crime and Inequality*. Stanford, CA: Stanford University Press.

Schäfers, B. (1998). *Sozialstruktur und sozialer Wandel in Deutschland*. Stuttgart: Enke.

Sennett, R. (1991). *Civitas: Die Großstadt und die Kultur des Unterschieds*. Frankfurt a. M.: Fischer.

Sennett, R. (1998). *The Corrosion of Character: The Personal Consequences of Work in the New Capitalism*. New York/London: Norton.

Siebel, W. (1997). Die Stadt und die Fremden. In J. Brech (Ed.), *Migration – Stadt im Wandel* (pp. 33–40). Darmstadt: Verlag für Wissenschaftliche Publikationen.

Stadt Frankfurt (Ed.). 1997. Erster Frankfurter Sozialbericht: Risiken für die soziale Stadt. Frankfurt.

Touraine, A. (1996). Das Ende der Städte? *Die Zeit*, 5.31. 24.

Wacquant, L. J. D. (1997). Vom wohltätigen Staat zum strafenden Staat: Über den politischen Umgang mit dem Elend in Amerika. *Leviathan*, Nr. 1, 50–66.

Wiley, N. F. (1970). The Ethnic Mobility Trap and Stratification Theory. In P. I. Rose and C. H. Page (Eds.), *The Study of Society: An Integrated Anthology* (pp. 397–408). New York: Random House

Wilson, W. J. (1987). *The Truly Disadvantaged: The Inner City, the Underclass, and Public Policy.* Chicago: University of Chicago Press.

Wilson, W. J. (1992). Ghettoisierte Armut und Rasse. In St. Leibfried and W. Voges (Eds.), *Armut im modernen Wohlfahrtsstaat* (221–236). Sonderheft der Kölner Zeitschrift für Soziologie und Sozialpsychologie.

6 From Street Children to All Children

Improving the Opportunities of Low-Income
Urban Children and Youth in Brazil

Irene Rizzini, Gary Barker, and Neide Cassaniga

Introduction

> The child is the beginning without end. The end of the child is the beginning
> of the end. When a society allows its children to be killed, it is because it has
> begun its own suicide as a society. When it does not love the child it is because
> it has failed to recognize its humanity. (Herbert de Souza, (1991:1 trans.)[1]

For much of the 1980s and 1990s, the national and international media
and local and international children's and human rights organizations focused considerable attention on the plight of "street children" in Brazil,
particularly on violence against street children by death squads and police.
The term *street children* generally refers to children and youth who work or
spend most of their time on the streets, as well as to the far smaller subset
who sleep in the streets and are no longer connected to their families and
communities. As portrayed in the national and international press and in
numerous research reports, the image of child poverty in Brazil is the street
child. But is this image accurate? And more importantly, does this image
of the street child point children and youth policies and programs in Brazil

[1] Herbert de Souza, known as *Betinho*, was one of Brazil's most important social activists in
the area of human rights in recent years. For his activism, he was forced into exile for several
years during the military dictatorship. During the 1980s until his death in 1997, he led an
important campaign on behalf of civic participation and citizenship that mobilized Brazil
during this period.
The authors would like to acknowledge the important support of the Chapin Hall Center for
Children at the University of Chicago in the development of this chapter. Both Neide Cassaniga
and Gary Barker benefited from international fellowships at Chapin Hall. In particular, thanks
to Rebecca Stone and Joan Costello for input.

in the right direction? Street children may be the most visible and in some cases the most obvious examples of poverty and inattention to the needs of children and youth, but there are millions of "invisible" children and youth who, although relatively more protected than children living or working on the streets, also lack important supports for their healthy development.

In this chapter we argue that the pervasive focus on street children – however well intentioned – deflects attention from the broader population of low-income children and youth. Of course Brazil's street children do have urgent and acute needs. Governmental and nongovernmental organizations as well as advocates and researchers working on behalf of street children in Brazil are carrying out vital work that has helped thousands of children and youth who need intensive and immediate assistance, protection, and caregiving. But this focus on street children means that most children's programs in Brazil have directed their attention to the relatively small number of children and youth in the most dire situations. Consequently, relatively little policy or program development has focused on assisting the far larger number of low-income children and youth who live with their families but nonetheless require additional support – support that may prevent them from becoming street children.

Brazil is not alone in focusing its child and youth policy on those at highest risk. However, Brazil offers compelling conditions to change the focus from street children to all children. In 1990, Brazil passed the Statute on Children and Adolescents, a progressive law based partly on the United Nations (UN) Convention on the Rights of the Child. The Statute calls on the state and civil society to provide developmental supports for all children and youth.

The Brazilian Statute codifies into national law the notion that all children and youth need special protection, care, and opportunities for growth, exploration, and education. Both Brazil's Statute and the UN Convention assert that such developmental supports are needed by all children and youth, not just those at risk of hardship, abandonment, or abuse.

Since its passage in 1990, the Statute, advocacy related to its provisions, and its implementation have carefully focused on child protection – specifically, responding to and protecting children and adolescents from abuse and abandonment. Although such advocacy has been crucial for improving community-based mechanisms for child protection, there is a need to take the Statute even further. In particular, we need to ask: What would be required to implement the concept of developmental supports for all children and youth as embodied in the Statute?

We use the term *developmental supports* to refer to community resources that offer young people safety; caring relationships; opportunities to develop skills, friendship, and self-confidence; and activities and services that contribute to the cognitive, social, creative, cultural, vocational, and emotional development of children and youth (see Ramphele, this volume). Although some of these supports may be provided in the formal education and health sectors, developmental supports generally comprise the constellation of resources available outside the public school and public health systems.

The idea of developmental supports for all children and youth may sound utopian. In developing countries like Brazil, with massive constraints on the public budget and unmet basic needs of much of its population (adult and child), this idea may appear unrealistic. Nonetheless, we will identify examples of programs in Brazil that have sought to implement community-based developmental supports for children and youth. We defend the idea that this phenomenon, which also occurs in other Latin American countries, may shift the thrust of interventions from their traditional emphasis on deviance and deficits among low-income young people toward perspectives that highlight their competencies and potential. Although we recognize the difficulties of implementing such universal supports for children and youth, we argue that such a paradigm shift in child and youth policy not only is possible, but is necessary to protect future generations from the dire consequences of social exclusion.

Overview of Low-Income Children and Youth in Brazil

Brazil has experienced tremendous economic growth since the 1960s and is currently one of the world's 10 largest economies. However, as in much of Latin America, economic growth in Brazil has been extremely uneven, producing wealth and financial stability for a few and poverty and financial insecurity for most. In the 1990s nearly half (47%) of Brazil's population of 160 million lived in poverty (UNDP, 1994; IBGE/UNICEF, 1997). According to 1997 World Bank statistics, Brazil has the worst income distribution among more than 60 countries for which data are available. As of 1989, the richest 10% of the population controlled 51.3% of total income, whereas the poorest 20% of the population had access to just 2.1% of total income (World Bank, 1997).

After rapid economic growth during the 1960s and 1970s, the 1980s was marked by recession, widespread economic instability, high external debt, high unemployment, and hyperinflation, which in 1989–1990 reached a staggering 1,500% per year (UNDP, 1993). This hyperinflation further increased income inequalities in Brazil. In 1994 the Brazilian government adopted a new currency, which appears to have succeeded in controlling inflation but caused some prices to stabilize at a level beyond the reach of much of the population. During this period of economic turmoil, the Brazilian government articulated a rhetorical commitment to the poor, but in practice the development models adopted have done little to address income inequalities. The proliferation of new *favelas*, the low-income settlements that ring Brazil's major cities, coupled with population increases in existing favelas, a growing homeless population, and a rise in urban violence are testimonials to widespread social exclusion and income inequality.

Chronic poverty in Brazil and in the rest of Latin America has had a direct impact on children. In 1990 more than half of Brazilian children and adolescents (53.5%) lived in families whose monthly per capita income was less than half of one minimum salary (or less than U.S.$75 per month). In absolute numbers, this amounts to roughly 32 million young people (IBGE/PNAD, 1990, in UNICEF, 1993). Brazilian poverty has also become more feminized as its concentration in female-headed households increased over time. The 1989 census reveals that mother-only families represent about 20% of all households, with higher concentrations among low-income, urban populations (Bruce et al., 1995).

The size of Brazil's child and adolescent population, and specifically its poor segment, presents tremendous challenges for the social services sector, and in particular the public education system. Nearly 50% of Brazil's population is under the age of 20. The public education system in Brazil can best be represented as a bottleneck with nearly universal enrollment at the primary level converging to dramatically reduced enrollment at the secondary and tertiary levels. The school enrollment rate in Brazil falls sharply from 84.2% at ages 10–14 (the primary, which is compulsory) to 56.8% at ages 15–17 (Oliveira, 1993). That only 22.5% of secondary school youth, ages 15–17, were enrolled in secondary school testifies to the high rates of grade retention and school failure.

One of the main reasons for high rates of school dropout and grade retention in Brazil, in addition to the lack of adequate infrastructure, is the need for children and youth to work. Household survey data from 1990 reveal that 50% of youth ages 15–17 and 17.2% of 10- to 14-year-olds were working (Rizzini, Rizzini, and Holanda, 1996). In both urban and rural areas, many low-income Brazilian children and youth are compelled to forgo school attendance to support themselves and their families (see McKechnie and Hobbs, this volume).

In the late 1980s, UNICEF, Childhope, and the International Catholic Children's Bureau estimated that as many as 7 million children and youth spent most of their time and/or slept on the streets in Brazil, but this estimate is now recognized as an overstatement (Barker and Knaul, 1991). During the past few years, several censuses and studies in Brazilian cities provided what seems to be a more reasonable estimate of the number of children and youth living on the streets. A 1995 study in Saõ Paulo found that 4,520 children and youth circulated in the streets during the day, but only 895 slept on the streets at night (Jornal do Brasil, 1995). In Salvador, Bahia, a 1993 study found 15,743 children and youth *working* in the streets and 468 living in the streets (Projeto Axe, 1993). Research in Fortaleza found only 184 children and youth living in the streets out of 5,962 children and youth working in the street (Secretaria de Ação Social, 1994).[2] Swart-Kruger and Chawla (this volume) also stress the distinction between children and youth who work and those who live in the streets. The consensus now emerging in Brazil is that the number of children and youth living in the streets is not nearly as large as once estimated and represents the tip of the iceberg of low-income children, the majority of whom continue to live with their families, but often in precarious situations that compromise their development.

The Path to the Statute on Children and Adolescents

To understand the potential of the Statute on Children and Adolescents as an advocacy tool to shift the policy and program paradigm from street children to all children, a brief overview of its history and impact to date is instructive. The Statute emerged from a confluence of historical trends and events, among them the drafting of the UN Convention on the Rights of the Child, the national and international mobilization on behalf of street children in Brazil, and the return to democratic rule in Brazil.[3] The Statute was one of the first successes of the social movements to emerge during the military regime, seeking to promote the participation of civil society in policymaking.

The history of children's policy in Brazil reveals that since the beginning of the 20th century, poor children wandering and/or working on the streets were placed in large prisonlike institutions. Justification for incarcerating

---

[2] Counting children who are by their nature mobile and who often go back and forth from their homes to the streets is a complicated undertaking. Although the reliability of these recent censuses of street children has been questioned, they do, nonetheless, provide more realistic accounts of the number of street and working children when compared with the "back of envelope" estimates that prevailed before any systematic attempts to count the children.

[3] Brazil was run by a military government that assumed power in 1964 and handed over rule to a civilian president elected by Congress in 1985. Direct presidential elections were held in 1989.

youth emphasized protection in the case of young children and "reeduca-
tion" in the case of teenagers. For most of the 20th century, the Brazilian
government's attitude toward poor children was ambivalent: Policies sought
to protect children and at the same time to protect society from so-called
antisocial youth.[4]

Until 1989, the codes for minors adopted in Brazil offered little variation in the treatment of poor children, particularly those working on the
streets, who were seen as a threat to society. Violence and maltreatment by
police and the institutions where they were placed without a hearing and a
general disregard for their rights were the general rule. Without due process, the state could summarily withdraw guardianship without notifying
either the children or their families. Furthermore, criteria for withdrawal of
guardianship were often subjective and discretionary. Poor children who
were on the streets or without the immediate protection of a guardian
were in effect considered delinquents unless proved otherwise (Pilotti and
Rizzini, 1995).

The massive migration from the poorest areas of the northeast to Brazil's
major cities during the 1970s and 1980s greatly increased the numbers of
the urban poor. Consequently, the number of children found wandering,
working, or living on the streets increased and became visible. The social
mobilization that resulted from this phenomenon led to a strong questioning
of the government. Starting in the mid-1980s, several nongovernmental
organizations (NGOs), university research and advocacy centers, grass-roots
movements linked to the Catholic church, and progressive policymakers
began collaborating to improve children's policies and programs. Media
reports on the often abysmal conditions in existing children's institutions
and the treatment of street children by police, coupled with strong child
advocacy by NGOs, resulted in a considerable national outcry on behalf of
street children.

A growing number of studies on street children also began to demystify
their backgrounds, finding that the majority were not delinquents, as commonly portrayed, but rather were low-income children and youth working
on the streets to support themselves and their families (Rizzini, 1986; Fausto
and Cervini, 1991). This movement on behalf of street children also involved

---

[4] This ambivalent view of the child – simultaneously in danger and dangerous – became one
of the dominant themes in the Brazilian debate over the need to create juridical reforms for
minors in the first three decades of the 20th century. Poor children and youth were clearly
defined in the legislation as potentially dangerous, and several articles were dedicated to regulating the situation of physically and morally abandoned minors and juvenile delinquents
(Rizzini, 1997a, 1997b).

children and youth themselves; in 1986, the First National Meeting of Street Children in Brazil, coordinated by the National Movement of Street Children in Brazil, included more than 500 children and youth participants, some of whom spoke on the floor of Brazil's Congress. The Statute on the Child and the Adolescent was born in large part of this national movement on behalf of street children.

The Statute and Children's Rights in Brazil

Until the Statute was passed, the concept of rights was not associated with childhood. The term *minor* as used in the Brazilian legal code was associated with the terms *delinquent* and *abandoned* or *without moral supervision* – connotations implying that the state had all the rights, and the child had none. The Statute introduced the notion that children were entitled not only to all human rights, but also to additional rights and protection as a result of their developmental needs. It is important to point out that in Brazil the notion of citizenship and rights began to resurface in the 1980s after having been repressed during the military rule, so the recognition of children's rights at this time is all the more impressive.

The Statute also introduces the concept of developmental supports for all children and youth (while not using that exact language) in recognizing that all children and youth – not just those of the middle class – are in a "special stage of development" and thus due special assistance, priority, and protection from the state in collaboration with civil society. The Statute includes codes for children who need special care, as in cases of abuse and abandonment, and provisions calling on the government to provide both preventive and developmentally appropriate health, recreational, and educational supports.

For implementation, the Statute stipulates the formation of two specific bodies. One is the Guardianship Council, which is established at the municipal level. These councils respond to individual cases of needy or at-risk children to ensure that they receive the best possible assistance. The Councils act as a point of entry into the children's services system and as an advocate for children and families within the state and nongovernmental service system. The Statute also calls for the creation of Municipal Children's Rights Councils, which are charged with coordinating children's policy and funding at the municipal level. As of 1992, two thirds of Brazil's states had created state-level Children's Rights Councils, as had slightly more than one-fourth of Brazil's municipalities (Rizzini et al., 1992). According to a national newsletter set up to promote the Statute, as of 1997, slightly less than half of

Brazil's 4,500 municipalities had Guardianship Councils (ECA em Revista, 1997).

The implementation of the Statute has been uneven, reflecting the vast regional differences in the country in terms of public administration and levels of public resources. A central tenet of the Statute is that municipalities have primary responsibility for all of their children and adolescents. Although this gives municipalities and local communities a tremendous say in the kinds of programs and policies for children, it also implies considerable responsibility. Some municipalities have risen to the challenge, whereas others have not reached the level of organization or political commitment required to make the system work.

The functioning of the Statute in general and the Guardianship Councils in particular depend on the existence of adequate local children's services, which by and large are scarce. In spite of the Statute's call for services and programs that support the integral development of all children and youth, program efforts in Brazil continue to offer mainly low-quality remedial services to low-income children. Nonetheless, at least at the level of remedial services, the Statute has succeeded in changing public attitudes about low-income children and youth in some municipalities, thereby contributing to a sense of optimism that socially excluded youth can be productively integrated into society and that municipalities can address the needs of their most disadvantaged children and youth (see Cassaniga, 1997). And, as we will see, in some municipalities, the State has provided the policy framework and support for the beginning of community-based developmental supports for children and youth.

Learning from the Experiences of Programs for Street Children

For many community-based organizations and NGOs working in child welfare or working in the social area in Brazil during the 1980s and 1990s, street children symbolized the worst examples of social exclusion. Although these programs have limitations, it is nonetheless useful to examine how these programs developed their impressive legacy via advocacy, research, and program methodology and philosophies. We do not provide an exhaustive analysis of the collective experience of programs working with Brazilian street children (and other children with special needs); however, aspects of these programs are worth highlighting because they offer insights for programs seeking to reach all children and youth.

The apparent increase in the number of children working and living on the streets of Brazilian cities fostered the creation of numerous organizations and efforts to assist them. Among these is the National Movement of Street Children (Movimento Nacional de Meninos e Meninas de Rua), a national umbrella advocacy and training organization that comprises individuals (including young people), NGOs, and governmental agencies working on behalf of street children. Several NGOs were founded in the 1980s to work with other populations of children needing special services, including working children, those exploited through prostitution, and victims of abuse. The common characteristic of all these programs is that they continue to offer services directly to children and youth who face some urgent and identifiable need or risk.

One of the most important lessons learned from these programs – and a lesson that applies to all youth developmental supports – is the emphasis on children as agents of their own development, or "agents of change in their own lives" (Myers, 1988:137). On the negative side, some programs for street children in Brazil have overdramatized them as little heroes, or resilient survivors. This emphasis has the unfortunate effect of making it seem as if they do not need assistance, or in some cases perversely glamorizes the poverty and hardships they have endured. However, the majority of programs working with street youth have sought to offer street children options, recognizing that the majority had few apart from work and survival. Thus, the cornerstone of most successful programs working with Brazilian street children has been working with them to reflect on, envision, and acquire an alternative future (see Swart-Kruger and Chawla, this volume). These programs have sought to help street children find or recover a sense of what it is they want to do with their lives. Thus, street educators (outreach workers) and other NGO staff typically work with youth individually and in groups to discover their personal interests and desires, and to design a program based on those interests.[5]

Another important legacy of street children's programs is that of developing a philosophy and a professional staff to work with street children, namely, the street educators. This educator, who is simultaneously outreach worker, advocate, and friend, may be either a volunteer or trained adult staff member or an older youth (in some cases street educators are former street children) who approaches the street children, befriends them, and works with them to resolve their immediate needs. Street educators generally

[5] Programs for street children in Brazil have sometimes drawn on the philosophical and theoretical underpinnings of Paulo Freire, who coined the phrase "pedagogy of the oppressed" and offered a framework for listening to the voices of the disadvantaged and increasing their awareness about their situation while also offering concrete skills, particularly literacy.

serve as the first point of contact to organizations and other institutions (education, vocational training, health services, income generation, etc.) that a given NGO or governmental program may offer.

Along with various youth-serving organizations, the National Movement for Street Children in Brazil developed training programs for street educators. In collaboration with universities, these organizations have sought to create the loosely defined profession of street educator. This effort is significant socially because it is the first time that a profession has been created in Brazil specifically to work with low-income children and youth. Of course, teachers, psychologists, and social workers, among other professionals, also work with children and youth, but the effort to create and define a field of work based on street education and street outreach is the first in Brazil (Castro, 1997; Chalhub, 1997). It is also noteworthy that street educators have had an important voice in structuring programs and policies on behalf of street children.

Brazil's programs for street children are also notable for their flexibility, their creativity, and their development of rules and timetables that flow from and accept children as they are, rather than trying to make them fit the programs. As such, they stand in sharp contrast to the public education system, which generally tries to make children fit its norms and structure. By contrast, successful programs for street children have tried to adapt to their norms. Thus, the admirable qualities of some street children's programs in Brazil include listening to children's voices, seeking to understand their realities, and striving to be nonjudgmental of their circumstances.

Brazilian street children have also benefited from an impressive body of research on their needs. Some research on the life course of children living and/or working on the streets provides insights about how to prevent others from ending up in the same situation. Research in the city of Goiania that compares the family situations of children who live on the streets and those who work on the streets finds that family cohesion is an important factor influencing who lives on the streets. As compared with families of working children, those with children living on the streets generally do not function as a coherent and cooperative unit; instead, individual family members seem to look out only for themselves (Fausto and Cervini, 1991; Rizzini et al., 1992). Research observing girls living on the streets and those exploited sexually through prostitution finds that being sexually abused in the home, particularly by a stepfather, was often a precursor to life on the streets (Vasconcelos, 1992). This kind of research offers important insights on what could be done to protect more children from life on the street by offering services such as family income support, employment possibilities, or family counseling.[6]

These programs and the movement for street youth in Brazil as a whole have been extremely important for the relatively small number of children and youth they have served. Unfortunately, the most impressive programs for street youth and other groups of at-risk children and youth in Brazil are, as Myers (1991) called them, "jewel boxes" – important for the small number of children and youth who benefit from them, but having a minimal impact on the well-being of the large number of low-income children and youth.

From Street Children to All Children: Prevention and Development Supports

During the last few years, most advocates working on behalf of street children have acknowledged the need to expand what they do to reach the much greater number of children and youth who are not yet living or working on the street but nevertheless require assistance to prevent them from doing so or simply to promote their healthy development. Several well-known NGOs working with Brazil's street children and youth have started prevention programs. Using their knowledge of and experiences with children already living or working on the streets, they have developed projects that seek to assist children and youth who are still connected to their families, and perhaps still enrolled in school, but who are at high risk of becoming street children.

Although the trend toward prevention has been growing, it remains extremely limited. The number of solid, ongoing community-based prevention efforts for children and youth in Brazil – and Latin America as a whole – is small. In particular, little has been done to develop community-focused efforts to assist children, youth, and families in those communities that produce large numbers of street children. Especially needed are efforts that reintegrate street children with their families. Equally important are programs and policies supported by the state that would enable low-income families to care for their children.

Prevention-based programs and policies represent an important paradigm shift away from focusing on a relatively small number of children and youth living and working on the streets, and they have several advantages that have yet to be fully explored. Prevention-based programs, for example, do not eliminate the need for remedial services for youth who

---

[6] For a review of some of this research, see Rizzini (1994, 1995, 1998).

have acute needs and problems, but in a situation of resource scarcity, the typically lower cost per youth of prevention programs means that more youth can be reached in a given budget (Barker and Fontes, 1996). However, as some street children's programs in Brazil have made this transition to prevention in recent years, another important question has emerged: Is prevention enough? Should programs for low-income children and youth focus on problem prevention and melioration of risks, or should they focus on supporting healthy development? And what is the difference?

In the United States and in Colombia there has been some debate at the policy and program levels over risk-based prevention programs versus programs that focus more broadly on youth development models, i.e., supportive services and activities that are open to all youth (Barker, 1996). Prevention or risk-based models have been criticized for focusing on the deficits of young people's lives instead of building on their competencies. Prevention and risk models also often stigmatize children and youth. For example, programs that seek to prevent girls from living on the streets may send an indirect and subtle message that the low-income girls it assists are potential street girls. This is a very different message from saying they are potential future citizens and equal partners in their families. Even when they do not stigmatize youth, prevention activities too often focus on a single cause of an undesirable activity, start too late, and end too early.

The prevention model is also questioned because of its assumption that youth who are free of problems or risks do not need help or special attention. In making a case for promotional and developmental activities for all youth in the United States, Pittman and Cahill (1991) state, "Problem-free does not mean fully prepared.... Youth development ... should be seen as an ongoing, inevitable process in which all youth are engaged and participate. The emphasis here is on constancy (ongoing) and inclusion (all youth)."

In Western Europe, many countries now accept the notion that all children and youth – regardless of their risk or income status – require and deserve special supports by virtue of their stage in development (Sherraden, 1992). Recognizing the major social differences between Western Europe and Brazil, though, how might this kind of model apply to Brazil? Should programs and policies for children focus on problem prevention, or should they focus on developmental support services and activities for all youth?

To most children's advocates in Brazil, the Statute advocates for developmental supports for all children and youth. The obvious questions become; What are the developmental supports that all children need? How can the state and civil society collaborate to provide these supports? One obvious starting point is to ask families and youth themselves what kinds of supports they need. Regardless of their income level, most parents if asked will say they want more for their children than that they stay out of trouble or not have to live on the streets. One useful way to explore this issue in Brazil is to examine middle-class families who through their own means typically provide a range of developmental supports and services for their children. Typical middle- or upper middle-income Brazilian families generally ensure that their children obtain a high-quality education by enrolling them in private schools and in private health insurance plans.[7] However, most middle-class parents recognize that private school does not by itself provide "holistic" development or keep their children occupied.

They typically also enroll their children in sports activities (private swimming classes, a soccer club, etc.) and recreational and cultural activities (such as ballet, arts, and music). If their son or daughter is having trouble at school or in another domain, they may engage a counselor or psychologist or another kind of specialist. Such families typically also pursue additional career-related activities, such as foreign language classes or computer classes. It is noteworthy that most middle-class families do not merely invest in activities that would prevent their children from getting in trouble but instead generally seek to promote their overall integrated development and happiness. Entire industries of private schools, tutors, psychologists, coaches, and art teachers exist in Brazil to provide these services, for pay, to millions of middle-class families. It is precisely these types of service and support networks that middle-class children and youth can access that should be advocated for low-income children and youth.

In discussions over children's policy in Brazil and throughout the world there is consensus that prevention is more cost-effective than remedial services. Policymakers and funders can be convinced to fund prevention programs if an evaluation confirms that they are successful. But the Statute requires us to look beyond mere prevention and to support integrated development for all children. One difficulty with broad-based developmental supports is that they are more difficult to evaluate and their long-term

---

[7] Preventing children from living and/or working on the streets also implies changes at the macrolevel, including improvements in the formal health and education sectors and transformation of economic systems that exclude or marginalize thousands of low-income families. However, even in Western European and North American countries, for example, where public sector social services and the public education sector offer more adequate services for the majority of the population, many governments have still recognized the need for additional services for children and youth that are developmentally appropriate and that link the school system and other social services. See for example, Sherraden (1992) and Whalen and Wynn (1995).

impact may be more diffuse. We contend that developmental supports do in fact prevent problems, but their long-term impact on child and adolescent well-being may be more akin to good nutrition than to immunization. Whereas immunization has a direct impact on lowering rates of infectious diseases, good nutrition has a more diffuse but nonetheless important impact on overall health throughout the life cycle. Similarly, the impact of developmental supports may be less direct, more difficult to measure, but nonetheless every bit as important as prevention-based services.[8]

Another pertinent issue for providing developmental supports is resource allocation. The traditional argument is that given limited resources, funds should be allocated to children with the most pressing needs. This concept also applies to developmental supports for children and youth: Namely, resources should be prioritized for those children and families who cannot pay for needed supports. The risks of this mind-set, however, are weak long-term political commitment and the potential for creation and perpetuation of a two-tier social service system. If developmental supports in Brazil are defined as government funds allocated only for poor children, middle-class families will continue to secure private services and supports for their children, thereby forcing the government to fund these services for the disadvantaged.

The lessons learned about providing developmental supports in the United States and Western Europe suggest that long-term political commitment is deeper when middle-class children and youth also benefit, that is, when the middle-class is also part of the system. Furthermore, the quality of these supports is higher when middle-class families participate because they typically have the political power to advocate for higher-quality services and in fact generally only use publicly funded services if their quality is on par with what they can obtain in the private sector.

A Developmental Support System for All Brazilian Children and Youth

> With the support of the states and the Federal Government, the municipalities will encourage and facilitate the directing of resources and spaces to cultural, sports and leisure programs oriented to childhood and youth. (Title II, Chap. 4, Art. 59, Statute of the Child and Adolescent, 1990)

---

[8] Private schools and private health plans are prohibitively expensive for the majority of the population. Considering that the current minimum monthly salary in Brazil is worth about U.S.$130, public school costs the equivalent of about four to six minimum salaries per month per child. Joan Costello, Chapin Hall Center for Children at the University of Chicago, personal correspondence, 1998.

Many advocates, program staff, policymakers, and members of the Municipal Children's Rights Councils in Brazil fully support the provisions in the Statute that call for developmentally oriented supports and services for all children and youth. For various reasons, though, these programs have not received the attention they deserve. One obvious reason is the lack of fiscal resources, but that is only a limited explanation. Historically, Brazil has invested in children and youth when they were perceived as representing a threat to the social order. Thus, on both sides of the social order question, the public has reacted to the needs of children in difficult circumstances – either calling for more repression or advocating their protection from the abuses of police and other authorities. The same kind of public attention has not been mobilized around low-income children and youth in general.

Many of the existing governmental agencies and NGOs have been reluctant to shift their focus from preventive services to developmental supports for all children and youth. In other cases, program planners may lack a vision of what community-based, developmentally oriented services for youth and children can and should be. Another barrier to the implementation of community-based programs for children and youth – in Brazil and throughout Latin America – is the reliance on central governments for such public policies, thereby impeding or usurping local leadership. This reliance stymies local empowerment of low-income communities. Thus, the concept of community as a participant in developing programs and services for children and youth has been absent. Communities are extremely important in the lives of children and youth in Brazil, providing informal supports in the absence of state-sponsored services and programs. However, few local communities have been empowered or involved in decision making about the needs of their children.

Politically, there is also a lack of commitment to the needs of all children and youth. Although the vast majority of Brazilian voters would agree that children should not be abused, for example, few voters are prepared to accept the idea – embodied in the Statute – that low-income children deserve, and that the government should provide, the same level of developmental supports as those enjoyed by most middle-class children.

Despite these barriers, there are several examples of community-based, developmentally oriented services for children and youth in Brazil and elsewhere in Latin America that involve growing community participation and local autonomy (Barker and Fontes, 1996). To illustrate what we mean by community-based developmental supports for children and youth, we have included three Brazilian examples. There are thousands of examples of community-based NGOs that provide services and carry

out developmentally supportive activities with children and youth in the
Latin American (and Caribbean) region. There are also numerous examples
of government-funded services and activities for children and youth. The
examples we include deserve special attention because of four important
factors: (1) they are all publicly funded efforts; (2) they seek to involve the
community, NGOs, as well as youth and families; (3) they seek to reach a
significant number of children and youth within the area where they operate; and (4) they take an integrated developmental approach to providing
for the needs of children and youth.

These three examples from Brazil are state- and municipality-funded
efforts to assist children and youth of low-income communities. All three of
the examples demonstrate an important degree of community participation
and leadership in the process, and all three seek to provide a range of activities and services to assist children and youth in their holistic development.

Case Studies

1. ABCs – Aprender, Brincar, e Crescer (Learn, Play, and Grow Centers): State of Ceará, North-East Brazil

Working with other state governmental organizations since 1991, the Social
Action Secretariat (the state-level social welfare ministry) in Ceará has
operated a program of community-based after-school centers that provide
a range of cultural, educational, recreational, and vocational training activities for children and youth of ages 7–17. The Secretariat offers services for
both enrolled and nonenrolled youth. As of 1996, these ABC centers provided activities to about 1,000 youth ages 7–17 per month in each of about
20 centers.

The overall goal of the ABCs was initially preventive: to strengthen family
and community ties with the goal of preventing the migration of children
and youth to urban centers (Neto, 1994), and in particular to Fortaleza,
the capital and largest city in Ceará. To prevent children from working or
living on the streets, the ABCs offer a combination of tutoring and literacy
courses, cultural and recreational activities, and vocational training, all with
the goal of attracting youth and offering them an alternative to the lure of the
city. The state government also offers services and activities for children and
youth who work and/or live in the streets and for youth who are involved in
prostitution.

The ABCs are notable for their steps to involve the community in the
design and implementation of each center. The original 20 ABCs began by
forming a community commission in each site that comprised five members

from existing and representative neighborhood associations. These commissions then planned the construction and implementation of the ABCs in their communities. All the centers have a similar array of activities and services, the exact mix determined by the local staff and community commission. In 1996, the ABCs were also negotiating with the InterAmerican Development Bank for funding to develop local information collection systems and public awareness campaigns to broaden community support and participation.

The ABCs have faced several obstacles, including difficulty of attracting local private sector support, which has been minimal; problems in cultivating and maintaining strong relationships with local schools; offering vocational training that is useful for the local job market; and experiencing high rates of staff turnover. Nonetheless, the ABCs have enhanced youth development in ways not possible if they did not exist because of their scope and levels of community participation. From 1992 to 1994, the number of children and youth enrolled and participating in all 20 centers totaled 56,901, of whom 15,949 received vocational training. The ABCs have succeeded and communities have responded to them because of the political climate in the state of Ceará. The state has received national and international recognition for its important public administrative reforms and its positive track record in decentralization. The ABCs were implemented during a period in Ceará's history when state government officials at the highest level rewarded and supported innovation, accountability, and cost-effectiveness (Neto, 1994; Barker, 1994, 1996). Whether other states can produce similar results remains to be seen.

2. Curumim Centers: State of Minas Gerais, South-East Brazil

Started by the Secretariat of Sports, Leisure, and Tourism in the state of Minas Gerais, the Curumim project rationale builds on the language of the Statute that all children have the right to play and to be children. The project seeks to provide low-income children with leisure and play activities as a complement, not a substitute, to the public school system. Focusing on low-income children, state officials insist that the program is a step toward the universalization of education in Brazil, referring to their goal of extending high-quality, publicly supported education to all children.

Curumim Centers are recreational centers that support after-school activities in low-income communities throughout the state of Minas Gerais. Each Curumim begins with a community-based needs assessment that involves evaluating needs and opportunities for children at the community level, including sports and leisure activities. When the evaluation is complete, an agreement is developed and signed by the local municipality and the state. The local municipality provides the space for the center; the state government provides construction materials and pays for ongoing operating expenses. The Centers offer an array of activities for children ages 6–12, including indoor and outdoor recreation, arts and crafts, and homework assistance/tutoring, as well as many opportunities for formal and informal social interaction. The main goal of the program is to offer children a safe place to play and "be children"; other objectives are to support children's educational attainment and to reduce rates of grade retention and repetition. As are the ABCs, the program is open to all children, but the location of Curumim Centers in the low-income communities disproportionately serves children at risk of abandonment. Between 1991 and 1995, 140 Curumim Centers were built in the state of Minas Gerais, 20 in the capital city of Belo Horizonte alone. As of 1995, these centers were serving approximately 40,000 low-income children. To date, a systematic assessment of their effectiveness has not been produced.

3. Cidade Mãe (Mother City): City of Salvador, Bahia, North-East Brazil

Cidade Mãe (Mother city) is a governmental youth-serving project founded in 1993 and operated by the city of Salvador, Bahia, with funding from both the municipal and state governments. The program's stated objectives are to improve the academic performance and employability of low-income youth and to lower the incidence of certain high-risk behaviors, such as drug abuse and teen pregnancy. The program provides community-based vocational training and after-school academic support activities, as well as health education, recreational activities, and counseling. The program operates in four low-income areas in Salvador, targeting youth ages 14–18 who are at risk of living in the streets and/or of dropping out of school.

Mother City's primary program strategy involves creating an integrated system of interventions to provide multifaceted support and vocational training to at-risk enrolled youth. Interdisciplinary teams develop case plans for youth based on individual assessments of their vocational training needs and then refer them to or connect them with appropriate services. Major challenges encountered by the program include the difficulty of involving the youth's families, who often lack time to participate in community activities and meetings; the bureaucracy involved and delays in receiving funding from the state government; and low staff salaries, which have contributed to a high staff turnover (Barker and Fontes, 1996). Although this customized approach to youth development appears to be rich and well founded on conceptual grounds, to date an assessment of program effectiveness has not been conducted, and it is unclear whether and how much the bureaucratic obstacles undermine project goals.

Comments on the Case Studies

In highlighting these programs we are not suggesting that their mere implementation will in any facile way overcome systems of exclusion and poverty. As Dewees and Klees (1995) remind us, we must avoid the simplistic idea of "technical rationality," that is, the belief that designing and replicating program models to resolve social problems will indeed solve these problems without ever addressing the underlying social problems and power structures. In their words (1995:80):

Technical rationality does not fail because of poor implementation, corrupt governments, or even the lack of good will or ideas. Instead, educational and other social policies do very little to solve social problems because there are interests that benefit from doing very little to the structures – capitalist, patriarchal, racist, and more – that favor these interests.

The three case studies are not examples of projects seeking to change the underlying power and income structure, yet they do represent small steps toward improving the lives of many low-income children and youth in the short run.

An important drawback of all three programs is that they perpetuate the division of social classes in Brazil. All are aimed at low-income communities, thereby allowing the possibility of maintaining second-class services for the poor while the middle class continue to use their personally and privately funded access to higher-quality services and programs. Brazil's legacy of discriminatory treatment of poor children (and in many cases, poor black children) can easily perpetuate class differences in access to support services. Thus, although it is true that the children participating in the ABCs or Curumim are not on the streets, they are also not participating in the same swimming classes or French classes as middle-class children.

The high residential segregation in Brazil and most of Latin America – as low-income children attend public schools and middle- and upper-income children attend private schools – has tremendous implications for the future of the region. In recent years, trends toward privatizing health and other public sectors have further exacerbated this social division. It is particularly disturbing that in recent years, many middle- and upper-income children (and their families) have begun to avoid public transportation and public spaces, fearing contact with low-income children and youth, whom they think of as street children (see White, this volume, for discussion of youth and public spaces). The long-term implications of this social partition are unknown, but given that the children of the middle and upper classes will likely govern the country in the future, their negative perceptions of poor children do not bode well for future policies.

What if, instead of constructing Curumim or ABC Centers only in low-income communities, a few of them were constructed in middle-class neighborhoods? As an issue of equity, the centers in middle-class neighborhoods might charge a sliding scale fee to families but would nonetheless receive governmental support. Even such a symbolic involvement of the middle class could have important long-term ramifications by ensuring long-term political commitment to the programs as well as potentially raising the overall quality of services rendered. Furthermore, involving families of different social classes would slowly change their perception and their children's perceptions of low-income children.

In these case studies, we have for the most part emphasized developmental supports that generally involved services and activities designed for and with children and youth. However, another component of youth developmental supports deserves special consideration, namely, the possibility of supports for entire families. In Western Europe and North America, such family support services include income subsidies, food or nutritional subsidies, in-home counseling, and crisis support services. Policy analysts need to determine what types of culturally appropriate services that ultimately benefit youth might be offered directly to Brazilian parents and families.

To be sure, community-based developmentally oriented programs for youth represent a move in the right direction. They signal a move away from focusing on street children to a recognition of the state's obligation to support the healthy development of all children. Indeed, the number of children and youth reached by preventive community-based projects is unprecedented in Brazil. Whether they will continue to proliferate and expand remains to be seen.

Finally, analysts and critics must be realistic about the short-term impact of community-based programs. The three case studies were sold to policymakers with the justification that they would prevent school failure or life on the streets. However, an after-school program may prove insufficient to prevent a child from failing in school or being abandoned to the streets. For most children, the causes of school failure, family stress, and abandonment are far more deep-seated, structural, and multifaceted than an after-school program can solve. The risk is that policymakers may hold these programs responsible for solving problems that are outside their control. Although youth programs must be accountable for their outcomes, their constraints deserve recognition. A 1997 evaluation of two of the largest youth-serving agencies in the United States provides an instructive warning:

> In an effort to adopt an accountability approach, many [youth-serving] organizations have been compelled to use outcomes over which they have no direct control (e.g., school completion, job attainment, healthy family formation) as their measures of success, primarily because the outcomes are at least measurable. The problem with the approach is that these ultimate outcomes, in fact, result from a diverse set of experiences (in the family, school, neighborhood, etc.); no one setting or experience alone can be expected to produce them. Focusing on the achievement of these future long-term outcomes does not provide a standard by which an organization or activity can be held accountable in the present. (Gambone and Arbeton, 1997:3)

Conclusions

> The child and adolescent have the right to protection of life and health, through effective implementation of public social policies that make possible . . . harmonious development in dignified conditions of existence. (Statute of the Child and Adolescent, Title II, Art. 7)

A comprehensive system of extracurricular, after-school community-based supports that includes recreation, health education, vocational counseling and training, tutoring, personal counseling, arts, and culture for all children and youth in Brazil may lie far in the future. Indeed, in promising as much as it does, the Statute runs the risk of proposing an unattainable utopia that can only generate pessimism about short-term outcomes. However, the Statute also offers a starting point toward pragmatic intermediary steps that can be implemented in the short run to reshape programs for low-income children and youth, while also laying the groundwork for a better system in the future. The best starting point offered by the Statute is the emphasis on community, family, and child participation. Indeed, in consulting communities, families, and children about their collective needs, the emerging system may come to resemble our typical middle-class family. It will likely include promotional services that focus on the strengths and potentials of children and youth rather than their shortcomings.

In making a case to support all children, we do not mean to suggest that the NGOs and governmental agencies assisting street children should cease or lessen their efforts. Instead, we are advocating that the focus should be shifted to include the needs of all children and youth. Many experiences of programs and advocacy organizations working with street children have provided important directions about the common needs of all children and youth in Brazil and elsewhere. Designers of future programs should learn from these experiences to understand both the enormous potential of Brazilian children and youth, as well as the supports and activities that are needed to ensure healthy, normative development. In that sense, the case studies presented here offer examples of viable initiatives in developmental supports. However, before recommending large-scale replication of any single model, we suggest systematic evaluation.

The Statute seeks to put Brazil's child support system on a par with notions of universal supports as established by the UN Convention on the Rights of the Child. The challenge before us is to use the Statute as a scaffold – as a way to move Brazil closer to that goal. A truly universal support system for all children and youth in Brazil, as envisioned by the Statute, also requires changing perceptions of children and youth and embracing the idea that every child has the right to healthy and harmonious development, regardless of his/her socioeconomic status, race, religion, political affiliation, and so on.[9]

Such a focus would require creating publicly funded, purposefully linked networks and structures that collaborate with the public education and public health systems to provide for the integrated development of all children and youth (1) to promote their individual potential, in reaching personal, educational, and vocational aspirations; (2) to promote their development, awareness, and full participation as citizens, present and future; and (3) to promote their ability to engage in meaningful and healthy intimate relationships. Such a system would require significant investment by the government in the futures of children and youth. However, this system can only be successful if the current health and education systems are improved.

Until appeals based on rights and social equality move policymakers to support services for all children and youth, models focused on poor youths' deficits or problems should not be invoked as justification for the existence of youth programs.

---

[9] As stated in the United Nations Convention on the Rights of the Child and the Statute of the Child and the Adolescent.

Focusing on the self-interest of Brazil as a country increases the chance that policymakers will appreciate that investing in children is investing in the future. As Brazil is becomes increasingly integrated in the global economy, competition requires more training in the use of technological tools and general technological literacy. Brazil will need citizens who are prepared for lifelong learning. Viewed in this light, shifting the focus from street children to all children is clearly not merely an issue of equity for Brazil, but in fact an investment in its future.

REFERENCES

Barker, G. (1994). *Assisting At-Risk Urban Youth in Northeast Brazil: A Project to Prevent Delinquency, Abandonment and Child Prostitution.* Brasilia: U.S. Agency for International Development (unpublished report).

Barker, G. (1996). *Integrated Service Models for Youth: An Analysis of Selected International Experiences.* Washington, DC: World Bank (unpublished working paper).

Barker, G., and Fontes, M. (1996). *Review and Analysis of International Experience with Programs Targeted on At-Risk Youth.* Working Paper No. 5. Washington, DC: World Bank.

Barker, G., and Knaul, F. (1991). *Exploited Entrepreneurs: Street and Working Children in Developing Countries.* Working Paper No. 1. New York: Childhope-USA.

Bruce, J., Lloyd, C., Leonard, A., Engle, P., and Duffy, N. (1995). *Families in Focus: New Perspectives on Mothers, Fathers, and Children.* New York: Population Council.

Cassaniga, H. (1997). The Guardianship Council in Blumenau, Santa Catarina. Personal correspondence.

Castro, M. R. (1997). *Retóricas da Rua: Educador, Criança e Diálogos* (Street rhetorics: the educator, the child and dialogues). Rio de Janeiro: EDUSU/AMAIS.

Chalhub, T. (1997). Homeless Children in Rio de Janeiro: Exploring the Meanings of Street Life. *Children and Youth Care Forum,* 26(3).

Dewees, A., and Klees, S. J. (1995). Social Movements and the Transformation of National Policy: Street and Working Children in Brazil. *Comparative Education Review,* 39(1), 76–100.

ECA em Revista (1997). "The Statute of the Child and Adolescent." São Paulo: Forum DCA. April/May.

Fausto, A., and Cervini, R. (1991). *O Trabalho e a Rua: Crianças e Adolescentes no Brazil Urbano in the 1980's* [Work and street: children and adolescents in urban Brazil in the 1980s]. São Paulo: Cortez.

Gambone, M., and Arbeton, A. (1997). *Safe Havens: The Contributions of Youth Organizations to Healthy Adolescent Development.* Philadelphia: Public/Private Ventures.

IBGE/UNICEF (Brazilian Institute of Geography and Statistics). (1997). *Indicadores sobre Crianças e Adolescentes* (Indicators on children and adolescents). Brasília/Rio de Janeiro: IBGE.

Jornal do Brasil (1995). Pesquisa Muda Teses sobre Meninos de Rua (Study changes theses on street children). Rio de Janeiro, May 17.

Myers, W. (1988). Alternative Services for Street Children: The Brazilian Approach. In A. Bequele and J. Boyden (Eds.), *Combating Child Labour*. Geneva: International Labour Office.

Myers, W. (Ed.). (1991). *Protecting Working Children*. London: Zed Books and UNICEF.

Neto, P. (1994). *Projeto de Reforma e Desenvolvimento Social: Avaliação do Projeto Setorial: Programa Vivendo e Aprendendo – Projeto ABC Comunitario* (Reform and Social Development Project: evaluation of the Program Living and Learning – ABC Community Project). Fortaleza, Brazil: Secretaria De Ação Social (The Social Action Secretary) (unpublished memo).

Oliveira, J. S. (1993). *O Traço da Desigualdade Social no Brazil* (Social inequality in Brazil). Rio de Janeiro: IBGE.

Pilotti, F., and Rizzini, I. (Eds.). (1995). *A Arte de Governar Crianças: A História das Políticas Sociais, da Legislação e da Assistência à Infância no Brasil* (The art of governing children: the history of social policies, legislation and child welfare in brazil). Rio de Janeiro: Instituto Interamericano del Nino, CESPI/USU, AMAIS Editora.

Pittman, K., and Cahill, M. (1991). *A New Vision: Promoting Youth Development*. (Commissioned Paper No. 3). Washington, DC/New York: Center for Youth Development and Policy Research, Academy for Educational Development.

Projeto Axe (1993). *Meninos que Vivem nas Ruas de Salvador – Mapeamento e Contagem* (Children living in the streets of Salvador – mapping and counting). Salvador, Bahia (unpublished mimeo).

Rizzini, I. (Ed). (1986). *A Geração da Rua: Um Estudo sobre as Crianças Marginalizadas do Rio de Janeiro* (The street generation: a study on the marginalized children of Rio de Janeiro). Rio de Janeiro: CESME/USU.

Rizzini, I. (Ed.). (1994). *Children in Brazil Today: A Challenge for the Third Millennium*. Rio de Janeiro: CESPI/USU.

Rizzini, I. (Ed.). (1995). *Deserdados da Sociedade: Os "Meninos de Rua" da América Latina* (Disinherited from society: "street children" in Latin America). Rio de Janeiro: CESPI/USU.

Rizzini, I. (1997a). *O Século Perdido: Raízes Históricas das Políticas Públicas para a Infância no Brasil* (The lost century: the historical roots of public policies for children in Brazil). Rio de Janeiro: EDUSU/AMAIS.

Rizzini, I. (1997b). Childhood and National Identity. Paper presented at the Urban Childhood Conference, Norwegian Centre for Child Research, Trondheim, Norway.

Rizzini, I. (1998). Poor Children in Latin America: A Case Example of Social Inequality. *Children's Legal Rights Journal*, 18(1), 50–70.

Rizzini, I., Rizzini, I., and Holanda, F. R. (1996). *A Criança e o Adolescente no Mundo do Trabalho* (The child and the adolescent in the world of work). Rio de Janeiro : EDUSU/AMAIS Ed.

Rizzini, I., Rizzini, I., Munoz-Vargas, M., and Galeano, L. (1992). Childhood and Urban Poverty in Brazil: Street and Working Children and Their Families. Florence, Italy: UNICEF International Child Development Centre.

Secretaria de Ação Social. (1994). *Report on Census of Street and Working Children*. Fortaleza: Sectretaria Estadual (Ceará) de Ação Social (State Social Action Secretary).

Sherraden, M. (1992). *Community-Based Youth Services in International Perspective*. Washington, DC: Carnegie Council on Adolescent Development.

Souza, H. (1991). Criança é Coisa Séria. In Murray, Rosane (Ed.), *Criança é Coisa Séria.* Rio de Janeiro: Ed. AMAIS/Memórias Futuras Edições.

Souza, H. (1994). *Criança é Coisa Séria* (Children are a serious matter). Rio de Janeiro: Amais Ed, 1992. English version in Rizzini, I., *Children in the City of Violence: The case of Brazil.* United Nations University Press.

Statute of the Child and Adolescent. (1990). Estatuto da criança e do Adolescente. Brasil, Lei N. 8.69, de 13 de julho.

UNDP Report (1993). *Human Development Report: People's Participation.* New York: United Nations Publications.

UNDP Report (1994). *Human Develpoment Report: New Dimensions of Human Security.* New York: United Nations Publications.

UNICEF. (1993). Situation Analysis – Country Programme 1994–2000. In *Children and Adolescents – Right to Have Rights.* Brasilia: UNICEF.

Vasconcelos, A. (1992). *Casa de Passagem Project.* Paper presented in the International Workshop on Strategies for Working with Children in Situations of National Violence, Bogota, Colombia March 24–27. Save the Children (UK).

Whalen, S., and Wynn, J. (1995). Enhancing Primary Services for Youth through an Infrastructure of Social Services. *Journal of Adolescent Research*, 10(1), 88–110.

World Bank. (1997). *World Development Report 1997: The State of a Changing World.* New York: Oxford University Press.

7 Youth Crime, Community Development, and Social Justice

Robert White

Introduction

This chapter provides a broad overview of social deviance and delinquency with a particular focus on urban young people. The first part of the chapter discusses the nature of youth offending, beginning with a brief description of *youth crime trends*. This is followed by a review of the *explanations for youthful offending*. I argue that beyond multifactoral analysis of the particular elements associated with criminality and antisocial behavior, there is a need to locate youth behavior and activity within a wider social structural context. In particular, the broader political economy, as related to distributions of poverty, is vital for a full appreciation of the social nature of juvenile offending.

How best to respond to youth offending is the focus for discussion in the second part of the chapter, which emphasizes *youth crime prevention*. After describing different approaches to crime prevention – the coercive, the developmental, and the accommodating – I outline a *strategic framework* for youth crime prevention. This framework summarizes key principles and programmatic concerns that might guide the development of local crime prevention initiatives. The chapter concludes with a discussion of the link between youth crime prevention measures and wider issues of social justice.

Thanks are due to Susan Reddrop and Sue Medlock for assistance in the preparation of this chapter.

The Nature of Urban Youth Crime

This section discusses general international crime trends, presents data drawn from particular national contexts, and provides information about specific kinds of youth offending. It also considers how the media portray youth crime and briefly outlines various explanations for youth offending.

Trends in Juvenile Offending

Data on the changing picture of juvenile convictions from a wide variety of jurisdictions around the world between 1990 and 1994 suggest that countries such as Slovakia, Italy, and Cyprus experienced significant increases in the number of juveniles convicted over this period. Alternatively, countries such as Japan, Myanmar (formerly Burma), England, and Wales witnessed decline in the number of convicted juveniles (United Nations Crime and Justice Information Network, 1998).

Interpreting such comparisons and trend analyses requires caution, however, because the nature of record keeping, definitions of juveniles, classification of crimes, and data-processing techniques vary greatly. Some countries record all arrests and court appearances; others record only convictions. This matters because many jurisdictions currently emphasize pre-court diversion programs and court-ordered diversion programs, and that emphasis affects the officially recorded number of convictions. A lower conviction rate, therefore, is no guarantee that youth crime is declining or that the number of young people who have contact with the criminal justice system is falling. Another area of concern is the nature of the offenses that may reach court attention and result in a conviction. In some jurisdictions, this may include offenses ranging from failure to pay a train fare to very serious criminal offenses. In others, there may be a more clear-cut distinction between minor offenses that can be resolved without court involvement and more serious criminal justice matters that end in court.

Another source of data on international offending is based on self-report studies. A review of the main findings of self-report studies in 13 Western countries concludes the following (Junger-Tas, 1994:371, 379):

- There is a great similarity in rates of delinquent behavior, as well as in the nature of the offenses that are most frequently committed (e.g., property offending, violence including vandalism, fare evasion, fights and riots, cannabis use, buying or selling of stolen goods).
- Drug use appears to be less prevalent in southern Europe than in western Europe and the United States.

- The ratio of boys' to girls' criminality is 1.5:1 for property offenses and drug use, but 2:1 to 4:1 for violence, with the largest sex disparity between violence against persons and violence against property.
- There is little difference between the sexes with respect to fare evasion, shop stealing, and problem behavior.
- The peak age for property offenses is 16–17 compared to 14–15 for vandalism and 18–19 for violence against persons.
- Less educated youth report higher rates of violent behavior.
- Early school leaving and unemployment are correlated with drug use.

Self-report studies also examine specific kinds of antisocial behavior, such as bullying (King, Wold, Tudor-Smith, and Harel, 1996). There is significant cross-sectional variation in reported rates of bullying, although there is consensus that more boys than girls engage in this antisocial behavior. Self-report studies also find a "striking disparity in delinquency self-reports of ethnic minorities and their overrepresentation in police statistics" (Junger-Tas, 1994:179). This disparity highlights the difference between actual offending behavior and rates (as represented in self-report studies) and the processes of criminalization whereby certain selected groups of teenagers are arrested, charged with, and convicted of offenses (as represented in official crime statistics). It also underscores unequal representation of particular groups in the criminalization process. For instance, in a survey of nine Western countries, Tonry (1997:1) observed:

Members of *some* disadvantaged minority groups in every Western country are disproportionately likely to be arrested, convicted, and imprisoned for violent, property, and drug crimes. This is true whether the minority groups are members of different "racial" groups from the majority population, for example, blacks or Afro-Caribbeans in Canada, England, or the United States, or of different ethnic backgrounds, for example, North African Arabs in France or the Netherlands, or – irrespective of race or ethnicity – are recent migrants from other countries, for example, Yugoslavs or Eastern Europeans in Germany and Finns in Sweden.

Comparative research on indigenous people and criminal justice in New Zealand, Canada, Australia, and the United States also finds similar patterns of over-representation in crime statistics (Hazelhurst, 1995).

In addition to supporting global generalizations about the ages at which certain offenses occur, the preponderance of young men in youth crime statistics, and the overrepresentation of some demographic groups in the criminalization process, international reviews provide useful selective documentation and comparison. For example, there is general argument that the crime rate in Japan lags far behind that of other industrialized countries such as Britain, France, Germany, and the United States and that offenses such as murder and robbery are extremely rare in statistical terms (Kurata and Hamai, 1998). By contrast, in Canada violent offenses constitute 21% of youth court cases. Moreover, Canadian juvenile murder arrest rates increased by 30% between 1986 and 1994, while robbery arrest rates increased by 56% (John Howard Society of Alberta, 1998). Likewise, U.S. crime trends reveal that over the 1990s major changes occurred in the patterns of juvenile offending (see Fox, 1997; Sickmund, 1997; Sickmund, Snyder, and Poe-Yamagata, 1997; Stone, 1998). For instance, whereas the juvenile arrest rate for property crimes remained stable, the number of juvenile arrests for violent crimes rose dramatically. Specifically, between 1985 and 1994 the rate of murder committed by U.S. youth ages 14 to 17 increased by 172% (although it declined in 1995). Although most female juvenile arrests were for nonviolent offenses, the 1981 to 1995 increase in female arrests for violent crimes (129%) was more than double the male increase (56%). The United States witnessed a disproportionate increase in court referrals for African American females in all offense categories.

Countries undergoing major economic and social changes have also experienced increases in youth crime trends. For instance, juvenile delinquency has been rising in China for several years, and the number of offenders under 18 years increased by 30% between 1985 and 1995. However, the ratio of perpetrators under 18 to the total number of perpetrators decreased from 23.8% in 1985 to 10.5% in 1995 (Yisheng, 1998). Chinese juvenile delinquency is not generally violent, as homicide accounts for only 0.75% of cases involving 14- to 17-year-olds and assault only 2.6%. Changes in the nature of youth offending are also apparent in Russia. An in-depth study of crime in Moscow also finds a 51% rise in the proportion of 14- to 15-year-old minors involved in criminal activity between 1988 and 1993, and a 46% increase for 16 to 17-year-olds (Alexeyeva and Patrignani, 1994). However, the share of 16- to 17-year-olds involved in specific crimes fell for all types, while the rate of criminality among 18- to 24-year-olds rose for all crimes, except hooliganism.

Broad crime trends across different jurisdictions provide some indication of national and regional similarity in delinquency and antisocial behavior. For example, in most jurisdictions the vast majority of young people are not serious and persistent offenders. The crimes most frequently committed by young people, for which they are arrested or charged, relate to property (usually of items of relatively low value) and public order (such as use of bad language or making noise in a public place), and in some jurisdictions such as the United States, drug and alcohol related offenses. Serious offenses, including homicide, are typically rare among young people, although actual rates vary across jurisdictions (Cunneen and White, 1995; Loeber and Farrington, 1998).

Nevertheless, a more fine-grained analysis of crime patterns is required to appreciate fully the nature of youth antisocial behavior. Although they constitute a relatively small share of all juvenile offenses, there is considerable public concern about perceived serious and violent youth offenses. Popular and media perceptions of youth criminality and police interventions in juvenile justice are, in turn, shaped by the specific features of juvenile offending itself. To wit, many aspects of juvenile offending relate directly to how young people use *public space.* Young people tend to hang around in groups, and youth crime is often committed by groups. Because the public congregation of young people makes them highly visible, youth crime becomes more easily detectable. Moreover, young people tend to commit crime in their own neighborhoods, where there is greater likelihood that they will be recognized and identified by observers. Also, youth crime tends to be episodic, unplanned, and opportunistic, often related to the use of public space (such as shopping centers and public transport) where there is more surveillance (see Cunneen and White, 1995). Consequently, the public visibility and group behavior of young people make them more prone to arrest for certain types of crimes than their adult counterparts.

Simultaneously, noncriminal behavior and less serious offending by young people are also subject to routine scrutiny by authority figures and other adults. This is partly due to the visibility of young people in public spaces and their tendency to congregate in groups. Furthermore, large congregations of young people may disrupt the flow of pedestrian traffic and, if accompanied by excessive noise, may disturb bystanders and shopkeepers. In addition, the adoption of unconventional subcultural styles marks teenagers in ways that call them to the notice of other users of public space. The very presence of young people, much less what they are actually doing, is often perceived as a problem.

Another important aspect of public order concerns conflicts within and between young people themselves. The congregation of youth groups from diverse social and cultural backgrounds occasionally flares into street conflicts, which range from name-calling through to more serious instances of personal harm. Mason and Tomsen (1997) report that violence against gay men and lesbians by groups of young men becomes a significant social problem in some places. Young women often feel intimidated or threatened by young men (and older men) when they use public spaces. There is also ample evidence of group fighting and violence in public spaces, both in relation to gangs and with respect to particular indigenous or ethnic minority groups (see Huff, 1996; Sanders, 1994; Gordon, 1995; Klein, Maxson and Miller, 1995; White 1999a). Street violence of this nature makes young people feel unsafe when they venture out of their homes and neighborhoods. Moreover, the perception and/or presence of criminal youth gangs further reinforces ideas that young people generate problems in their use of public spaces.

In addition to theft offenses, minor assaults, and public visibility, many studies focus on youth vandalism. Although few vandals actually get caught (Geason and Wilson, 1990), urban environments are replete with wall graffiti, broken windows and street lights, damage to playground equipment, smashed telephone boxes, and carving on park benches, which presumably are attributable to youth. Canadian research claims that although "some vandals may be antisocial youths who deliberately seek ways to express themselves in costly rampages of destruction – as is believed by the public and portrayed by the media – many are ordinary youths who do their damage spontaneously and with little thought of its costs or consequences" (LaGrange, 1996:140). This view concurs with self-report data on juvenile offending in Australia, suggesting that vandalism is more uniformly spread across the youth population than arrest figures indicate (Cunneen and White, 1995; Mukherjee, 1997). Nevertheless, specific types of vandalism warrant closer attention because some studies suggest quite different motivations, contexts, and definitions of vandalism, particularly in regard to graffiti (see, for example, Carrington, 1989; Forrester, 1993; Ferrell, 1997).

The issue of vandalism is intrinsically related to youth's use of public space in that it is highly visible, is ubiquitous across the urban landscape, and appears to confirm the worst fears of adult society that young people are "out of control." Whereas the actual cost of vandalism tends to be overstated (LaGrange, 1996), its prevalence reinforces the belief that young people's use of public space requires close monitoring. Interestingly, Hollands (1995:65) found that only 13% of the young people interviewed in his English study admitted to ever being involved in any kind of vandalism, with the vast majority of acts involving petty crimes (such as stealing street signs or traffic cones). I return to this theme of public spaces in proposing a proactive approach to youth crime prevention.

Portrayals and Explanations of Youth Crime

The representation of young people in media and in political and academic discourse has a major influence on how youthful offending is dealt with at policy and program levels. Popular views about youth crime are very much influenced by media portrayals, and juvenile crime is big news in some countries. The persistence and pervasiveness of such reporting not only reinforce stereotypes, but also make adults unnecessarily fearful and suspicious of young people.

Hogg and Brown (1998) identify several distortions of youth behavior that often are perpetuated by the media. These include beliefs that crime rates are soaring; that crime is worse than ever; that the criminal justice system is "soft" on crime; that the greater satisfaction of victims demands more retribution through the courts; and so on. Crime is sensationalized in the media by giving more emphasis to atypical, unusually violent crimes than to common crimes. Focusing on "street crime," youth deviance is presented as random and thus a threat to everyone in the same way (see Grabosky and Wilson, 1989; Ericson, Baranek, and Chan, 1991).

In the specific case of youth crime, the media are saturated with stories about "young thugs," "hooligans," "ethnic youth gangs," "school vandals," and "lazy teenagers" (see, for example, Bessant and Hil, 1997). These representations acquire meaning in the context of a wider discourse about "youth" (with the dominant image that of criminality) and "law and order" (with the dominant image of rampant crime and major threats to personal safety). As the language of the media emphasizes the criminality of young people (gangs, drugs, violence), it also incorporates ideas of child protection (youth in moral or physical danger). In a study of how the media and the "antiyouth lobby" portray young people in Canada, Schissel (1997:16) notes that the agenda is invariably one of extending social control: "Most youth-focused crime panics urge others either to protect children or condemn them." In either case, the result is to reinforce the notion that "youth are the problem." As such, it is not surprising that opinion polls and surveys in Canada in the 1990s show a consistently high and growing number of adults who claim that youth behavior has been getting worse and that youth gangs or youth violence is a major crime problem (John Howard Society of Alberta, 1998).

The widespread distortion of young people's lives in the United States has been powerfully criticized by Males (1996). Whether in relation to drug use, teenage pregnancy, or criminal violence, certain categories of young people have been roundly condemned by the mainstream media and politicians of the major political parties. This is so despite historical analyses and empirical trends showing either that the problem is smaller than portrayed or that the reasons for any particular trend are not age-specific. In the words of Males (1996:21):

Efforts to frame violence as a "teenage problem" as officials and a compliant media have done, fail before the stark reality that race, class, gender, era, family background, and locality are far greater predictors of violence than young age. In fact, when such factors are fully accounted for, young age doesn't predict much of anything about violence.

Nevertheless, young people in Western countries feature prominently in media stories about violence, crime, antisocial behavior, and all manner of social ills. It is true that young people account for a fair share of property crimes, such as shoplifting, and various nuisance activities relating to their presence in public spaces. However, these problems are exaggerated in terms of their seriousness, and that emphasis is often misplaced when it comes to actual perpetrators and crime contexts.

Media treatment of young people as threats and pariahs, coupled with commercial pressures to publish "crime news," further entrench the law and order common sense among leading politicians and criminal justice officials. Consequently, government responses to youth behavior, and especially youth criminal behavior, are heavily influenced by the media's message of "moral panic" and images of youth. Not surprisingly, jurisdictions and policymakers often respond with punitive and controlling measures, although simultaneous efforts to introduce softer crime prevention measures sometimes accompany the coercive practice. Whereas media images of youth offending stress willful and flagrant disregard for law and decisions to commit crime, the criminological literature deemphasizes problem youth per se and instead underscores the problems of youth.

Theories and studies of juvenile offending point to a wide range of circumstances that illustrate how the problems youth confront eventuate in crime (Cunneen and White, 1995). For example, in a review of research on the correlates of offending, Farrington (1996) identifies the key "risk factors" associated with youth crime (see also Rutter, Giller, and Hagell, 1998). The many factors identified include (1) hyperactivity and impulsivity (e.g., hyperactivity–impulsivity–attention deficit, inhibition); (2) intelligence and attainment (e.g., low nonverbal intelligence, abstract reasoning, cognitive and neuropsychological deficit); (3) parental supervision, discipline, and attitude (e.g., erratic or harsh parental discipline, rejecting parental attitudes, violent behavior); (4) broken homes (e.g., maternal and paternal deprivation, parental conflict); (5) socioeconomic deprivation (e.g., low family income, poor housing); (6) peer influences (e.g., male group behavior, delinquent friends); and (7) community influences (e.g., high residential mobility, neighborhood disorganization, physical deterioration, overcrowding, type of housing). In isolation, these circumstances do not produce youth delinquency. Rather, several factors combined explain variation in the propensity for criminal behavior and/or criminalization among young people.

Who is actually *criminalized* (i.e., labeled and processed as a criminal) nevertheless tends to follow a distinctive social pattern. Although most young people do something illegal at some stage in their lives, only certain categories of youth reach the deepest parts of the juvenile justice system. The criminal justice system screens young people on the basis of both offense categories (serious/nonserious; first time/repeat offending) and social characteristics (family background, income, employment, education). A profile of youth who enter detention looks remarkably similar across countries: single, urban young men, aged 14 to 18, with low educational attainment, from poor families, and often with no fixed address (see Braithwaite, 1989). Some categories of young people (poor, indigenous, ethnic minority) tend to be overrepresented for both males and females. Stated differently, the most disadvantaged and vulnerable youth receive the greatest attention from justice officials at all system levels, ranging from police through to detention center staff. This pattern reveals as much about the operation of the juvenile justice system as it does about young offenders (see Miller, 1996). Moreover, the overrepresentation of vulnerable youth in the criminal justice system has implications for explanations about group differences in offending by type of offense. As well, this tendency directly influences public perceptions about youth offending behavior.

Researchers continue to identify a range of risk factors and protective factors that influence propensity to engage in criminal or antisocial behavior (Catalano and Hawkins, 1996), but the wider societal context ultimately shapes the life chances and experiences of young people (Wyn and White, 1997). The social ecology of poverty, and prevalence of youth unemployment in particular, is crucial for understanding the precise nature and extent of juvenile offending in particular locales. Youth unemployment is the foundation for criminality (witness the social background of most juveniles in detention), but when it is part of a larger structure of adversity, its impact is most profound. More generally, the extent of inequality in access to community resources, especially income opportunities, is essential to youthful offending (Polk and White, 1999).

Research in the United States, Australia, and Britain points to the devastating social impact of high concentrations of unemployment within local areas (Gregory and Hunter, 1995; Green, 1995; Wilson, 1996). Youth labor market patterns are often marked by high levels of unemployment, dramatic increases in insecure part-time and casual positions, and declines in real earnings from both paid work and government benefits (see McKechnie and Hobbs, this volume). The problems associated with the precarious nature of work and income are accentuated in the context of concentrated unemployment (Reiss, 1986). That is, the geographical concentration of unemployed young people increases individual difficulties in gaining paid work. These circumstances have obvious implications not only for the economic well-being of young people, but also for their perception of themselves and their future prospects.

The social status and crime rate of a neighborhood also influence the chances that youth will become involved in offending behavior, independently of their specific socioeconomic status (Reiss, 1986). For example, a young person with a low-income background living in a high-crime-rate area is far more likely to engage in offending behavior than a youth of similar income in a low-crime neighborhood. Community context is crucial for explaining variation in the propensity of unemployed youth to commit crime (Wilson, 1996; Vinson, Abela, and Hutka, 1997; White, Aumair, Harris, and McDonnell, 1997; Hunter, 1998). The systematic marginalization of youth involves disintegration of connections with mainstream social institutions (such as school and work) and a tenuous search for meaning in an uncaring and unforgiving world (see Heitmeyer, this volume). Thus, the quality and quantity of youth crime are heavily overlain by geographical location in that local economic resources, social networks, and the spatial organization of (un)employment shape the choices available for young people.

Youth lacking adequate economic resources encounter strong pressures to take the possessions of others (Adamson, 1998). Exclusion from the legitimate spheres of production (i.e., paid work) and thereby from other forms of legitimate identity formation (i.e., as workers) channels attention to alternative sites to forge social identities (see Heitmeyer, this volume). If social identity and membership are rendered problematic by exclusion from paid work and commodity consumption, then "street" culture becomes an appealing substitute. The presence of groups of youth hanging out in the public domains of the streets, shopping centers, and malls manifests their search for social connection.

Entrenched economic adversity has been accompanied by state attempts to intervene in the lives of marginalized groups, usually by coercive measures, which reflect a shifting role of the state from concerns with social welfare to renewed emphasis on repressive solutions to youth rebellion. State intrusiveness generally is biased toward marginalized youth, as reflected by overrepresentation of minority youth in the criminal justice system in Australia (Luke and Cunneen, 1995; Cunneen and Macdonald, 1996), Europe (see Heitmeyer, this volume), and the United States (Miller, 1996). Because economic structural transformations are refracted socially in ways that reinforce negative images and repressive law enforcement practices directed at the most vulnerable youth, these processes further entrench the unemployability, alienation, and outsider status of minority young people.

How then ought one respond to issues of youth offending, especially given the trends, explanations, and developments outlined? A balanced response requires a solid appreciation of crime prevention currently in use, a topic to which we now turn.

Youth Crime Prevention
This section discusses trends in youth crime prevention, with a focus on intervention strategies that provide positive frameworks for dealing with young people's offending behavior. It also raises questions about the connection between crime prevention and the underlying issues of social inequality and social injustice.

Before discussing particular approaches, it is useful to comment briefly on the use of terminology in the broad area of youth crime prevention. The substantive content and philosophical orientation of specific approaches vary considerably, even when similar labels are used to describe particular programs and interventions (see Tonry and Farrington, 1995; O'Malley and Sutton, 1997). A developmental approach may target specific individuals by addressing deficits (Tonry and Farrington, 1995). Developmental approaches may also refer to programs that assist communities to use their resources to improve their social and economic conditions (Lincoln and Wilson, 1994).

There is some debate over whether crime prevention necessarily conflicts with the idea of social development (see Hil, 1996; Hill and Sutton, 1996). Coventry and associates (1992) note that crime prevention is mainly oriented toward rectifying the troublesome behavior of young people rather than fostering positive institutional change. These conceptions of crime prevention are tied to a controlling and behavioral modification agenda. Defined in more holistic and broadly social developmental terms, crime prevention is also used to challenge the traditional law and order discourse that imposes coercive and controlling measures on young people. From this perspective, the principles of youth crime prevention are entirely consistent with progressive practices and interventions that address the structural issues of unemployment and inequality conducive to offending behavior, and that recognize the importance of community consultation and youth participation in prevention. For present purposes, social development and crime prevention are seen as compatible and interlinked concepts.

Models of Youth Crime Prevention

There are three distinctive approaches to the prevention of juvenile crime: coercive, developmental, and accommodating. Table 7.1 summarizes the key elements of each approach schematically. Although these approaches need not be mutually exclusive, use of coercion as a *strategy* rather than a specific measure is contrary to the principles of the other two approaches (White, 1998a, 1998b). In many places coercion is the favored crime prevention to "keep young people in line." The privileged position of coercive measures is reinforced by a combination of law and order media hype, situational crime prevention strategies oriented first and foremost to crime control

Table 7.1 Models of Youth Crime Prevention

Coercive approach
  Emphasis: crime control
  Concepts: deterrence, opportunity reduction, and exclusion of troublemakers
  Main players: police, security guards, transit police
  Perspective: young people seen as a problem or threat
  Methods: heavy street policing, youth curfews
  Key problems: offense displacement, denial of youth rights, stigmatization of young
    people

Developmental approach
  Emphasis: dealing with social problems
  Concepts: youth participation, opportunity enhancement, and inclusion of all
    young people
  Main players: schools, local councils, parents, young people
  Perspective: young people seen as part of the community and part of the solution
  Methods: development of positive options in school, work, leisure
  Key problems: lack of resources, multiagency coordination, encouragement of youth
    action

Accommodating approach
  Emphasis: dealing with immediate conflicts
  Concepts: negotiation, stakeholder interaction, multiagency cooperation
  Main players: shopkeepers, local councils, police, young people
  Perspective: young people seen as legitimate stakeholders and users of public spaces
  Methods: open lines of communication, use of youth advocates, provision of youth
    services
  Key problems: issue of community spaces and private interests, commercialization of
    leisure

(rather than community building), and a disregard for young people's basic civil and human rights (see White, 1999b).

The crime fighting terminology adopted in many jurisdictions is that of zero tolerance, which refers both to a broad philosophical stance about how best to counter street crime and to specific methods of intervention deemed most effective in combating crime. Rhetoric about "taking crime seriously" by getting "tough on crime" at its source translates to preemptive police action in city "hot spots" and against specific targets, such as youth in groups. This coercive approach involves stepped-up surveillance of specific areas and categories of people, along with active use of force or arrest, for even relatively minor offenses (e.g., street littering, offensive language). Any behavior or group deemed to be antisocial is subject to sanction. This approach, which relies heavily on police intervention to maintain public order in public spaces, is the most pervasive form of crime prevention targeted at young people. Proponents of zero tolerance policing advocate preventing juvenile crime through proactive interventions to constrain youth behavior and presence in public spaces.

Deliberate reconfiguration of public spaces in ways that restrict access to designated users is another strategy to regulate behavior in the interest of crime prevention. Many towns and cities across the United States, Canada, Australia, and Britain now have an extensive array of closed-circuit cameras in inner-city business districts as well (Davis, 1994; United States National Crime Prevention Council, 1996).

Youth curfews represent a third way to clear the streets of young people, irrespective of their orderly or disorderly behavior. Informal youth curfews are widespread in the United States, and curfew ordinances are in effect in a majority of the largest U.S. cities (Bilchik, 1996). Support for curfews has also been suggested in the United Kingdom as a solution for juvenile crime (Jeffs and Smith, 1996). More recent research, however, indicates that curfew programs are ineffective unless accompanied by a range of proactive services (Bilchik, 1996). The success of the youth curfews resides not in their regulatory dimension, but rather in the developmental resources offered in some locales, such as recreation centers and counseling services. The presence of community supports is decisive in shaping the operation of the curfew and its perception by adults and youth alike.

There are several problems and limitations with the coercive approach to youth behavior in the interest of crime prevention (see White, 1998b). Most crucially, these approaches ignore the problems of poverty, unemployment, and racism that lie at the core of youth disadvantage and criminality. Juvenile crime prevention that is respectful of young people, while not criminalizing their activities and presence in public domains, demands a different response altogether. Rather than deriving from the perspective of law and order, such concerns are generally expressed in terms of social crime prevention.

Developmental approaches are directed at enhancing the opportunities of young people by encouraging their participation in activities that are age-appropriate and respond to needs of maturation. The core idea is that young people deserve ownership and responsibility for solutions to youth problems and that various local constituencies should collaborate to broaden opportunities for youth involvement, including the most marginalized groups (Polk, 1997). This means that young people should be included in crime prevention strategies rather than perceived as threats to their communities, by emphasizing ways to enhance productive opportunities for youth involvement and reforming institutional processes that disadvantage and marginalize young people. Another core idea behind the developmental approach involves providing space for young people to acquire a greater sense of competence, usefulness, belonging, and agency (Polk and Kobrin, 1973). To assist the development of young people requires strategic action to improve the performance of social institutions that work with youth.

Methods of developmental crime prevention revolve around problem solving. Operationally this means strategies designed for youth to acquire legitimate identities in school, work, and politics, while reducing their access to illegitimate identities associated with the criminal justice system (Polk and Kobrin, 1973). Developmental approaches generally are holistic in that they involve multiagency collaboration among youth and community workers, local councils, the police, and other interested parties.

There is much support for the adoption of developmental crime prevention approaches within the criminological community. For example, the Youth Justice Committee of the National Crime Prevention Council of Canada conducted numerous consultations across Canada between May and August 1995 to identify the most effective programs and methods in preventing youth crime. From these activities, the Council recommended a constellation of effective programs and best practices. These include programs that set the stage for community-based prevention (such as abuse prevention and public education programs), early intervention programs (such as parent support and child abuse programs as well as high-quality child care), and preventive support activities for older children and youth (such as recreational and job creation programs). The Council underscored that broad-based community involvement is essential to development of effective prevention programs, and that youth must be involved.

These concerns and proposals have been echoed in other countries as well. In Britain, for example, a Home Office report that examined various programs designed to reduce youth criminality (Utting, 1996) evaluated programs in three main areas: family, schools, and sport and leisure. The most effective programs were practical, straightforward plans based on careful assessment of local needs and with clearly defined outcomes. Another critical ingredient is involving youth in planning, implementation, and evaluation so that they can appreciate and own their benefits from the program (Utting, 1996:85). Projects that work best are targeted geographically, have a strong commitment to multiagency cooperation, and build on detailed knowledge of local problems and resources.

In the United States, the United States Coordinating Council on Juvenile Justice and Delinquency Prevention similarly concludes, "Improving education and youth employment opportunities, enhancing social skills, and providing youth with mentors and adult role models are essential components of delinquency prevention" (1996:55). Ensuring that all community stakeholders collaborate and take responsibility for the health and well-being of youth is a key ingredient for success (see also, Bowes and Ingersoll, 1997; United States Office of Juvenile Justice and Delinquency Prevention, 1995). The same themes are also evident in crime prevention policies and programs put forward in Australia (see Brown and Polk, 1996; O'Malley and Sutton, 1997; Developmental Crime Prevention Consortium, 1999).

The primary challenge confronting developmental approaches is the inadequate community investment in developmental institutions (e.g., education, welfare services, health, and especially community services). This, in turn, makes interagency collaborative work very difficult. Government cutbacks in needed public services, changes to rules guiding service provision and benefit allocation for youth, and high adolescent unemployment all restrict local ability to solve problems that originate in wider political and economic changes. Important partner institutions, such as the police, can likewise be evaluated from the perspective of fiscal decisions and political priorities. The internal allocation of resources (e.g., education and training packages in the area of police–youth relations) and staffing (e.g., number and training of youth liaison personnel) involves conscious choices about departmental policy and best use of limited resources.

Disagreements about how to implement preferred methods often stymie the developmental approach (see Stokes and Tyler, 1997). For example, multiagency collaboration often begs the question of leadership to coordinate the process and criteria to use for evaluating outcomes (Hughes, 1996).

Differences in the conceptualization of developmental strategies can also pose difficulties. Tonry and Farrington (1995) distinguish among "developmental prevention," "community prevention," and "situational prevention." The first refers to interventions designed to prevent the development of criminal potential in individuals; the second, to strategies designed to change the social conditions that influence offending in residential communities; the third, to measures that prevent crimes by reducing opportunity to offend and increasing the risks of doing so. The ideal mode of intervention establishes the links between individual circumstance and community social life and focuses on how to improve both.

An *accommodating* approach is not concerned with either coercion or developmental issues per se (White, 1998a). This approach arose from youth–adult conflicts, particularly in relation to the uses of public spaces such as shopping centers and malls. In this sense, the accommodating perspective originated as a reaction to a social problem, rather than being institutionally tied to wider communal projects such as law enforcement or socialization processes. Negotiation is the key concept of the accommodating approach, which is premised on the idea that there may be diverse and competing perspectives about the use of public resources. Public consultation is required to accommodate the needs and desires of various stakeholders and users, such as shopping center managers, retailers, developers, older people, architects, and town planners.

The accommodation approach uses participatory methods as a strategy to reduce youth crime, antisocial behavior, and fear in particular settings. That young people are considered as legitimate stakeholders satisfies a key premise of the developmental approach, namely, the opportunity to participate and take partial ownership of solutions to problems in a multiparty collaboration. Importantly, the approach acknowledges that young people have legitimate concerns, particularly over their treatment in public spaces, and that these should be represented in compromises. Rather than attempting to exclude young people – as users of certain public spaces, as active participants in community life, as citizens with rights – this approach favors social inclusion. In some instances, the approach may be linked to developmental strategies insofar as provision of youth services and youth-friendly spaces can result from the negotiation process.

Several examples of the accommodating approaches that deal specifically with malls and commercial street areas are noteworthy. In the American city of Santa Monica, California, for instance, the local council redesigned a neighborhood mall to encourage different types of activity by providing ample space for public seating (Sandercock, 1997). In this instance, the public area was planned and designed from the start as a "community space" – open and accessible to residents and visitors from a wide range of backgrounds. The emphasis was on a mix of activities, low-level and tolerant police presence, encouragement of street performers without controlling them (they do not have to audition), and improvement in the general streetscape. In the resulting socially *inclusive* environment, there is very little street crime.

In Australia, the Brisbane City Council in the state of Queensland turned its attention to management practices within major shopping centers, including security arrangements (Heywood, Crane, Egginton, and Gleeson, 1998). In reviewing public space issues, the Council recommended that centers develop clear, fair, and nondiscriminatory rules that apply to all users. Protocols were developed to provide guidance for managers, police, security, and youth in resolving difficulties. In addition to these general protocols, the Council recommended the development of a specific code of practice for security personnel when dealing with young people and specific training of security staff. Center managers were encouraged to adopt a customer-oriented security provision and abandon the law enforcement approach.

In the Dutch city of Rotterdam, dealing with serious forms of youth crime and vandalism at the Zuidplein shopping center likewise included the adoption of rules of conduct for the center. These rules were conveyed to district youth by the police through the local school (Hoefnagels, 1997). Furthermore, a street youth worker was appointed to assist in enforcement, jointly financed by the city and the employers' association. Two tolerance locations were established at the shopping center, and the youth worker was responsible for organizing support and activities for young people who use the center. When problems arose, the worker discussed them directly with the parties involved, fostering productive communication between shopkeepers and youth. As a consequence of these measures, both vandalism and stealing declined appreciably.

In Berkeley, California, the response to street-level violence involved deploying large numbers of police officers into the busy Telegraph Avenue area. This tactic not only cost the city more than it could afford, but had the undesirable consequence of scaring away tourists and customers who frequented the local restaurants and shops (Noguera, 1996). In response, a community task force that involved youth was created and a steering group that included youth from various racial and ethnic backgrounds was formed. Their task was to help provide nonthreatening, nonconfrontational security in the area. The steering group provided a youth escort service and monitoring patrol and mediated conflict and promoted safety. Measures were also taken to expand the range of options for youth to use public spaces, such as midnight basketball and supervised weekend parties at venues throughout the community. Consequently, crime diminished substantially in the area. To some degree, the intervention succeeded because young people who used the street for socializing felt that they received respect, not harassment, from the patrol group, who were, in fact, their peers.

These examples provide concrete, low-cost practical measures that offer effective ways to reduce both the fear of crime and crime itself. Clearly, a successful crime prevention program based on the accommodation approach must take into account specific aspects of the physical environment, as well as the social dynamics of public life. The accommodating approach explicitly recognizes the importance of involving the private commercial sector in noncoercive forms of youth crime prevention. It also recognizes that much police–youth contact and conflict occurs in the precincts of shopping centers and malls and that a large share of youth offending involves theft offenses. The accommodating approach occurs in the context of privately owned public space; therefore, it is important to explore possibilities to transform such spaces from use for relatively narrow commercial purposes to broader communal objectives. Inherent in this posture are questions about how best to extend public access, public control, and public ownership over community spaces regardless of whether the current managers are state governments, local councils, or private companies.

In analyzing the pros and cons of each crime prevention perspective, their limits and possibilities of receiving institutional support must be appreciated, along with the conflicts and debates regarding crime prevention matters. Given the very difficult social, economic, and political climate within which many young people make sense of their world, approaches to crime prevention that do the least amount of harm to young people are preferable (see Wyn and White, 1997). Regardless of existing conceptual difficulties and practical limitations, it is clear that the developmental and accommodating approaches offer the most constructive avenues for positive and socially inclusive forms of youth crime prevention.

Community Action for Social Justice
Acknowledgment of the rights, worth, and dignity of youth is integral to successful approaches to problem behavior. Young people share many commonalities, including lack of adequate resources, a dearth of youth-friendly amenities, frequent harassment from authority figures, fear of being victimized, and exclusion from decision-making processes. These circumstances constitute a recipe for resentment, frustration, alienation, and

retaliation. In unpleasant social environments, these responses are reflected in both the perceptions of crime (e.g., fear of crime) and the realities of crime (e.g., vandalism, disrespect for authority). The provision of legitimate alternative activities is a vital ingredient for successful youth crime prevention. This requires that governments, communities, and commercial enterprises give priority to providing resources and facilities for youth. Such investments for youth not only benefit the entire community, but also encompass values about social cohesion, personal safety, public order, and commercial gain.

Although the principle of respect for the rights of young people, coupled with a recognition of their needs in relation to public spaces, provide the strategic base for improving existing relationships, both must be translated into concrete measures at a practical level. Several general prescriptions suggest themselves in terms of evidence reviewed (see White, 1999b). For example, young people need a *diverse range of options*. This includes facilities and spaces that are multifunctional or that offer a range of uses and that do not become the exclusive domain of any single group (e.g., skateboard ramps tend to have limited appeal to groups of young men). A second key ingredient is provision of *youth outreach services* that allow them to connect with youth advocates, adult mentors, and service providers. Assistance in the form of welfare, counseling, health, and legal support as well as mediators is also highly desirable. Provision of *youth-oriented public transport services* is vital as well. Besides ensuring that public transportation matches the entertainment needs of young people (as in the case of cinema closing times), ideally special services for weekend late night travel or special events (e.g., concerts or sports carnivals) should be available. Moreover, public transport personnel should be prepared to deal with and respect young users.

In developing options, spaces, services, and facilities for young people there is a clear and pressing need to take into account the *social differences among youth*. Offering flexible usage of public spaces to accommodate different groups with varied interests (e.g., young women and young men) permits for social interaction in comfortable and safe environments. Providing age-appropriate amenities (e.g., game parlors, cafe-style shops) will serve developmental tasks of youth.

A *range of communication strategies* is required when working with teens and children whose needs and interests vary. Because sensitive issues (e.g., relating to illegal drugs) and conflicts (e.g., relating to racism or sexual harassment) can have large impacts on how public spaces are used, *safe and confidential consultation methods* are essential. Allowing both *formal and informal means of participation* is possible via youth councils or similar types of participatory bodies (as part of local councils, local youth services, or site management committees).

Strategic intervention builds on the *development of competencies* in young people to ensure better use of resources and facilities. At times youth need instruction on how to use facilities, as well as to learn new skills in order to take advantage of community offerings (e.g., sports, computers). To ensure a suitable environment for such learning, *clear guidelines and codes of conduct involving young people* are essential. And, building on insights from the accommodation and development approaches to youth prevention, youth participation in establishing boundaries of acceptable or unacceptable behavior, particularly in public spaces (e.g., shopping centers, city skating zones), should be encouraged. Youth can and should play a major role in ensuring the effective and fair application of rules and in creating defined avenues of appeal when conflicts arise over rules.

It may be necessary to reserve spaces for the *exclusive use* of certain groups of young people. Young women, indigenous youth, and ethnic minorities may require or desire exclusive access to space for specific needs or interests, and/or as a result of safety concerns (e.g., Muslim women and use of swimming pools). There is also scope for undertaking *proactive campaigns* that attempt to break down social stereotypes and barriers about selected sociocultural groups. Youth reconciliation projects that foster understanding provide another way to improve intergroup relationships.

The development of specific projects or youth programs needs to take into account these concerns, especially in light of the common problems faced by youth. However, there are particular groups and issues that warrant further attention. As previously noted, the profile and social location of youthful offenders indicate gross disparities in life chances and community circumstances among youth. The marginalization and criminalization of the most vulnerable population groups constitute a complex process that is couched in racism, gendered behavior, and political disenfranchisement. Underpinning much youthful criminality and the forging of criminal careers are deeply embedded forms of social inequality and social injustice. Therefore, the challenge is to construct youth crime prevention strategies in ways that allow system transformation. The formulations and examples of progressive practice described here provide important alternatives to the dominant law and order and enforcement approaches. Still needed, however, are measures that can bridge the gap between "harm minimization" approaches and those leading to substantive political and economic change. Just as youth crime can be analyzed from the viewpoint of community resources and social ecology, action on crime prevention must bear a relationship to wider social processes and systemic power relationships. The process of empowerment implies both reconnecting people within and across communities and challenging dominant ideologies and repressive structures. To reduce youth offending behavior, it is necessary to move beyond measures that focus on the management of unequal social relationships to strategies that transform them.

To some extent this can be achieved by working through many of the prescriptions and suggested courses of action identified in the course of this chapter and recasting them in overtly transformative directions. For example, the first task of crime prevention is to *rebuild communities*, and as part of this to foster the ideas of solidarity and cooperation. This can initially be approached through the democratization of decision making at the neighborhood level, and by inclusion of young people, especially young offenders, in the process. The proposals put forward jointly by the Bloods and the Crips shortly after the Los Angeles riots illustrate the seriousness and creativity of even the most violent and alienated youth, who care greatly about what happens to their lives and their communities (Lusane, 1992). Their proposals included spending on hospitals and health clinics, school improvements, and support for minority businesses. Also suggested was the idea of creating a community-based police buddy system involving former gang members who, after receiving training, work with the L.A. police to make the local neighborhoods safe and secure. That the proposals were not implemented clearly implicates *political will*, rather than entrenched social deviance, as the core problem.

There also exist ample opportunities for transcommunal cooperation among diverse ethnic, religious, and racial groups (Childs, 1997). Building *social alliances* is crucial for connecting residents throughout the community, thereby fostering cohesion, and forging proactive campaigns on social and economic issues, such as economic redevelopment, antiracism, and unwanted intrusions by the state. To take control of the community is to establish alternative community structures. This might involve, for example, the promotion of protocols and procedures of accountable behavior, whereby generally agreed rules are used to guide interaction within the community, including those involving criminal justice officials. Giving all members a stake in the community means not only encouraging participation in decision making, but ensuring that viewpoints carry some social weight.

As political pressure and calls for greater government program and funding assistance are necessary ingredients in campaigns to redevelop local neighborhoods, creative thinking is needed to use existing *community resources* effectively. Mapping assets, capacities, and skills at the local and regional levels indicates the stock of resources to build on. Attention should not be solely on "deficits" (whether of the individual or of the neighborhood), but on existing competencies and strengths. In most cases, there is great potential for alternative uses of existing physical and social infrastructures. For example, schools might be used as multipurpose community resources, rather than solely as age-specific or function-limited centers. Developing a variety of physical sites to connect residents is an important component in rekindling community pride and neighborhood spirit. Such sites also act as avenues for providing programs and services that connect youth and adults. In a similar vein, cultural forms and practical activities such as computer use, dance, art, music, storytelling, and fashion design embody skills and activities that are often quite remarkable in their breadth and depth and represent important community assets. Taking account of the perspectives of youth is a sure way to guarantee that an activity has meaning for them. This core observation also applies to issues of safety and crime prevention. Young people who know and use the streets are logically in the best position to become agents of public safety. Indeed, the idea of street monitors and of development of prosocial street activity suggests that there may be many novel ways of encouraging youth participation in precisely these areas.

Conclusion

Devastated communities, not criminal individuals, are at the heart of rising youth offending. Few young people are truly malevolent, and even fewer consider themselves master criminals. Most youth offenders are responding to circumstances outside their immediate control. Given the social context of youth crime and the varied responses of governments to so-called problem youth, crime prevention interventions ought to be based on a premise of social justice rather than social control. This premise requires a fundamental paradigm shift – from dealing with young offenders solely as criminals and deviants to viewing the central problem as one of system transformation. Reshaping the lives of urban youth can be thought of as a political process that requires evaluation of whether specific programs are effective in altering their life situations.

The origins of the most serious youth offending lie in the changing dynamics of community life itself. Unemployment and social marginalization are not simply youth issues; rather they are social problems that now pervade the lives of millions of people worldwide. Yet, governments have generally persisted with the neoliberal social and economic policies that engender further social polarization and the spatial concentration of poverty and that fuel demands for ever more intrusive and punitive law and order interventions (see Heitmeyer, this volume).

Redressing these social imbalances will require a different kind of political will of governments and communities, as well as the development of alternative visions regarding the good society and how best to attain it. Most governments have tended to view globalization as both the major goal and the central constraint on national development. In this context, it is even more vital that the push for reform and change derive from the grass roots. The creation of positive crime prevention strategies, which accord young people dignity, respect, and participant status, can be an important stimulus for broad social transformations. If the structure of society is implicated in the dynamics of why some young people offend, then the answer to youth crime, and by implication social injustice, must lie in changing that very structure.

REFERENCES

Adamson, C. (1998). Tribute, Turf, Honour and the American Street Gang: Patterns of Continuity and Change since 1820. *Theoretical Criminology*, 2(1), 57–84.

Alexeyeva, M., and Patrignani, A. (Eds.) (1994). *Crime and Crime Prevention in Moscow*. Publication No. 52. Rome/Moscow: United Nations Interregional Crime and Justice Research Institute.

Bessant, J., and Hil, R. (Eds.) (1997). *Youth, Crime and the Media*. Hobart: Australian Clearinghouse for Youth Studies.

Bilchik, S. (1996). *Curfew: An Answer to Juvenile Delinquency and Victimization?* Washington, DC: Office of Juvenile Justice and Delinquency Prevention.

Bowes, D., and Ingersoll, S. (1997). *Mobilizing Communities to Prevent Juvenile Crime*. Washington, DC: Office of Juvenile Justice and Delinquency Prevention.

Braithwaite, J. (1989). *Crime, Shame and Reintegration*. Cambridge: Cambridge University Press.

Brown, M., and Polk, K. (1996). Taking Fear of Crime Seriously: The Tasmanian Approach to Community Crime Prevention. *Crime & Delinquency*, 42(3), 398–420.

Canada National Crime Prevention Council. (1996). *Mobilizing Political Will and Community Responsibility to Prevent Youth Crime*. Ottawa: NCPC.

Carrington, K. (1989). Girls and Graffiti. *Cultural Studies*, 3(1), 89–100.

Catalano, R., and Hawkins, J. (1996). The Social Development Model: A Theory of Antisocial Behavior. In J. Hawkins (Ed.), *Delinquency and Crime: Current Theories*, pp. 149–197. Cambridge: Cambridge University Press.

Childs, J. (1997). The New Youth Peace Movement: Creating Broad Strategies for Community Renaissance in the United States. *Social Justice*, 24(4), 247–257.

Coventry, G., Muncie, J., and Walters, R. (1992). *Rethinking Social Policy for Young People and Crime Prevention*. Discussion Paper No. 1. Melbourne: National Center for Socio-Legal Studies, La Trobe University.

Cunneen, C., and McDonald, D. (1996). *Keeping Aboriginal and Torres Strait Islander People out of Custody: An Evaluation of the Implementation of the Recommendations of the Royal Commission into Aboriginal Deaths in Custody*. Canberra: Aboriginal and Torres Strait Islander Commission.

Cunneen, C., and White, R. (1995). *Juvenile Justice: An Australian Perspective*. Melbourne: Oxford University Press.

Davis, M. (1994). *Beyond Bladerunner: Urban Control and the Ecology of Fear*. Open Magazine Pamphlet Series No. 23. Westfield, NJ.

Developmental Crime Prevention Consortium. (1999). *Pathways to Prevention: Developmental and Early Intervention Approaches to Crime in Australia*. Canberra: National Crime Prevention, Attorney General's Department.

Ericson, R., Baranek, P., and Chan, J. (1991). *Representing Order: Crime, Law and Justice in the News Media*. Toronto: University of Toronto Press.

Farrington, D. (1996). The Explanation and Prevention of Youthful Offending. In J. Hawkins (Ed.), *Delinquency and Crime: Current Theories*, pp. 68–148. Cambridge: Cambridge University Press.

Ferrell, J. (1997). Youth, Crime and Cultural Space. *Social Justice*, 24(4), 21–38.

Forrester, L. (1993). Youth-Generated Cultures in Western Sydney. In R. White (Ed.), *Youth Subcultures: Theory, History and the Australian Experience*, pp. 107–113. Hobart: National Clearinghouse for Youth Studies.

Fox, J. (1997). *Trends in Juvenile Violence*. Washington, DC: Bureau of Justice Statistics, U.S. Department of Justice.

Geason, S., and Wilson, P. (1990). *Preventing Graffiti and Vandalism*. Canberra: Australian Institute of Criminology.

Green, A. (1995). The Changing Structure, Distribution and Spatial Segregation of the Unemployed and Economically Inactive in Great Britain. *Geoforum*, 26(4), 373–394.

Gordon, R. (1995). Street Gangs in Vancouver. In J. Creechan and R. Silverman (Eds.), *Canadian Delinquency*, pp. 311–321. Toronto: Prentice-Hall.

Grabosky, P., and Wilson, P. (1989). *Journalism and Justice: How Crime Is Reported*. Sydney: Pluto Press.

Gregory, R., and Hunter, B. (1995). *The Macro Economy and the Growth of Ghettos and Urban Poverty in Australia*. Discussion Paper No. 325. Canberra: Center for Economic Policy Research, Australian National University.

Hazelhurst, K. (Ed.) (1995). *Perceptions of Justice*. Aldershot: Avebury.

Heywood, P., and Crane, P., with Egginton, A., and Gleeson, J. (1998). *Out and About: In or Out? Better Outcomes from Young People's Use of Public and Community Space in the City of Brisbane*. Brisbane: Brisbane City Council, Community Development Team West.

Hil, R. (1996). Crime Prevention and the Technologies of Social Order – A response to Philip Hill and Adam Sutton. *Just Policy*, 6, 59–62.

Hill, P., and Sutton, A. (1996). Crime Prevention: Not Just Neighbourhood Watch and Street Lighting. *Just Policy*, 6, 54–58.

Hoefnagels, P. (1997). *The Prevention Pioneers: History of the Hein Roethof Prize, 1987–1996*. The Hague: Ministry of Justice.

Hogg, R., and Brown, D. (1998). *Rethinking Law and Order*. Sydney: Pluto Press.

Hollands, R. (1995). *Friday Night, Saturday Night: Youth Cultural Identification in the Post-industrial City*. Newcastle upon Tyne: University of Newcastle, Department of Social Policy.

162   Robert White

Huff, R. (Ed.) (1996). *Gangs in America*, 2nd ed. Thousand Oaks, CA: Sage.

Hughes, G. (1996). Strategies of Multi-Agency Crime Prevention and Community Safety in Contemporary Britain. *Studies on Crime & Crime Prevention*, 5(2), 221–244.

Hunter, B. (1998). Addressing Youth Unemployment: Re-Examining Social and Locational Disadvantage within Australian Cities. *Urban Policy and Research*, 16(1), 47–58.

Kurata, S., and Hamai, K. (1998). Criminal Justice System at Work: Outline of Crime Trends, Criminal Procedure and Juvenile Justice System in Japan. Japan Criminal Policy Society. Internet: http://www.jcps.ab.psiweb.com/con1.htm.

Jeffs, T., and Smith, M. (1996). Getting the Dirtbags off the Streets: Curfews and Other Solutions to Juvenile Crime. *Youth and Policy*, 53, 1–14.

John Howard Society of Alberta (1998). Youth Crime in Canada: Public Perception vs. Statistical Information. Internet: http://www.johnhoward.ab.ca/PUB/PDF/C16.pdf.

Junger-Tas, J. (1994). Delinquency in Thirteen Western Countries: Some Preliminary Conclusion. In J. Junger-Tas, G.-J. Terlouw, and M. Klein (Eds.), *Delinquent Behavior Among Young People in the Western World: First Results of the International Self-Report Delinquency Study*, pp. 371–379. Amsterdam: Kugler Publications.

King, A., Wold, B., Tudor-Smith, C., and Harel, Y. (1996). *The Health of Youth: A Cross-National Survey*. World Health Organization Regional Publications, European Series No. 69. Geneva: World Health Organization.

Klein, M., Maxson, C., and Miller, J. (Eds.) (1995). *The Modern Gang Reader*. Los Angeles: Roxbury.

La Grange, T. (1996). Marking Up the City: The Problem of Urban Vandalism. In G. O'Bireck (Ed.), *Not a Kid Anymore: Canadian Youth, Crime and Subcultures*, pp. 131–142. Toronto: Nelson.

Lincoln, R., and Wilson, P. (1994). Questioning Crime Prevention: Towards a Social Development Approach. *Transitions*, 3(3), 7–11.

Loeber, R., and Farrington, D. (Eds.) (1998). *Serious and Violent Juvenile Offenders: Risk Factors and Successful Interventions*. Thousand Oaks, CA: Sage.

Luke, G., and Cunneen, C. (1995). *Aboriginal Over-Representation and Discretionary Decisions in the NSW Juvenile Justice System*. Sydney: Juvenile Justice Advisory Council of New South Wales.

Lusane, C. (1992). Gang-Banging and Budget-Writing. *Crossroads*, 6, 5.

Males, M. (1996). *The Scapegoat Generation: America's War on Adolescents*. Monroe, ME: Common Courage Press.

Mason, G., and Tomsen, S. (Eds.) (1997). *Homophobic Violence*. Sydney: Hawkins Press.

Miller, J. (1996). *Search and Destroy: African-Americans in the Criminal Justice System*. Cambridge: Cambridge University Press.

Mukherjee, S. (1997). The Dimensions of Juvenile Crime. In A. Borowski and I. O'Connor (Eds.), *Juvenile Crime, Justice and Corrections*, pp. 4–24. Melbourne: Longman.

Noguera, P. (1996). Reducing and Preventing Youth Violence: An Analysis of Causes and an Assessment of Successful Programs. *In Motion Magazine*. Internet: http://www.inmotionmagazine.com/pedro3.html.

O'Malley, P., and Sutton, A. (Eds.) (1997). *Crime Prevention in Australia: Issues in Policy and Research*. Sydney: Federation Press.

Polk, K. (1997). A Community and Youth Development Approach to Youth Crime Prevention. In P. O'Malley and A. Sutton (Eds.), *Crime Prevention in Australia: Issues in Policy and Research*, pp. 185–199. Sydney: Federation Press.

Polk, K., and Kobrin, S. (1973). *Delinquency Prevention through Youth Development.* Washington, DC: U.S. Department of Health, Education and Welfare.

Polk, K., and White, R. (1999). Economic Adversity and Criminal Behavior: Rethinking Youth Unemployment and Crime. *Australian and New Zealand Journal of Criminology,* 32(3), 284–302.

Reiss, A. (1986). Why Are Communities Important in Understanding Crime? In A. Reiss and M. Tonry (Eds.), *Communities and Crime,* pp. 1–34. Chicago: University of Chicago Press.

Rutter, M., Giller, H., and Hagell, A. (1998). *Antisocial Behavior by Young People.* Cambridge: Cambridge University Press.

Sandercock, L. (1997). From Main Street to Fortress: The Future of Malls as Public Spaces – or – "Shut Up and Shop." *Just Policy,* 9, 27–34.

Sanders, W. (1994). *Gangbangs and Drive-Bys: Grounded Culture and Juvenile Gang Violence.* New York: Aldine De Gruyter.

Schissel, B. (1997). *Blaming Children: Youth Crime, Moral Panics and the Politics of Hate.* Halifax: Fernwood Publishing.

Sickmund, M. (1997). *Offenders in Juvenile Court, 1995.* Washington, DC: Office of Juvenile Justice and Delinquency Prevention.

Sickmund, M., Snyder, H., and Poe-Yamagata, E. (1997). *Juvenile Offenders and Victims: 1997 Update on Violence.* Washington, DC: Office of Juvenile Justice and Delinquency Prevention.

Stokes, H., and Tyler, D. (1997). *Rethinking Inter-Agency Collaboration and Young People.* Melbourne: Language Australia and University of Melbourne, Youth Research Center.

Stone, S. (1998). Track I: Changing Nature of Juvenile Offenders. *Juvenile Justice,* 4(1), 1–5. Washington: Office of Juvenile Justice and Delinquency Prevention. Internet: http://wwwncjrs.org/ojjdp/conference/track1.html.

Tonry, M. (1997). Ethnicity, Crime, and Immigration. In M. Tonry (Ed.), *Ethnicity, Crime, and Immigration: Comparative and Cross-National Perspectives.* Chicago: University of Chicago Press, pp. 1–30.

Tonry, M., and Farrington, D. (1995). Strategic Approaches to Crime Prevention. In M. Tonry and D. Farrington (Eds.), *Building a Safer Society: Strategic Approaches to Crime Prevention,* pp. 1–19. Chicago: University of Chicago Press.

United Nations Crime and Justice Information Network. (1998). Results from the 5th UN World Crime Survey. Rome: UNCJIN. Internet: http://www.uncjin.org/Statistics/WCTS/WCTS5/wcts5.html.

United States National Crime Prevention Council. (1996). *Working with Local Laws to Reduce Crime.* Washington, DC: NCPC.

United States Coordinating Council on Juvenile Justice and Delinquency Prevention. (1996). *Combating Violence and Delinquency: The National Juvenile Justice Action Plan.* Washington, DC: OJJDP.

United States Office of Juvenile Justice and Delinquency Prevention. (1995). *Guide for Implementing the Comprehensive Strategy for Serious, Violent, and Chronic Juvenile Offenders.* Washington, DC: OJJDP.

Utting, D. (1996). *Reducing Criminality among Young People: A Sample of Relevant Programs in the United Kingdom.* Home Office Research Study 161. London: Home Office.

Vinson, T., Abela, M., and Hutka, R. (1997). *Making Ends Meet: A Study of Unemployed Young People Living in Sydney.* Uniya Research Report No. 1. Sydney: Uniya Jesuit Social Justice Center.

White, R. (1998a). Public Space and Youth Crime Prevention: Institutions and Strategies. In C. Alder (Ed.), *Juvenile Crime and Juvenile Justice*, pp. 16–23. Research and Public Policy Series No. 14. Canberra: Australian Institute of Criminology.

White, R. (1998b). Curtailing Youth: A Critique of Coercive Crime Prevention. *Crime Prevention Studies*, 9, 93–113.

White, R. (1999a). Youth Gangs. In R. White (Ed.), *Australian Youth Subcultures: On the Margins and in the Mainstream.* Hobart: Australian Clearinghouse for Youth Studies.

White, R. (1999b). *Hanging Out: Negotiating Young People's Use of Public Space.* Canberra: National Crime Prevention, Attorney General's Department.

White, R. (1999c). Public Spaces, Social Planning and Crime Prevention. *Urban Policy and Research*, 17(4), 301–308.

White, R., with Aumair, M., Harris, A., and McDonnell, L. (1997). *Any Which Way You Can: Youth Livelihoods, Community Resources and Crime.* Sydney: Australian Youth Foundation.

White, R., and van der Velden, J. (1996). Class and Criminality. *Social Justice*, 22(1), 51–74.

Wilson, W. J. (1996). *When Work Disappears.* New York: Knopf.

Wyn, J., and White, R. (1997). *Rethinking Youth.* Sydney: Allen & Unwin.

Yisheng, D. (1998). Are the Wolves Really Coming? An Alternative View of Juvenile Delinquency (China). *Crime & Justice International*, 14(14), 1–3. Internet: http://www.acsp.uic.edu/oicj/pubs/cjint1/1414/141413.shtml.

8   Youth Violence Prevention in America

Lessons from 15 Years of Public Health Prevention Work

Deborah Prothrow-Stith

Introduction

Motivated by the increase in youth homicide in the United States, this chapter provides a short history of the efforts within public health to address youth violence, defines and describes the problem, and illustrates examples of public health approaches to violence prevention. The magnitude of the U.S. homicide problem is extremely disturbing when compared to that of other industrialized nations not at war. The United States has a problem with youth violence that is unlike that in any other country in the world. The U.S. homicide rate for young men is eight times that of Italy (the country with the next highest rate), and 100 times greater than that of Japan, the industrialized country with the lowest rate (CDC, 1997). Homicide is also the second leading cause of death of young people between the ages of 15 and 24, and the leading cause of death of African American youth in the same age group (FBI, 1995).

The public's demand for solutions to violence in the United States has generated multidisciplinary attention to a problem that goes beyond the traditional criminal justice responses of punishment and deterrence. Since the 1980s we have witnessed a dramatic effort led by public health professionals to confront violence, and youth violence in particular. Leadership has emerged from the Centers for Disease Control and Prevention (CDC), officials of the Surgeon General's offices, and many state and local health officers and workers determined to lower the youth mortality rate from violent aggression. As a result of these efforts, a national movement to prevent violence using standard epidemiology, community outreach, screening, community-based programs, health education, behavior modification, public awareness, and education campaigns is under way. Every aspect of the U.S. Public Health Service is involved. The movement to prevent violence in the United States is similar to the multidisciplinary efforts to prevent lung cancer deaths, heart disease, and fatal car crashes.

Though embryonic and comprising thousands of separate programs scattered across the country, the violence prevention movement has the potential for the success public health professionals attained in reducing smoking and drunk driving. The analogy between violence prevention and other public health problems is not flawless, yet two decades of experience employing comparable techniques and strategies indicate sufficient parallels for success.

Definition and Classification

The Injury Control and Prevention Center at the CDC classifies both unintentional injuries (accidents) and intentional injuries (violence) as public health problems. Intentional injuries consist of self-directed violence (suicides and suicide attempts) and interpersonal violence (assaults and homicides). The CDC defines *violence* as "the threatened or actual use of physical force or power against another person, against oneself, or against a group or community that either results or is likely to result in injury, death, or deprivation."[1]

There are at least four reasons interpersonal violence became an important concern for U.S. public health professionals; (1) the dimensions of the problem, (2) the characteristics of victims and perpetrators, (3) the contact health professionals have with the victims and perpetrators of violence, and (4) the opportunities to apply public health strategies to both understanding and preventing violence. I discuss each reason in turn and then discuss public health professionals' unique approach to violence, and its contributions as well as promise to address the problem.

[1] The estimates of the probability of dying as a result of homicide for 1991 and 1997, calculated directly from the CDC's *Compressed Mortality Files*, are not currently available for years after 1997. However, to account for the change in murder rates between 1997 and 1998, CDC analysts combined data from the FBI's latest *Uniform Crime Reports* for 1997 and 1998 with the rates derived from the 1997 CDC mortality data to produce a preliminary estimate of the impact of 1998 murder rates on African American life expectancies.

The Magnitude of the Problem

The Federal Bureau of Investigation (Bureau of Justice Statistics, 1995, 1996) estimates that 1.8 million Americans are victims of violence each year. Adolescents are more likely than any other age group to be victims of violence, mostly that of their peers. Since 1999, politicians and the media have been heralding a decline in violent crime in the United States, however our youth homicide rates remain incredibly high compared to those of other industrialized nations. A complete representation of the extent of violence is not possible because reliable and consistent measures of nonfatal episodes of violence do not exist. Homicides are more accurately measured because they are mandatorily reported to the FBI by local police departments. Other countries make their homicide rates available through the World Health Organization.

Of the 20,738 murder victims in 1996 (CDC, 1997), 92% of Black victims were killed by Black offenders and 83% of White murder victims were killed by White offenders. Firearms were used in 7 of 10 murders (FBI, 1996). But the U.S. epidemic of youth violence is not limited to homicide. Police arrest data reveal an increase in nonfatal episodes of adolescent violence, despite the limitations of the administrative data. The 1980s witnessed a 19% increase in the juvenile violent crime arrest rate for Blacks, a 44% increase for Whites, and a 53% decline for the "other race" category, which includes a large increase in Asian youth (FBI, 1992). The escalation of adolescent violent crime rates in the last several decades cuts across race, class, and life-style, despite a common perception that it is an urban Black problem. It is unclear why the arrest rates for violence differ so much by race, but a possible explanation for the increases in white juvenile arrests is expansion of what was initially a problem in urban poor communities to other geographical areas. The rise in immigrant populations that are not yet acclimated to America's culture of violence may also account for the aggregate decline in arrest rates.

Adolescent Violence

Violence involving youth has reached alarming levels in the United States. In 1996, homicide was the second leading cause of death for youth 15–24 years of age (20.3 deaths per 100,000, second only to motor vehicle accidents) and stood at almost twice the rate of the overall U.S. population (10.4) (CDC, 1997). Furthermore, trends in adolescent mortality rates indicate that while overall death rates and death rates due to motor vehicle crashes decreased for youth aged 10–24 years between 1979 and 1988, homicide death rates for this age group increased by 6.7%. The CDC estimates that by the year 2003, more Americans will die of firearms-related injuries than of motor vehicle accidents. In eight states, this is already true (CDC, 1994). Even for nonfatal violent victimizations, the 1990 National Crime Survey finds that age is one of the most important single predictors of an individual's risk of being a victim of violence. This risk peaks at age 16 to 19 for both men (95 per 1,000) and women (54 per 1,000) (BJS, 1992, 1993).

School Violence: More Lethal

Violence in schools is not new, but it is increasingly more severe and lethal, as evidenced by the recent tragic episodes of school violence in Arkansas, Mississippi, Kentucky, and Oregon. In the 1999 Youth Risk Behavior Surveillance System (YRBSS) survey conducted by the CDC, 17% of U.S. students enrolled in grades 9–12 in the United States and the U.S. Virgin Islands reported carrying a weapon and 5% reported carrying a gun at least one time during the 30 days prior to the survey (CDC, 2000). Seven percent said they had been threatened or injured with a weapon while on school property during the 12 months before the survey. Twelve percent admitted to having carried a weapon onto school property within the month before the survey, and 16% had been involved in a physical fight on school property within a year of the study (CDC, 1993). According to a Metropolitan Life and Louis Harris Associates Poll of Youth and Guns survey conducted in 1993, 59% of students in Grades 6 through 12 said they could get a handgun if they wanted one (Metropolitan Life, 1993). The addition of weapons to the typical school brawl has contributed significantly to the greater severity and mortality rate of school fights.

Economic Costs

In 2000, the U.S. government spent about 8 billion dollars for youth violence-related criminal justice interventions (National Economic Council, 2000). These figures reflect only the monetary costs of violence, not the pain, suffering, and lost quality of life for victims. They do not reflect the cost of safety measures – the inability of children and adults to walk or play in their own neighborhood, the cost of guard dogs and guns for "protection," and an immeasurable sense of fear of crime victimization. In considering the broad social impact of violence, it is also important to note these costs of violent crimes.

Miller and colleagues (1993) developed a framework to quantify costs of violent crime that incorporates direct losses other than property losses (medical, mental health, emergency services, insurance administration), productivity losses (wages, fringe benefits, housework), and nonmonetary losses (pain, suffering, lost quality of life). Costs to victims of crimes resulting in injury were estimated to be $60,000 for rape survivors, $22,000 for assault survivors, and almost 2.4 million dollars per murder (in 1989 dollars). Moreover, the lifetime costs of criminal victimizations for persons 12 years and older were estimated to be $10 billion for rape, 96 billion dollars for assault, and 48 billion dollars for murder (Miller et al., 1993). However, these figures do not include property losses incurred during violent acts nor the mammoth costs incurred by collective society's reactive response to violence, including law enforcement, adjudication, victim services, and correctional expenditures. In 1993, the cost of direct medical spending, emergency services, and claims processed for the victims of gun violence nationwide totaled approximately 3 billion dollars. Average hospital charges for treating one child wounded by gunfire were more than $33,000.

The Characteristics of Youth Violent Offenders and Victims

Contrary to the stereotype of violence as predominantly being stranger-related or occurring in the context of criminal behavior such as racial harassment, robbery, or drug dealing, much of the violence experienced in the United States occurs in the context of personal or acquaintance relationships (Spivak, Prothrow-Stith, and Hausman, 1988). CDC statistics reveal that a typical homicide usually involves two people who know each other. Only 15% of homicides occur between strangers. Thirty-eight percent of homicides occur between acquaintances and 13% among relatives. For 35% of all homicides, the relationship between offender and victim is unknown (CDC, 1997).

The perpetrator and victim of violence share many traits. They are likely to be young, male, and of the same race. They are likely to be poor and to have been exposed to violence in the past, particularly family violence. They may be depressed and use alcohol and/or other drugs (Prothrow-Stith and Weissman, 1991). The incongruity between public perception and actual circumstances of violence has generated demands for resources and solutions that address only part – possibly the smaller part – of the problem, namely, the extreme cases that reach the attention of the medical establishment and the criminal justice system. Although certainly established anticrime and antiviolence strategies should not be discarded, the diversity of violent circumstances that exist require a broader base of efforts that not only respond to violent events, but, more importantly, focus on preventive services as well.

A closer look at demographic characteristics reveals certain noteworthy factors contributing to a complex picture of adolescent violence that has implications for the needed prevention services. For example, in 1996, homicide rates were considerably higher among 17- to 19-year-olds (692 murders for the year) and 20- to 24-year-olds (1,669 murders) as compared to 13- to 16-year-olds (81 murders) (FBI, 1996). Also, with the exception of sexual assault, boys greatly exceed girls in the number of violent victimizations and are also more likely than girls to be violent offenders and witnesses of violence. However, girls are increasingly participating in violent offenses. The U.S. Department of Justice reported that in 1993 nearly one fourth (24%) of juvenile arrests for violent crimes involved girls. Between 1989 and 1993, the relative growth in juvenile arrests involving girls was more than double the growth for boys (OJJDP, 1996).

There also exist extremely large racial differences in violence rates among young Americans. In 1996, homicide was the number one cause of death for Black youth aged 15–24; the homicide rate for Black youth (both sexes) was more than seven times the rate for comparably aged Whites (approximately 74 versus 10 per 100,000) (CDC, 1996). National statistics concerning other ethnic minority groups, such as Hispanics, Asian Americans, and Native Americans, are scant. Race differences are not indicative of any biologic or genetic factors because they are confounded by socioeconomic status, income inequality among communities, urban living, gun availability, and racism. Using family income as the primary indicator of socioeconomic status, the National Crime Survey found an inverse relationship between income and the risk of violent victimization (BJS, 1992). In 1988, the risk of victimization was 2.5 times higher in low-income (under $7,500 per year) than in high-income families ($50,000 + per year) (Reiss, 1993).

Despite these well-documented correlates of violence, the relationship between violence and social factors is complex and not well understood. For example, studies employing multivariate analyses document complicated interactions among race, socioeconomic status, and violence. That is to say, at low socioeconomic levels Blacks have a higher risk of homicide than Whites. At higher socioeconomic levels, however, the race difference disappears. William Julius Wilson's work on neighborhood poverty offers a possible explanation (Wilson, 1987, 1997). Because poor Blacks are much more likely than poor Whites to live in neighborhoods where the majority of the residents are poor, they are exposed to much higher rates of victimization.

In fact, other studies suggest that, in fact, socioeconomic status is the major predictor of violence and victimization, and race is merely a marker for violence (Reiss, 1993). One study that used several correlates of poverty, including housing density, finds that overcrowded Whites have a domestic homicide rate comparable to that of overcrowded Blacks. Less crowded

Blacks and Whites both exhibit equally lower rates of violence (Centerwall, 1984, 1993). Moreover, gun-related homicides for African American males living in core urban areas occur at an alarming rate of 143.9 per 100,000 (Furlong and Morrison, 1994).

Heritage Foundation analysts examined the data for young African American men who reside in eight of the nation's largest urban communities. The jurisdictions examined were Baltimore, Maryland; Brooklyn, New York; Chicago, Illinois; Detroit, Michigan; Los Angeles, California; New Orleans, Louisiana; Philadelphia, Pennsylvania; and Washington, D.C. The analysis of 1991 and 1997 homicide data from these communities demonstrates that, despite some progress, urban black males continue to face a high risk of dying from homicide even after accounting for the decline in homicide rates in the mid- to late 1990s.[2] On the basis of 1998 data for the eight communities studied (U.S. Bureau of the Census, 1999), a male 15-year-old urban African American faces a probability of being murdered before reaching his 45th birthday that ranges from almost 8.5% in the District of Columbia to just under 2.0% in Brooklyn, New York. The fact that by comparison the probability of being murdered by age 45 is 2.21% nationally for all male U.S. Blacks and 0.29% for all male Whites implicates the overarching influence of situational and economic factors in their high rates of violence.

Identification of Risk Factors

Major risk factors for youth violence can be broadly categorized into environmental and psychological factors. The major environmental risk factors include firearms, alcohol and other drugs, and situational factors, such as being a victim of child abuse, witnessing family violence, and being exposed to media violence and to high levels of peer and community violence. Corporal punishment is a controversial environmental factor that may be related to risk for violence. Other environmental risk factors for adolescents include peer pressure, the crack epidemic, and policing practices. Poverty is a consistent and strong environmental risk factor for homicide. The mechanism for this influence is not well understood; it may include (1) the anger and frustration associated with not having money and the essential commodities relative to others; (2) the experience of class antagonisms; (3) the likely absence of adult male role models; (4) the scarcity of neighborhood

---

[2] Based on data from the FBI's 1997 and 1998 *Uniform Crime Reports* and the CDC's 1997 *Compressed Mortality Files.*

recreational, extracurricular, and after school activities; and (5) the greater exposure to violence on television.

In its extreme form, abuse increases the risk of delinquency. Therefore, efforts to improve parenting and to reduce child abuse often focus on alternative disciplinary strategies. Several studies document associations among child abuse, neglect, witnessing of violence, and subsequent adolescent and adult violence. A retrospective comparison of violent and nonviolent juvenile delinquents shows a significantly higher rate of physical child abuse among the former. Interviews with violent delinquents and medical chart reviews indicated high levels of victimization, such as skull fractures, emergency trauma visits, and other physical injuries (Lewis et al., 1987). Similarly, a cohort study of abused or neglected children reveals greater risk for delinquency, adult criminal behavior, and violent criminal behavior compared to that of nonabused or nonneglected children, even though the majority of abused or neglected children do not demonstrate these behaviors. Abused children have a higher number of offenses and begin delinquent behavior at earlier ages, regardless of race and sex (Widom, 1989).

For Black adolescents ages 11 to 19 living in or around an urban housing project, self-reported use of violence was associated with exposure to violence and personal victimization, hopelessness, depression, family conflict, and previous corporal punishment. Youth with a higher sense of purpose in life and less depression were better able to handle the exposure to violence in the home and community (Durant et al., 1994).

The links between childhood exposure to media violence and subsequent youth and adult violence have been firmly established since the 1960s and are considered conclusive by the American Psychological Association (1993). Therefore, I provide only a brief synopsis of these findings. Several experimental studies suggest that exposure to media violence results in an increased risk for future violence and violent crimes. These studies include a wide spectrum of experiments, ranging from laboratory studies of individual children to large population studies. Centerwall (1992) shows that in three different countries (the United States, Canada, and South Africa), homicide rates double approximately 10–12 years after the introduction of English-language television. In the United States homicide rates doubled first among the population segments exposed to television first (White urban dwellers), and only later among those segments of the population who later had access to television. He attributes approximately 10,000 U.S. deaths annually to exposure to media violence (Centerwall, 1992).

Taken together, these studies meet the criteria for establishing a causal relationship as set forth in the Surgeon General's 1964 report on smoking and health (U.S. Department of Health, Education and Welfare, 1964) and establish that exposure to media violence places children at risk for subsequent violence. Public debate flourishes about the influence of video games and violence-oriented music in encouraging violence, but definitive data on these issues are sorely lacking.

Firearms
The United States has more firearms than other industrialized nations not at war, and the facts regarding their increased prevalence are astounding:

- The overall firearm-related death rate among U.S. children under 15 years of age is nearly 12 times higher than that of children in 25 industrialized countries (CDC, 1997).
- Firearms are used in more than 80% of teenage homicides and about 68% of homicides over all ages.
- Guns are used in 60% of all teenage homicides. The youth firearm rate in an American city with minimal restrictions on gun ownership is more than three times higher than that in a Canadian city with strict gun control laws (The Carter Center, 1994).

Given these differences, it is not surprising that teen and young adult homicide is a uniquely American problem. The high U.S. youth homicide rate has been attributed to the higher prevalence of gun ownership. But a similar association obtains in other countries. An international study of gun ownership and homicide finds positive correlations between the rates of household gun ownership and the rates of gun-related homicide (Lester, 1988; Killias, 1993).

Handguns are widely accessible to adolescents in the United States. The national 1999 Youth Risk Behavior Surveillance System survey shows that about 1 in every 20 high school students carried a firearm at least once in the 30 days preceding the survey. The incidence was higher among males, 9% (CDC, 2000). In another study of inner-city youths, as many as 35% of males carried a gun outside school (Sheley et al., 1992). Handgun availability appears to be playing an increasingly important part in homicides among U.S. youth.

In addition to the young people directly injured by violence, increasing attention is being given to the scores more who are affected indirectly, as witnesses to violent acts or by exposure to chronically violent environments (Groves et al., 1993). Pynoos and colleagues (Pynoos et al., 1987) examine the appearance of posttraumatic stress disorder (PTSD) symptoms in children who experienced a fatal sniper attack on their elementary school. They find a significant association between the type and number of PTSD symptoms and proximity to the violent incident, and even more severe symptoms in children who knew the deceased child.

Beyond acute incidents, other studies identify correlations between exposure to chronic violence and distress symptoms (Fitzpatrick and Boldizar, 1993; Freeman et al., 1993; Lotion and Saltzman, 1993; Martinez and Richters, 1993; Osofsky et al., 1993). Lotion and Saltzman (1993) describe anecdotal reports from their research participants, as well as from teachers and administrators, about children living in violent settings who arrive at school in distress, are unable to concentrate or maintain appropriate behavior in class, and who hide in the classroom because they are afraid to return home or take the bus. These studies document the pressing need to address not only the physical threat of violence, but also the potential for psychopathological and/or emotional disturbances in both victims and bystanders (Emde, 1993; Durant, 1994).

Public Health and Criminal Justice Approaches to Violence Prevention: Interdisciplinary Challenges

Historically, society has relied almost exclusively on the criminal justice system both to respond to and to prevent violence. This fact is rooted in the beliefs that violence is criminal, that those who commit violence should be punished, and that the threat of punishment is a potential deterrent to violent acts. A large, elaborate set of institutions has been developed to achieve these goals. This system includes police, prosecutors, public defenders, judges, probation officers, and prison guards. It is principally designed to respond to crimes after they have been committed by identifying, apprehending, prosecuting, punishing, and controlling the violent offender. The system is guided not only by the practical goals of reducing crimes of all types (including violence), but also by the normative goal of assuring justice to victims and accused.

The public health and criminal justice systems have been historically separate in their conceptualization of approaches to violence and the development of activities to reduce or prevent violence. The public health field has approached the issue through efforts to identity the risk factors related to violent behavior. Public health workers study violence in terms of the magnitude of intentional injuries observed in health care settings. The criminal justice system approaches violence through efforts to identify and assign blame for criminal behavior, maintain public safety, and remove violent offenders from the community.

Viewed from the perspective of those interested in reducing violence, the criminal justice system's responses have had only limited success. Partly this stems from inherent limitations in the overall approach of the criminal justice system. First, it is more reactive than preventive in its basic orientation. Although deterrence may prevent some crime, the criminal justice system largely seeks to rehabilitate offenders through special programs in prisons, and to prevent children from becoming violent offenders through the juvenile justice system. Nonetheless, the criminal justice system comes into play only after a crime occurs.

Second, the criminal justice system – and particularly the police – focuses primarily on the predatory violence that occurs among strangers on the street. Violence that emerges from frustrations and disputes in intimate settings is more difficult for the criminal justice system to deal with than is stranger-inflicted violence that arises from greed or desperate need and occurs in public. Robbery, burglary, and their violent underpinnings are more traditional and central to the business of the criminal justice system than aggravated assaults among friends in bars, lovers in bedrooms, or teenagers at dances.

Unfortunately, the collaboration of public health and criminal justice in the area of violence prevention has been wrought with tension. Some stems from a basic failure in violence reduction, which puts both disciplines on the defensive – criminal justice for its failure to control the problem and meet societal expectations, and public health for its slowness in recognizing and addressing the problem. However, much of this tension also derives from divergent perspectives of the disciplines, which are exacerbated by inadequate resources directed to violence reduction, thereby forcing them to compete rather than collaborate.

Public health primarily focuses on prevention through identifying causality (or its approximation) and intervening to control or reduce risk factors. It has little interest in assigning blame or meting out punishment and is not very concerned with labeling victim and perpetrator. The public health community may agree that justice must prevail but is not professionally committed to the process.

The criminal justice system, on the other hand, is deeply and morally rooted in "justice" through having criminal offenders properly identified and punished. There is less emphasis on the precursors or factors that precipitate violent events. The criminal justice system is less likely than the public health system to consider external factors that undergird violence because these issues are largely irrelevant to judgment of guilt and innocence.

This tension is a barrier to progress in the violence-prevention field. The tenuous relationship between the criminal justice and public health systems undermines collaboration and precludes opportunities to pool resources and expertise. Healing this rift requires a more cooperative spirit of both disciplines. The public health "purists" must transcend their focus on science and recognize the invaluable contributions and practical experiences of the criminal justice professionals. In turn, the criminal justice "moralists" must recognize the limitations of assigning blame and assuring that justice is done as a primary agenda.

Transcending these initial reactions and successfully meshing the complementary qualities of these two approaches to violence requires setting aside professional differences. More importantly, clearer definitions of perspectives, roles, and expertise will not only lead to a more creative process, but also establish productive working partnerships.

Primary, Secondary, and Tertiary Prevention

A conceptual framework that can alleviate interprofessional tension, clarify roles and responsibilities, and assist in developing a broader perspective on programmatic strategies requires breaking the spectrum of violence into levels representing different points of intervention. This framework, used frequently in public health circles, structures approaches to problems into three stages: primary prevention, secondary prevention (or early intervention), and tertiary prevention (or treatment/rehabilitation). These distinctions have proved valuable when thinking about medical intervention efforts, even though the boundaries among the levels are not discrete. In this discussion, it might be best to view these distinctions as concentric circles that widen out in space and time from a central point, which in this instance is the occurrence of some violent event.

Primary prevention, which by definition addresses the broadest level of the general public, might seek to reduce the level of violence shown on television or to promote gun control. Such efforts can be directed toward public values and attitudes that encourage the use of violence.

Secondary prevention is distinguished from primary prevention in that it identifies relatively narrowly defined subgroups or circumstances that are at high risk of being involved in or occasioning violence. Thus, secondary prevention efforts might focus on urban poor and/or young men who are at particularly high risk of engaging in or being victimized by violence. This may be accomplished by educating them in nonviolent methods of resolving disputes or displaying competence and power.

Tertiary prevention attempts to reduce the negative consequences of a particular event after it has occurred or seeks ways to use the event to reduce the likelihood of similar incidents' occurring in the future. Thus, one might think of improved trauma care, on the one hand, and increased efforts to rehabilitate or incapacitate violent offenders, on the other hand, as tertiary prevention instruments in the control of or the response to violence.

The relative risk level of groups or circumstances is a continuum – with some people and circumstances at very high risk (e.g., a person who has been victimized by violence in his or her own home, also surrounded by violence in school, entering a bar in which members of a rival gang are drinking), and others at relatively low risk (e.g., a happily married professor, who owns no weapon more lethal than a screwdriver, writing on her computer at home). Fortunately, the higher-risk groups are smaller than the lower-risk groups.

Primary prevention instruments can influence large populations at relatively low cost. Indeed, the need to reach very large populations requires that primary prevention efforts be low in cost per capita. Thus, primary prevention instruments tend to provide information and education about the problem of violence through the popular media – such as Bill Cosby's recruitment to the cause of using the media to prevent adolescent violence or Sarah Brady's efforts to advocate for gun control laws and educate the public about the risks of handguns. Of course, the ultimate long-term primary prevention goals, which are related to eliminating some of the root causes of violence, are not affected by primary prevention strategies.

This public health model can be very useful when applied specifically to the issue of interpersonal violence. In the past, the criminal justice system has addressed each of the three points of intervention to varying degrees. Yet, the bulk of its efforts respond to serious violent behavior, with moderate attention to early identification and intervention and limited efforts in the area of primary prevention.

The major activities of the criminal justice system have historically involved the roles of the police, the courts, and the prison system in responding to criminal or violent events. Most fiscal resources are spent investigating and punishing criminal behavior, whereas tertiary prevention generally involves incarceration. Secondary prevention efforts focus on early intervention with youthful offenders. Unfortunately, youth are frequently ignored by the courts and probation system until their criminal behavior becomes serious. Primary prevention efforts usually attempt to control "criminogenic" commodities such as guns, drugs, and alcohol or establish elementary school drug and violence prevention education by police.

With the more recent involvement of the public health system, attention has been broadened with enhanced efforts in the prevention arena. The public health agenda emphasis on prevention and early intervention plays only a minor role in the treatment of individuals with serious violence-related problems. Because the violence-related activities of the public health system are newer and less extensive, they are therefore less developed than those of the criminal justice system. Traditionally, public health responded by treating the violence-related injury in the emergency setting – just as the criminal justice system responds intensely after a violent incident.

The regular contact that physicians and nurses have with victims of violence, particularly in emergency departments, has fostered their involvement in prevention. Not only are nonfatal violent episodes inadequately measured with police data, but the greater contact of health providers with victims presents an opportunity to offer public health prevention and intervention strategies in the emergency department. Such programs have been started at Boston City Hospital in Massachusetts; Cook County Hospital in Chicago, Illinois; Harborview Hospital in Seattle, Washington; and Grady Memorial Hospital in Atlanta, Georgia.

Today a new generation of committed health practitioners, community violence-prevention practitioners, social workers, and community activists have devised numerous intervention programs to serve medium- to high-risk adolescents. At the primary prevention level, efforts have focused on gun control and safety, and enhanced public awareness of risk factors and dominant characteristics of violent acts to dispel myths and modify societal values relating to the use of violence. Additionally, some educational interventions (e.g., violence prevention curricula) have been applied in broader, lower-risk settings. Because much of this work is relatively recent, it has not yet established a long track record to assess its effects fully. Finally, public health has applied its analytical expertise to enhance general understanding of risk factors greatly, allowing for a broader vision in the planning and development of preventive approaches (Spivak, Prothrow-Stith, and Hausman, 1988; Prothrow-Stith and Weissman, 1991).

In the area of secondary prevention, public health has developed educational interventions focused on behavior modification of high-risk individuals, particularly children and youth. Various curricula addressing both the risks of violence in solving problems and conflict resolution techniques are currently in use (Spivak, Prothrow-Stith, and Hausman, 1988; Prothrow-Stith and Weissman, 1991).

More recently, the criminal justice system also has increased its involvement with primary and secondary prevention efforts. For example, some criminal justice professionals are involved in gun control initiatives. In 1974, the Juvenile Justice and Delinquency Prevention Act gave the Justice Department primary responsibility for delinquency prevention programs. The Office of Juvenile Justice and Delinquency Prevention was designed in part to encourage development of model delinquency prevention programs. One such program is the Boys Clubs of America Gang Prevention/Intervention through Targeted Outreach. Other community groups refer to the program at-risk boys, who are then recruited to the initiative.

Evaluations of these programs are promising. Feyerherm, Pope, and Lovell (1992) conducted a process evaluation of 33 different Boys & Girls Clubs of America (B&GCA) gang intervention programs. Their examination focused on the degree to which the clubs implemented the gang intervention model and the extent to which clients received the various treatment components. The researchers concluded that "the youth gang prevention and early intervention initiative by Boys & Girls Clubs of America is both sound and viable in its approach." The researchers also collected descriptive information on risk factors and found that 48% of participants showed improvement in school (more than one third of the youth improved their grades, and one third improved their school attendance). B&GCA has also expanded this program in recent years to reach out to youth who have become involved with gangs.

Mentoring programs have also been shown to reduce juvenile alcohol and drug use, reduce antisocial behavior, improve school performance, and prevent youth from getting involved in crime and violent behavior. Probably the best-known mentoring program in the United States is Big Brothers/Big Sisters of America. The highlights of an Office of Juvenile Justice and Delinquency Prevention (OJJDP) Research Bulletin, *Mentoring – A Proven Delinquency Prevention Strategy* (Grossman and Garry, 1997), demonstrate that youth involved in the Big Brothers/Big Sisters mentoring programs were 46% less likely to experiment with drugs, 27% less likely to experiment with alcohol, and almost 33% less likely to hit someone than youth not participating in the program. Participating youth also skipped school less often than youth not participating in the program and showed a modest grade improvement in academic performance.

These types of interventions reflect an important interface between the criminal justice and public health professions. With further attention and the dedication of more public health system resources to this issue along with a broadened vision of criminal justice, a more reasonable balance between prevention and treatment can be achieved. Optimally, the emphasis of the public health system will be on prevention and the priority of the criminal justice system on the response to violence, and the disciplines will work together across the spectrum.

Lessons from Success with Cigarette Smoking Reduction

To illustrate the advantages of this approach, it is instructive to review how it succeeded in other areas. One example, which on the surface appears to be quite different from violence, is the multidisciplinary approach developed to deal with tobacco use. This example, which illustrates a collaboration between public health and the medical care system, represents a useful analogy for the possible collaboration between public health and criminal justice.

Smoking is a major contributing factor to death and disability in the United States and many countries. Significant inroads have been made in turning the tide on this health threat. What was once a valued, sexy, and socially acceptable behavior is now viewed as a disgusting, unhealthy, and socially unacceptable behavior. Heroes in the media used to smoke all the time; now they rarely do. Nationally, the number of smokers has declined dramatically. Smoking was and remains a learned behavior – one that can be unpleasant or distasteful to begin, but extremely difficult to stop.

The strategy to deal with smoking involved a three-pronged approach: primary prevention for those not yet smoking to explain the reasons and support the decision not to start; secondary prevention to encourage stopping or reducing use for those who already started smoking (often this involves helping individuals identify alternative behaviors to replace the smoking behavior); and treatment in the form of surgery, chemotherapy, and other medical interventions for those smokers who have cancer or other health consequences of their behavior. Broad public initiatives to alter the societal values that encouraged smoking were also established to support the three-pronged approach. This has been accomplished through legislation (package labeling, advertising constraints, restrictions on sales to minors, establishment of smoke-free environments), public education, and pressure on media to change images and role models. This example of a public health/medical care interface represents an important success that is instructive for contemplating the possibilities of a public health and criminal justice collaboration to address violence.

A similar approach could and should be taken with respect to violence. Primary prevention strategies and more targeted secondary prevention efforts that proactively value and teach nonviolent behaviors in response to anger and conflict can be developed and applied. This is particularly important given the mounting evidence that violence is a learned behavior (Bandura et al., 1963; Allen, 1981; Huesmann et al., 1984; Slaby and Guerra, 1988; Prothrow-Stith and Weissman, 1991; Vissing et al., 1991). Well-child health visits in neighborhood health centers provide an ideal window of opportunity for early intervention. Dr. Peter Stringham, a pediatrician at the East Boston Neighborhood Health Center, incorporates a violence prevention protocol for families from the newborn visit through the teenage years.

Teaching social skills is as important to our children as teaching the academic subjects we now emphasize in our society. This will in no way eliminate the underlying societal stresses that influence violent behavior but can influence and direct reactions to social stressors from antisocial to prosocial behavior. Curricula that emphasize decision making, nonviolent conflict resolution, and development of self-esteem currently exist but are terribly underutilized and viewed as an "add-on" in academic settings rather than a basic component of intergroup relations. Placing more emphasis on the use of such curricula coupled with enhanced investments in social and support services for both families and youth are important steps toward reducing youth violence. Such a move would also require that the education, human service, and public health institutions join forces to foster these changes in our communities.

Recognition that teaching nonviolent behaviors might be an important element of a combined public health/criminal justice response to youth violence reminds us that the modern view of how the law operates on social behavior has become far more narrow than it once was. Modern conceptions of the law imagine it as operating on individual behavior primarily through its incentive effects – the promise of punishment – for misconduct, which are made concrete and credible through individual prosecutions.

Classic writings on law devote considerable attention not only to the passage and application of laws to individual cases, but also to their promulgation throughout society (Friedman, 1975). Extensive efforts to explain and educate citizens about the need for laws served to ensure both justice and efficacy. Unless citizens understood the law – its spirit as well as its letter – they could not reasonably be held accountable for disobedience. Voluntary compliance (which is crucial to the law's effect) is not reasonable when the purposes are unclear.

Building on these insights, the public health community focuses on the importance of educating the public about violence as well as the existence of sanctions for violating laws in its nonviolence education. It also incorporates an important insight about the promulgation of obligations, namely, that it is often far easier to persuade people to fulfill an important obligation by showing how and why it is in their best interest to do so. Persuasion and assistance are often more effective tools than accusation and blame. A broad social rule against violence that is included in the context for the education often helps in persuading and assisting. Thus, behavioral change requires a combination of education and laws.

Gun control legislation further illustrates the interconnection between education and laws. Although there is growing support for increased hand-gun ownership restrictions as a primary prevention strategy, legislation alone is unlikely to create great change in violent injury rates in the fore-seeable future. One quarter of adults in the United States own a gun and only about one in six Americans (16%) owns a handgun. That means that five of six Americans do not own a handgun (Diaz, 1999). With 60 million handguns in circulation in the United States (Miller, 2000), understanding and accepting the risks of handgun ownership and carrying are as important as legislative restrictions to reduce intentional handgun injuries.

Secondary level strategies require a more targeted effort, including the early identification of individuals at high risk for or already beginning to ex-hibit violent behavior, along with the development of treatment services for them. These strategies represent an important interface between the human service and criminal justice systems because the early identification of indi-viduals at high risk for violence requires considerable collaboration. Points of early identification occur in schools, health facilities, police departments, courts, and a variety of other community institutions. Professional training in early identification and appropriate evaluation and treatment is essential to properly identifying at-risk youth. Professional definitions and institu-tional boundaries that encourage limited, one-dimensional approaches have been established.

Treatment interventions (tertiary prevention) for the most seriously af-fected individuals represent a key focal point for the criminal justice sys-tem. Violent behavior cannot be condoned; punishment is an appropriate response to violent crimes or episodes, and some individuals who have serious disorders require firm intervention to ensure safety within commu-nities. Although tertiary prevention occurs most extensively in the criminal justice realm, public health has a role working with the prison system in the area of rehabilitation. Without increased attention to rehabilitative ef-forts, including supportive services for those returning from prison to the community, most will continue to leave the prison system without the skills to avoid violent behaviors. Public health must advocate for and support drug and alcohol treatment services, job training efforts, conflict resolution and violence prevention skills, as well as the development of more extensive behavior change interventions. That successful rehabilitative efforts remain limited further reinforces the need for more involvement of the public health system in this area.

Promising Prevention Programs Using Public Health Strategies

There is a common tendency among expert police to provide explanations for increases and decreases in violence. For example, the Boston Strike Force, a unique partnership between police and probation officers, and the Cease Fire Program, a creative policing effort with federal officers to decrease access to guns, have been given well-deserved credit for contributing to the decline in juvenile homicides. But to limit our understanding of effective interventions to policing seriously ignores the thousands of school-, church-, and other community-based programs around the country that can and do impact children's lives successfully.

The researchers Joy G. Dryfoos and Lisbeth Schorr agree that the most effective programs must be comprehensive, family- and community-oriented, and collaborative in nature. Some schools, communities, social agencies, and politicians have incorporated this formula for success and have developed strategies to help children and their families prevent or cope with violence. These programs offer opportunities to learn from their successes and failures.

The Boston Violence Prevention Program

The Boston Violence Prevention Program, an intensive community-based outreach and education effort run by Boston's Department of Health and Hospitals, was launched in 1986 as part of its Health Promotion Program for Urban Youth. Much of its early work focused on training teachers and youth services staff how to teach adolescents about the risks of violence and to discuss measures that can be employed to prevent fights. The core text for this program is *Violence Prevention Curriculum for Adolescents* (Education Development Center, 1987). Teachers, health workers, street outreach workers, and peer workers are offered regular training. Peer leaders are trained and actively participate in training sessions offered by the Program. A mass media campaign, "Friends for Life Don't Let Friends Fight," was developed to create a new community ethos in support of violence prevention. The program has been part of the city budget since 1995 and has generated several spin-off activities.

Resolving Conflict Creatively Program
The Resolving Conflict Creatively Program, a holistic school-based conflict resolution program in New York, California, and Alaska, works with the entire school system to create safe schools. Developed and refined since 1986, the K–12 curriculum requires support from school administrators, though it does not mandate that every teacher be trained. Each of the 32 school districts in New York City that use the curriculum maintains some autonomy to grant decision-making power to the school community. After intense 40-hour curriculum training, teachers incorporate the methods in their classrooms. The program also invites and encourages the participation of parents. Both teachers and administrators in these schools document fewer fights. Moreover, students become peer mediators and receive special training to negotiate and mediate arguments during school hours.

In this program, not only do students develop leadership skills and a sense of responsibility for peace and respect, but teachers and administrators find practical use for conflict resolution skills in their daily lives. The program also offers regular advanced training sessions in topics such as helping students deal with death and grief. A walk through the hallways of the Satellite Academy High School in the Bronx gives the sense that despite unsafe surroundings, the school offers an oasis of safety – a place of mutual respect – where learning can occur. Program evaluations show that both teachers and students notice a positive change in the school climate.

Save Our Sons and Daughters
Clementine Barfield Chism, executive director of the community-based program for Detroit public schools Save Ours Sons and Daughters (SOSAD), works daily to restore a sense of safety in a community that regularly experiences violence. She is one of the first in this country to recognize the feelings of children after a violence episode. In her words, "They are scared. They see violence is a way of life so they act out. It is normal." She cringes when hearing about inner-city children's experiences with posttraumatic stress disorder. To her, it is not a disorder, but a natural response to the chaotic violence around them. After losing her son to violence, she founded SOSAD to provide grief counseling to her other sons. Over the past years, SOSAD activities have grown to include a K–12 curriculum, named the Peace Program, which was implemented in the Detroit schools most devastated by violence. The Peace Program teaches age- and culturally appropriate conflict resolution and helps children and adolescents find a sense of empowerment by establishing and maintaining peace in their school and by teaching them to become peacemakers. It also deals with the grief and pain that follow losing someone to violence.

The Peace Program schools proudly display a peace chain, which is constructed by linking the children's signed peace pledges together. Early assessments indicate that teachers report improved school climates and that children are excited with their roles as peacemakers and peacekeepers. The teachers of one particularly tough group of freshman girls, known for their physical fighting at one of Detroit's high schools, affirm the success of this program. These girls have made a pledge not to fight and are fully engaged in learning and practicing the skills of peace.

Boston City Hospital Violence Prevention Programs
In 1990, Boston City Hospital Program began a project of visiting and providing special violence prevention counseling to adolescents admitted to the hospital for gunshot wounds and stab wounds. This program eventually grew to involve the patient's friends and family. A safety plan is developed for each patient, and follow-up includes far more than attention to the physical wound. In 1992, Boston City Hospital initiated a special program for children who witness violence. The Harvard Community Health Plan Foundation has sponsored parent information brochures on television watching and disciplinary techniques in addition to their "Think – Violence Is for Those Who Don't" campaign.

Overcoming Obstacles
The Los Angeles–based Overcoming Obstacles is an education, employment, and entrepreneurship program that teaches young people the skills needed (1) to succeed in education, (2) to find jobs, (3) to develop entrepreneurial skills, and (4) to involve themselves productively in their community. It illustrates business partnering with a community program to enhance students' chances of succeeding.

This three-phase program includes coursework that has several objectives:

- To improve self esteem
- To develop a sense of personal responsibility
- To instill a sense of pride in community
- To set realistic goals
- To develop communication and conflict resolutions skills
- To gain employment seeking and retention skills

An evaluation demonstrated positive behavior change in successful students during the school year and after graduation. After the first educational phase, high school students move to a job placement phase. Through a network, students secure part-time and summer employment and full-time employment is offered for program graduates. One example is a special program with ARCO Product Company/Prestige Stations, Inc. Students working for this company receive a salary subject to increases and bonuses based on performance, and they have an opportunity to attend college, which is paid for by ARCO. Phase three encourages students to learn to become managers and owners of a business.

Coordinating Coalitions

The Contra Costa County California Health Department is widely known for its efforts to develop comprehensive programs that harness existing resources to alleviate poor health outcomes. Rather than designing and implementing their own stand-alone projects, Contra Costa County Program (CCCP) coordinates and develops existing programs to meet identified community needs. It serves as a lead agency for several health-related issues, including violence prevention. CCCP programming builds on the premise that coalitions

- offer more resources for less money,
- can reach more people than a single organization,
- provide greater credibility than single organizations,
- offer more political clout,
- serve as a community networking function, and
- offer more diverse opinions and talents.

They also insist that coalitions should include

- prevention efforts involving home, school, and community coordination;
- program evaluation measures that are integrated into the program design; and
- new programs that build on prior successes.

These premises have been incorporated in the Safe Schools Project of the Pittsburgh Public Schools, a model for a multidisciplinary violence prevention coalition. Members of the Pittsburgh Public Schools, the Jewish Healthcare Foundation, the Western Psychiatric Institute and Clinic, the Center for Injury Research and Control at the University of Pittsburgh, and the Boys & Girls Club of Western Pennsylvania formed a working group that produced a Blueprint for Violence Reduction in Pittsburgh Public Schools, an action plan based on a sound theoretical framework, data collection and analysis, a commitment to understanding the causes of violence, and an analysis of state-of-the-art school violence prevention programs. The blueprint reviews the project's components and discusses each step in a manner that lends itself to replication in other school districts. It also includes a set of valuable guiding principles for school-based program implementation.

Conclusion

The contributions made by public health professionals' efforts to prevent violence have been tremendous. The continued application of public health strategies to the understanding and prevention of violence assures more success than the criminal justice system achieves alone. The public health campaign to reduce smoking took 30 years after the first Surgeon General's report to reduce smoking. Violence reduction can be expected to take at least as long and requires as many, if not more, diverse strategies.

REFERENCES

Allen, N. H. (1981). Homicide Prevention and Intervention. *Suicide and Life Threatening Behavior*, 11, 167.

American Psychological Association Commission on Violence and Youth. (1993). "Violence and Youth: Psychology's Response," Summary Report of the American Psychological Association Commission on Violence and Youth, Vol. 1. Internet: http://www.apa.org/pi/pii/violenceandyouth.pdf.

Bandura, A., Ross, D., and Ross, S. (1963). Vicarious Reinforcement and Imitative Learning. *Journal of Abnormal Social Psychology* 63, 601–607.

BJS (Bureau of Justice Statistics), U.S. Department of Justice. (1992). *Criminal Victimization in the U.S., 1991.* Washington, DC: U.S. Department of Justice.

BJS (Bureau of Justice Statistics), U.S. Department of Justice (1993). *Criminal Victimization in the U.S., 1992.* Washington, DC: U.S. Department of Justice.

BJS (Bureau of Justice Statistics), U.S. Department of Justice. (1995). *Guns Used in Crime: Firearms, Crime and Criminal Justice – Selected Findings.* Washington, DC: U.S. Department of Justice.

BJS (Bureau of Justice Statistics), U.S. Department of Justice. (1996). *Firearm Injury from Crime.* Washington, DC: U.S. Department of Justice.

Bureau of Alcohol, Tobacco, and Firearms. (1991). *Firearm Census Report.* Washington, DC: U.S. Treasury Department.

CDC (Centers for Disease Control and Prevention). (1993). Morbidity and Mortality Weekly Report 42(2). January 22, 1993. Internet: ftp://ftp.cdc.gov/pub/Publications/mmwr/wk/mm4202.pdf.

CDC (Center for Disease Control and Prevention). (1994). Morbidity and Mortality Weekly Report 43(3). January 28, 1993. Internet:ftp://ftp.cdc.gov/pub/Publications/mmwr/wk/mm4303.pdf.

CDC (Centers for Disease Control and Prevention). (1997). Rates of Homicide, Suicide, and Firearm-Related Death among Children in 26 Industrialized Countries. *Morbidity and Mortality Weekly Report*, 46(5), 101–105.

CDC (Centers for Disease Control and Prevention). (2000). CDC Surveillance Summaries. Morbidity and Mortality Weekly Report 49(SS-5). June 9, 2000. Internet: http://www.cdc.gov/mmwr/preview/mmwrhtml/ss4905a1.htm.

Centerwall, B. S. (1984). Race, Socioeconomic Status, and Domestic Homicide, Atlanta, 1971–72. *American Journal of Public Health*, 74(8), 813–815.

Centerwall, B. S. (1992). Television and Violence: The Scale of the Problem and Where to Go from Here. *Journal of the American Medical Association*, 261 (22), 3059–3063.

Diaz, T. (1999). *Making a Killing: The Business of Guns in America*. New York: New Press.

Dryfoos, J. G. (1998). *Full-Service Schools: A Revolution in Health and Social Services for Children, Youth and Families*. San Francisco: Jossey-Bass.

Durant, R., Pendergast, R., and Cadenhead, C. (1994). Exposure to Violence and Victimization and Fighting Behavior by Urban Black Adolescents. *Journal of Adolescent Health*, 4, 311–318.

Education Development Center. (1987). Prothrow-Stith, D. (Ed.). *Violence Prevention Curriculum for Adolescents*. Newton, MA: Education Development Center.

Emde, R. N. (1993). The Horror! The Horror! Reflection on Our Culture of Violence and Its Implications for Early Development and Morality. *Psychiatry* 1, 119–123.

Eron, L., and Huesman, L. R. (1984). Television violence and aggressive behavior. In B. Lahey and A. Kazdin (Eds.), *Advances in Clinical Psychology*. New York: Plenum Press.

Farrell, C. (1993). The Economics of Crime. *Business Week*, December 13, 72–80.

FBI (Federal Bureau of Investigation), U.S. Department of Justice. (1992). *Crime in the U.S., 1992*. Uniform Crime Reports. Washington, DC: Government Printing Office.

FBI (Federal Bureau of Investigations), U.S. Department of Justice. (1995). *Crime in the U.S., 1995*. Uniform Crime Reports. Washington, DC: Government Printing Office.

FBI (Federal Bureau of Investigation), U.S. Department of Justice. (1996). *Crime in the U.S., 1996*. Uniform Crime Reports. Washington, DC: Government Printing Office.

Feyerherm, W., Pope, C., and Lovell, R. (1992). Youth Gang Prevention and Early Intervention Programs (unpublished final research report, Portland, OR, Portland State University).

Fitzpatrick, K. M., and Boldizar, J. P. (1993). The Prevalence and Consequences of Exposure to Violence among African-American Youth. *Journal of the American Academy of Child and Adolescent Psychiatry* 2, 424–430.

Freeman, L., Mokros, H., and Poznanski, E. (1993). Violent Events Reported by Normal Urban School-aged Children: Characteristics and Depression Correlates. *Journal of the American Academy of Child and Adolescent Psychiatry*, 2, 419–423.

Friedman, L. M. (1975). The Legal System – a Social Science Perspective, pp. 56–66. New York: Russell Sage Foundation.

Furlong, M. J., and Morrison, G. M. (1994). School Violence and Safety in Perspective. *School Psychology Review*, 23, 139–150.

Grossman, J. B., and Baldwin, J. (1997). Mentoring: A Proven Delinquency Prevention Strategy. *OJJDP Bulletin*, April.

Grossman, J. B., and Garry, E. M. (1997). U.S. Department of Justice. *OJJDP Juvenile Justice Bulletin*, 1.

Groves, B., Augustyn, M., Parker, S., and Zuckerman, B. (1993). Silent Victims: Children Who Witness Violence. *Journal of the American Medical Association*, 2, 262–264.

Huesmann, L. R. et al. (1984). Stability of Aggression over Time and Generations. *Developmental Psychology*, 20:1120–1134.

Killias, M. (1993). International Correlations between Gun Ownership and Rates of Homicide and Suicide. *Canadian Medical Association*, 10, 1721–1725.

Lester, D. (1988). Firearm Availability and the Incidence of Suicide and Homicide. *Acta Psychiatrica*, 20, 387–393.

Lewis, D. O., Pincus, J. H., Lovely, R., Spitzer, E., and Moy, E. (1987). Biopsychosocial Characteristics of Matched Samples of Delinquents and Nondelinquents. *Journal of the American Academy of Child and Adolescent Psychiatry*, 26(5), 744–752.

Lotion, R. P., and Saltzman, W. (1993). Children's Exposure to Community Violence: Following a Path from Concern to Research to Action. *Psychiatry*, 1, 55–65.

Martinez, P., and Richters, J. (1993). The NIMH Community Violence Project. II. Children's Distress Symptoms Associated with Violence Exposure. *Psychiatry*, 60, 22–35.

Metropolitan Life and Louis Harris and Associates. (1993). *Violence in America's Public Schools*. New York: Metropolitan Life Insurance Co.

Miller, T. C. (2000). Bush Announces Free Gun Trigger Lock Program. *Los Angeles Times*, May 13, A1.

Miller, T. R., Cohen, M. A., and Rossman, S. B. (1993). Datawatch, Victim Costs of Violent Crime and Resulting Injuries. *Health Affairs*, winter, 187–197.

Murphy, S. L. (2000). Deaths: Final Data for 1998. *National Vital Statistics Report*, 48 (11). DHHS Publication No. (PHS) 2000–1120. Hyattsville, MD: National Center for Health Statistics.

National Economic Council (2000). "Background on Programs and Themes Announced in the Address: Fiscal Discipline and Nearing The Longest Economic Expansion in U.S. History. Supplement to President William Jefferson Clinton's State of the Union Address. 27 January 2000. Internet: http://clinton4.nara.gov/textonly/WH/EOP/nec/html/2000SotuBookFinal.html.

OJJDP (Office of Juvenile Justice and Delinquency Prevention). (1996). Female Offenders in the Juvenile Justice System, June.

Osofsky, J., Wevers, S., Hann, D., and Fick, A. (1993). Chronic Community Violence: What Is Happening to Our Children? *Psychiatry*, 56, 36–45.

Prothrow-Stith, D., and Weissman, M. (1991). *Deadly Consequences: How Violence Is Destroying Our Teenage Population and a Plan to Begin Solving the Problem* (pp. 1–203). New York: HarperCollins.

Pynoos, R. S. et al. (1987). Life Threat and Post traumatic Stress in School-age Children. *Archives of General Psychiatry*, 44, 1057–1063.

Reiss, D. (1993). The Long Reach of Violence and Aggression. *Psychiatry*, 56(2), 163–165.

Sang, F., Schmitz, B., and Rasche, K. (1993). Developmental Trends in Television Coviewing of Parent-child Dyads. *Journal of Youth and Adolescence*, 22(5), 531–543.

Satcher, D. (1985). The Public Health Approach to Violence. National Education Association National Conference, Los Angeles, California, April 8.

Schorr, L. B., and Wilson, W. J. (1998). *Common Purpose: Strengthening Families and Neighborhoods to Rebuild America*. New York: Doubleday

Sheley, J., McGee, Z., and Wright, J. (1992). Gun-Related Violence in and around Inner-City Schools. *Journal of Diseases of Childhood*, 146, 677–682.

Slaby, R. G., and Guerra, N. G. (1988). Cognitive Mediators of Aggression in Adolescent Offenders. 1. Assessment. *Developmental Psychology*, 24, 80–88.

Spivak, H., Prothrow-Stith, D., and Hausman, A. (1988). Dying Is No Accident: Adolescents, Violence, and Intentional Injury. *Pediatric Clinics of North America*, 35, 1339–1347.

U.S. Bureau of the Census, Population Estimates Program, Population Division. (1999). Counties Ranked by Black Population in 1998, table CO-98-16. September 15. Washington, DC: Government Printing Office.

U.S. Department of Health, Education, and Welfare. (1964). *Smoking and Health: Report of the Advisory Committee to the Surgeon of the General Public Health Service.* Washington, DC: Government Printing Office.

Vissing, Y., Straus, M., Felles, R., and Harrop, J. (1991). Verbal Aggression by Parents and Psychological Problems of Children. *Child Abuse and Neglect*, 15, 223–238.

Widom, C. S. (1989). The Cycle of Violence. *Science*, 244, 160–166.

Wilson, W. J. (1987). *The Truly Disadvantaged: The Inner City, the Underclass, and Public Policy.* Chicago: University of Chicago Press.

Wilson, W. J. (1997). *When Work Disappears: The World of the New Urban Poor.* New York: Knopf.

9 Social Learning and Community Participation with Children at Risk in Two Marginalized Urban Neighborhoods in Amman, Jordan

Curtis N. Rhodes, Jr., Haytham A. Mihyar, and Ghada Abu El-Rous

Increasing numbers of Jordanian youth face growing value conflict and restlessness, partly as a result of profound social and demographic changes that have refashioned the urban landscape. Since the mid-1970s, the ratio of urban to rural population shifted from 20:80 to 80:20. With a rate of natural increase of 3.6%, Jordan's youth population is growing rapidly, and over half of all persons are currently under 20 years of age. Economic pressures stemming from inflation, declining purchasing power, and high unemployment have imposed hardships on all families, but especially those living in low-income urban neighborhoods. Parents now confront situations that were unprecedented in their past experience raising children, particularly if they moved from rural to urban areas during the period of rapid social change.

In this chapter, I review the promise and pitfalls of neighborhood interventions planned and implemented with at-risk youth that were based on a pilot program conducted in Amman, Jordan. The program involved youth in devising and implementing strategies for neighborhood improvements in two economically and socially marginalized urban communities. The neighborhood is the central locus within which youth develop relationships with adults and adult-mediated structures and events.

In what follows I elaborate the character of social change in Jordan, describe the two sites in which the intervention was implemented, and draw systematic comparisons between the two neighborhoods as contexts for prosocial youth development. Subsequently, I describe the intervention to transform the two sites and create prosocial communities by providing youth with opportunities to develop their talents in a safe environment. The final section draws lessons from the experience and summarizes the key findings.

Social Context of Jordanian Youth

Jordan has witnessed a rapid pace of social and economic change as it develops into a modern, urbanized society. The most striking changes include a large youth population, an unprecedented movement from rural to urban settings, underdeveloped social institutions, and a shift away from an authoritarian, patriarchal social system that has created a generation gap between youth and their elders.

Movement from rural areas to towns began during the 1950s and continued through the 1960s as farm families sought to enter a wage-based economy, and as traditionally nomadic people settled into stationary communities. The pace of migration quickened by the 1980s, such that 80% of the population resided in urban areas in the 1990s as compared to 20% in the 1960s. Furthermore, a population growth rate of 3.6% has resulted in a youthful society: Fifty-five percent of Jordanians are under the age of 20, and at least 43% are under the age of 15.

The return-migration of Jordanians (particularly after the Gulf War of 1991) decreased outside remittances to families whose members once provided income from jobs abroad. Jordan's economy was not prepared to absorb large numbers of employable individuals; consequently, living costs increased and incomes stagnated for large segments of the population during the 1990s.

By international standards, Jordan is a patriarchal society. Authority lies in the hands of the head of an institution, whether it is the family or a formally constituted social organization, and relationships among people are authoritarian in nature (Hasan, 1997). In families, the father is the seat of authority and sons assume family responsibility and make decisions. In the tribal structure of this society, men with status make decisions for larger groups of related individuals.

Until the relatively recent rapid urbanization of Jordanian society, communities of extended families and clans existed in a context of localized trust – one in which actions were based on shared knowledge and experience. These communities were *facework* communities, in which relations of trust were sustained by or expressed in social connections established in the presence of all significant persons (Giddens, 1990). These communities stabilized social relations over time through kinship. Major community activities took place within familiar sites and were organized by using local resources. Meaning was rooted in tradition.

Despite these stabilizing forces, urban youth confront different circumstances. In the modern city of Amman, institutions play more active roles than do parents in raising children. A child may spend more time in school, on public transport, and in street play than in the family home. Because the institutions in this rapidly urbanizing city are overwhelmed with demands for services while the roles of parents and local communities are shrinking, the social supports needed for normative youth development are eroding.

Young Jordanians who have been exposed through modern mass media to different models of life – sexuality and gender relations, child–parent relations, student–teacher relations, and citizen–bureaucracy relations – find that modern viewpoints often conflict with local models. In their socialization process, young Jordanians are also exposed to conflicting influences: traditionalism versus modernism, tribalism versus nationalism, authoritarianism versus freedom. These tensions place stress on them as they seek to build their value systems and form new cultural expectations.

Adjustment to change is accompanied by conflict between the new and the old values and life perceptions. Moreover, in settings that are rapidly changing, it is difficult for the elder generation to provide the young with meaningful guidance. Therefore, young people look for their life paths alone in untried, uncertain directions. Internal and external value conflicts lead to feelings of restlessness, hesitation, dependency, and failure (Hasan, 1997).

Background for Case Studies

In 1994, two types of urban neighborhoods were selected as learning sites within which to discover capabilities of at-risk youth and to encourage actions for improving their living circumstances. Selection of youth was based on their history, their social characteristics, and the various attributes that isolated them from productive social relationships within the community and with external agencies. In both communities youth were alienated from adults and socially isolated from the urban mainstream. Youth perceived adults as unsympathetic, threatening, and unwilling to understand their viewpoints; adults viewed children's behaviors as problems. Neighborhood residents viewed municipal authorities and social agencies as unresponsive and unaware of their problems, and municipal authorities viewed the poor neighborhoods as intransigent obstacles to urban improvement. In turn, alienation produced antagonism and estrangement between children and adults and also between adults and municipal authorities and representatives of social agencies.

The Questscope social learning project sought to understand the consequences for children and youth living in distressed neighborhoods. The intervention project described here was designed to assess and improve the situation of youth by transforming their neighborhoods to make them child-friendly (prosocial). Special emphasis was placed on male youth ages 6–14, who were followed for 4 years while the project was active. To accomplish this goal, neighborhood residents were involved in identifying factors that supported or undermined their children's development and subsequently taking action to alter those circumstances that prohibited children's participation as valuable members of their community.

Two Types of Urban Neighborhoods

Two sites were selected to represent different types of low-income under-served communities in the social landscape of Jordan – a typical poor urban neighborhood and a "quasi-urban neighborhood." The former functions much as do urban ghettos throughout the world, whereas the latter is a type of urban village, where gemeinschaftlike relations maintain the rural character of the original communities. For convenience and for differentiating between them, hereafter we refer to the conventional urban neighborhood as *a ghetto*, and the quasi-urban site as *an urban village*.

Residents in the ghetto are not linked through social relations or kinship ties, and their children are an obvious source of annoyance and often in trouble with legal and institutional authorities. Residents in the urban village are closely bound by kinship ties, clan loyalty, and traditional social practices. Parents discourage children from interacting with individuals and institutions outside their geographical boundaries, thereby reinforcing social isolation while perpetuating rural traditions. Both sites are densely populated with large low-income families and weak social institutions. In both sites, youth experienced a high risk of neglect and abuse (Questscope, 1995).

The Ghetto. The urban ghetto is populated by refugees (established after the "1967 War") and rural migrants. When the project began, youth were alienated from their parents and other adults and there was little cooperation among families. Residents were marginalized from mainstream social institutions, and consequently also from the benefits enjoyed by mainstream society, such as employment, income security, and social participation. Many poor families were trapped there and unable to move.

Despite these problems, several factors made the site attractive to families. Low rental and construction costs allowed low-income families to build or rent a house. The proximity of the neighborhood to work and public transportation reduced time and travel costs. There were job opportunities for nonskilled work in a busy nearby commercial area, including parts of the city where young boys (ages 10 to 17) collected cans, glass, and scrap iron from the trash. An underground economy (related to drugs and prostitution) operated in and around the area, and some individuals had life-styles that benefited from the anonymity afforded by the crowded neighborhood.

Although a strong entrepreneurial spirit existed among neighborhood residents, the lack of capital and appropriate skills (including vocational training, personal life skills, and small-business acumen) prevented them from actualizing their economic potential. Low-wage unskilled labor provided the main income source, but many children supplemented family income when they worked for daily wages or collected materials for resale from the trash.[1] Several small grocery stores and service shops (tailors, etc.) also provided day to day income for some families. Most adult breadwinners were unable to compete for jobs that required moderate or high skills. Public assistance to alleviate poverty was not available. Externally, this neighborhood was considered an offensive urban problem that was best "cleaned up." All residents were aware of the neighborhood's problems, but there were no mediating structures to help them envision that they belonged to something worth improving. Therefore, to manage these circumstances, families adopted one of two strategies: To protect youth from the problems of the streets, many isolated their children indoors; others simply allowed youth to grow up in the streets.

Children living in the poor urban neighborhood lacked the basic necessities for normative development. "Family" meant a place to sleep and serious problems, such as adult unemployment, alcoholism, and mental illness. By the age of 6, many children shouldered the responsibility of increasing family income by collecting aluminum cans, selling chewing gum in the streets, cleaning car windshields, or begging at traffic lights. Young men ages 10 to 18 typically assumed parental responsibilities that ranged from breadwinning to making important family decisions. Many children suffered abuse from intoxicated fathers who spent meager earnings on alcohol and gambling, leaving little or nothing for the family. Most mothers were uneducated, and their main concern was providing food for their children. Because many mothers had to work to make ends meet, they often did not know where their children were during the day (or night) or what they were doing.

Young boys searched for affection, protection, and security in gangs of other children with similar needs. But belonging to a gang meant a loss of autonomy and agency. When the gang collected cans throughout the night, all members had to do so as well. When the gang sold the cans, everyone

---

[1] The underground economy provided income, but only to certain types of families, and the amount and nature of this income were outside the scope of the study.

had to sell to the same vendor. When gang members sniffed paint thinner or glue or drank alcohol, all members participated. They stole together, and they shared affection and sex with each other. Their fights were each other's fights. In return, the gang was "family" for each member. Each "family" had a leader who gave orders; to disobey was to risk physical beating.

Youth from the ghetto easily differentiated between patronizing behavior and serious concern for them as individuals. Feeling rejected by their community, they resorted to aggression and violence as a way to establish their presence within the neighborhood. Many carried switchblades and concealed razors to defend themselves. As one of the adult volunteers mentioned during the initial community assessment, "Violence is our language."

The Urban Village. This neighborhood in Amman is an urban "village" that comprises families who migrated over a period of more than 40 years from a single rural village in the south of Jordan. They have maintained their clan and kinship structures, traditions, and values almost intact. Because their site was established before land ownership issues were settled, the entire neighborhood (around 12,000 residents) was considered a "special case." The municipal authorities were in a difficult position because provision of services to this community would represent "de facto" recognition of ownership of land that was legally owned by other parties.

These residents maintained their "subsociety" by kin's living in close proximity to each other. Their strategy involved building more and more dwelling units (sons' apartments atop fathers' houses) within the same neighborhood (about 1 km^2). This practice reached its limits, as there is now little space (either vertical or horizontal) in which to expand. Because the houses were small and families large (averaging seven to nine children), many children lived on the streets during the daytime.

Residents earned relatively low wages through public sector employment as teachers or civil servants and in army service. In the past, these jobs provided relatively adequate incomes for living in a low-cost neighborhood (because land was not purchased and houses were built adjoining relatives' houses). However, the rising cost of living and contraction of public-sector employment created a crisis in the viability of this strategy.

Extensive clan obligations had created a highly integrated "social safety net" for residents. In the past, marriages, deaths, religious events, and holidays were accompanied by the exchange of money and goods. As incomes fell, the base for this internal support system did not keep pace with the demands made on this social network. Youth assisted their families by selling home-prepared sweets, tea, and so on, in public squares near the neighborhood. Although the young were not alienated from their neighborhood, the traditional strategies for keeping the community intact had reached the limit of their ability to accommodate the needs of youth.

Nevertheless, there was a relatively high level of social capital in this neighborhood. Every family participated in a variety of social networks, which were usually of a religious or traditional nature. Although the presence of these networks represented a potential for concerted community action, in practice there were few relationships with national organizations that could assist them with their growing problems. In part, this resulted because the internal solidarity of this community had created an isolated (and sometimes alienating) stance toward the larger city and its institutions.

In the urban village, practically all the children attended school, including those who were obligated to augment family income. Male youth lived in two worlds – the traditional and authoritarian world of their fathers and adult male relatives and the modern world of the larger city that required a different set of personal competencies. They could not be like their fathers because the life-style their parents knew no longer existed. They also were not prepared to meet the demands imposed by city life.

Inside the neighborhood behavior was carefully regulated. Adult males controlled the social environment. The only space for children was the street, where they developed their own games and activities to fill time. The most remarkable difference between the urban village and the ghetto is that the street was considered safe for youth and the peer groups were largely made up of relatives and cousins. Relationships within the household were warm and nurturing but conformed to traditional lines of authority: Boys did not interrupt their fathers when they were speaking or even talk in the presence of fathers or uncles. A male child could go where he wanted only after informing his father. Girls did not leave the house without an accompanying male relative (husband, brother, or father) except to attend school. (Most of the girls were enrolled in school.) Community norms also accepted women's working as teachers and in some types of public sector employment.

All the institutions to which youth might relate were located outside the neighborhood, including schools. When youth were obligated to leave the neighborhood, they were keenly aware that external conditions were different. Both adults and children considered school attendance dangerous because it put them at risk in the city. Therefore, boys who ventured into the city in groups developed an elaborate system of whistles and "call signs" that allowed them to be located and surrounded by their peers whenever they perceived danger. Furthermore, all of the male children carried switchblades, concealed razors, or sharpened objects.

Creating Prosocial Communities

The goal of the Questscope program is to develop prosocial communities that reinforce prosocial behavior among children and youth by developing positive attitudes and practices within the community (Tyler, 1997). However, given the lack of effective institutions to provide assistance to the community, it was necessary to emphasize residents' roles in guiding its direction. Awareness that troublesome children could change their behavior provided an incentive to collaborate with external resource providers. Once the prosocial behavior of individual children and youth was observed and understood, the neighborhood was positioned to create a healthy environment for normative youth development.

Participatory interaction within the community fostered discussion about social issues down to the grass-roots level. Neighborhood residents discussed social issues and problems, identified priorities, and subsequently took action to improve conditions. In turn, these outcomes provided a strong base for building informed, self-directed volunteerism, which proved vital in rapidly growing urban centers where the voices of poor, young citizens were seldom heard or even sought.

The intervention used three complementary approaches to building prosocial communities. Together they have a cohesive prosocial effect because they create collaborative and enhanced roles for everyone (Tyler, 1997). The first approach was locality development. Consensus among neighborhood members grew as they identified common concerns and planned collective solutions. Community members were trained in the use of social assessment tools to create their own vision of their community, establish their own priorities, and develop a plan for action. They used their skills and resources to work with providers of external resources to strengthen volunteer capabilities within the community.

The second approach to building prosocial communities entailed building collaborative linkages, such as involving local experts to assist in problem solving by jointly designing and implementing interventions. External experts treated community members as active collaborators rather than as passive clients (Tyler, 1997). Expert providers were able to suggest and implement programs that suited the community environment as they became aware of the community's constraints. Accordingly, they tailored their roles to reshape the social environment and to develop competencies that suited youth's needs.

Social action was the third strategy used to change the local social context in which youth are reared. Mainly, this entailed attracting the attention of urban leaders and managers who could modify policies that created hardships and prevented cooperation between the community and broader urban structures. Since marginalized communities have traditionally been invisible to policymakers, the project began to capture their attention.

Components of the Questscope Program

Program staff identified five important constraints operating on or within the two marginalized urban neighborhoods. These served as arenas for implementing the program to build prosocial communities. The five constraints were (1) frustrated aspirations, (2) changed family relations, (3) neighborhood deterioration, (4) truncated roles of youth, and (5) ineffective institutions (Szanton Blanc, 1994). Emergent strategies were developed to address improvements in each of these areas, and the strategies were oriented around locality development, establishment of linkages, and social action.

(1) Frustrated Aspirations. Frustrated aspirations (the results of psychological and subjective causes) reflect bleak futures and a protracted inability to satisfy material longings. In the world of the information highway and satellite superchannels, everyone is cultivated as a market for consumption through beautiful advertisements by beautiful people for beautiful products.[2] The media make youth aware of what others have and the limited possibilities to acquire what is advertised, thereby creating frustrations. Children in both neighborhoods were made aware of material deprivation through television and through proximity to an affluent urban environment just beyond their neighborhoods.

In the ghetto, a high percentage of male children abandoned school between the ages of 9 and 12, thereby exposing themselves to a future of limited employability and social marginalization as adults. In the urban village, the high value placed on education by adults did not motivate the youth to remain in school because they understood all too well that a high school certificate (the *tawjihi*) no longer guaranteed a job that would pay enough to survive in the city. Not even college completion could ensure a living wage. Moreover, economic demands of their families drove many youth from marginalized urban neighborhoods to engage in petty informal

---

[2] The proliferation of the means of information dissemination (satellite dishes) as part of the modernization of Jordan ensures media coverage throughout the kingdom. The delivery of the same message to a vast and varied number of people is one aspect of globalization that enhances urbanization and is enhanced by it.

activity, like collecting cans for resale. This responsibility did not, however, gain them a respected role in their local neighborhood and in the broader society. Rather, the inability of parents to fulfill basic needs led children to seek support in peer-group structures that encouraged alienating behaviors, such as substance abuse and early unprotected sexual experiences.

The initial approach to address the problem of frustrated aspirations involved identifying the risk factors that were present in young people's lives (substance abuse, early unprotected sexuality, truancy and dropout from school, gang behavior, etc.) by involving neighborhood volunteers in participatory community assessments (Questscope, 1995). The goal was to create more child-friendly atmospheres by creating activities that were beneficial to children and youth. Such activities were based on young people's expressed desires and were designed to reduce the sense of "not belonging." Once youth were involved in constructive activities such as studying or reading in a library, working in a computer lab, or participating in sports programs, a foundation was established from which to cultivate positive links with the rest of the neighborhood.

In the ghetto, provision of new activities increased the time spent in the social center by "troublesome" boys. Initially, this led to new problems because the problem youth carried their aggressive behaviors into the center. Adult staff and volunteers in the center were initially unprepared to handle these problems because they had been selected to operate narrowly defined programs (preschool day care, embroidery and sewing classes, etc.), and their main recourse was to hold lectures in the center on topics they selected.

At this point in the Questscope program, staff established ties with a researcher and two graduate students affiliated with a university counseling center. They took counseling roles in a 1997 summer camp for "troublesome" young men (ages 10–17) designed to help them understand what motivated their positive and negative behaviors. This counseling camp enabled adults to understand their roles in creating an environment that provided positive reinforcement for alienated youth. The young men themselves gained an understanding of options for relating to others apart from violence and aggression.

The staff of the camp were drawn from individuals who lived in the site and who worked in the local center, from Questscope staff, from the counseling center, and from two cooperating government agencies, namely, the Juvenile Department of the Ministry of Social Development and the Housing Organization. Everyone was surprised at the ability of the troublesome young men to adjust their behavior to the structure required in the camp (regular schedule, physical activities, kitchen and clean-up duties, community service projects, etc.). Although the young men were aggressive toward each other, they never expressed aggression toward adults who interacted with them in the camp or later in the neighborhood.

At the end of the camp, everyone was surprised that the young men considered themselves partners with the staff. Upon their return to the neighborhood, the young men organized themselves and arranged to meet for coffee with the juvenile authorities and to talk over their problems. In the past, their only relationship with authorities was related to juvenile justice and detention. This loose self-organization has continued because the gang leaders identified a new direction in which to lead their protégés, which involves more constructive relationships with adults and adult-mediated structures. This activity allowed them to cultivate identities and social roles that are recognized and respected.

The urban village was isolated from the surrounding city partly because of the residents' desire to keep their own identity and traditions alive. In fact, every weekend (Friday, the day for Muslim worship), most of the residents departed to their home village. It was in the village where young women enacted social roles that matched expected behavior that allowed them a measure of freedom of movement and association that was not possible in the city. For residents, maintenance of their village atmosphere in the city had the cost of social isolation, but isolation by choice (Caincar and Abunimah, 1998).

(2) Changed Family Relations. Shifting relationships within and beyond the family can create an emotional poverty that is devastating for children. Social relations, particularly within the family, represent both the cause of and a potential remedy for a great many disturbances affecting young people. Focusing on these relationships highlights the importance of the loving capacities developed in the child–adult relationship and identifies problems that transcend those of poverty.

Urban living is wage-dependent because city dwellers do not grow their own food and have few noncash resources to fall back on in case of unexpected demands. Increased cost of housing in a growing city means smaller homes and more crowding, and less opportunity for extended family members to live together. As urbanization accelerated the shift from patriarchy to less authoritative families, parents had to provide increased resources of time, money, energy, patience, and institutional linkages on behalf of youth while also exercising less traditional control over them.

Few institutions were prepared, either with mandates for programs or with experience in communities, to assist families in accommodating to the dramatic social transformation brought about by rapid urbanization. Parental responsibilities – even the understanding of what constitutes good parenting – also became more difficult to comprehend. As parents proved unable to provide their children an adequate livelihood, there was growing pressure on youth to shoulder family responsibilities. In the ghetto, fathers with traditional expectations encouraged their sons to leave school and contribute to family support. One father refused his son entrance to the house if he failed to meet his daily income target (approximately U.S.$4.25). The 14-year-old son slept on the doorstep of the house. These pressures, coupled with a densely crowded urban environment and little or no support from national institutions, led ultimately to a crisis for children.

Therefore, the Questscope intervention program placed a very strong emphasis on establishing volunteer committees for children's issues from the outset. Organizers assumed that the presence of motivated community members who were oriented to action to improve the neighborhood environment for their children was a key component of a strategy for change. After the initial community-based assessments in each site, the volunteer committees began to establish priorities for activities for their children.

In the ghetto, women volunteers observed the benefits of personal and group counseling for male children. The counseling team was aware that many of the boys' problems could not be addressed unless parents provided information about the specific backgrounds of their children. Women volunteers willingly met with the counselors to discuss the problems youth faced. When it became apparent that youth's interpersonal relationships within families were beyond the scope of the project, group sessions on family issues were gradually discontinued.

In the urban village, family issues were not discussed with "outsiders"; therefore, the process of involving women and girls in participatory assessments was much slower. Allowing women and girls to join in open discussions and to think of activities for both boys and girls was possible only after a social center was established for children. Residents observed that something significant beyond "just talk" was possible.

A first step involved assisting adults to listen to young people, but progress in responding to children's concerns slowed when adults demanded immediate tangible results. Two lessons stem from observing children's responses to building (or rebuilding) healthy relationships with adults (parents or others). One is that a person-to-person relationship with a caring adult can bring about a remarkable shift in the attitudes and behaviors of these children. The other is that all caring, concerned adults can have positive, encouraging relationships with young people if they take the time to understand the individual child. An adult's role as a mentor can be vital, particularly if there is a program to support that relationship. If caring adults are from the young person's neighborhood, the impact of the supportive relationship not only enhances the youth's development, but also augments adult competencies needed to cope with the consequences of poverty. As a result of these observations, Questscope developed a program to train volunteers to acquire mentoring capacities and implemented it in a subsequent project.

(3) Deteriorated Urban Neighborhoods. Cities are not designed with children in mind. The physical environment – pollution, traffic, noise, poor housing, insufficient social spaces outside the homes and off the streets, and insufficient green areas – contributes to the social isolation of children. The organizational environment of inadequate, unresponsive, or inaccessible social services contributes to this social isolation and creates myriad hardships.

Deterioration of urban neighborhoods is a difficult problem for an intervention to address. When youth from the ghetto were asked about changes they would like to see in their neighborhood, staff assumed that their first priority would be a playground. Instead they indicated that a playground would only make life more dangerous for them. They felt that problems associated with gang-related fights and being hurt by razors, and so on, had to be solved first, before making any changes to the physical space. The school setting was equally inhospitable because the institutions were unable to cope with the large numbers of youth entering the system. Many of the children from the poor urban ghetto were unwelcome in school – a learning environment critical for normative development.

The urban village witnessed another type of neighborhood decay, namely, overcrowding. Three or four generations of families had built apartments composed of sons' homes atop fathers' houses, until no vertical or horizontal space remained. Yet, the 12,000 members of this closely knit community bound by kinship and clan linkages did not wish to live elsewhere. The collective strategy for raising children entailed keeping them in the neighborhood (bounded by three streets, about 1 km^2) to protect them from the corrupting influences of the wider city. Because of the rapid demographic growth, the sheer numbers of children – composing 60% of the community – created a crisis of space and resources, which strained families' ability to cope with the growing pressures of urban life.

Nevertheless, when approached by Questscope, community leaders were willing to focus attention and resources on their children and were very active in the initial appraisal of young people's needs. The crucial issue for them was maintaining leadership and involvement in community change. The establishment of a community center and the development of a plan for action through a local committee were turning points in their ability to manage the deteriorating environment. First, a group of adults with experience in assisting their own children served as community leaders. Subsequently they took the initiative to increase linkages to and cooperation with national providers of services and assistance. This represented a major behavioral change for a community that had become culturally isolated by design.

Neighborhood physical quality was a major concern for residents of both sites involved in this project. In the ghetto, no organization was responsive to these concerns, partly because of ambiguous land ownership and the legality of housing construction. The owner of the land (upon which squatters had settled) was often not the owner of the house. Furthermore, the owner of the house was often not the tenant in the rented house. Consequently, the neighborhood lacked legitimacy in presenting its concerns.

During the period of the Questscope project, municipal authorities flattened about a third of the buildings in the neighborhood to complete a long-planned highway. Displaced families received only minimal compensation for the destruction of their houses. Even more devastating was the challenge that displaced residents faced in rebuilding a new life in a resource-poor environment. Destruction of homes placed particular stress on those young men who were involved in the neighborhood programs designed to give them new roles, respect, and a hope for the future.

In the urban village, project staff focused attention on microimprovements, such as building a wall around the social center to make it safe for children. The library and computer learning lab were attractive facilities in an otherwise resource-scarce center. Other activities, such as sports and camping, helped to alleviate some of the pressures on children anticipating loss of their homes and to enrich their lives devastated through prosocial experiences. Once the bulldozers arrived to complete the building of the highway, more emphasis was placed on programs to strengthen young men's involvement in community service, sports, and camping.

In the urban village, a social center to sponsor activities and to gain the support of the community was established first. This was essential to address the priorities expressed in the initial participatory assessment. The social center was a novelty in this community, and its presence drew attention to the need and ability of the community to organize itself for social goals. The leaders of the voluntary action committee for children capitalized on this opportunity to interest the municipal authorities in considering a larger multipurpose building that could be used for broader social goals and activities. Project staff developed programs to assist residents to engage in community improvement.

The ability to attract the attention of a government agency to act on needs and priorities of the urban village was due largely to its success in improving the social environment for children. This illustrates a successful relationship for social action fostered by residents engaged in a deliberate path of change. The process was fragile, because it depended on the motivation and patience of local residents, as well as the political will of outsiders to recognize their enabling roles in opening up opportunities for positive change.

(4) Truncated Roles of Children – Growing Up Marginalized. The alienation and isolation of children living in marginalized urban communities are exacerbated when children shoulder adult responsibilities without the requisite capabilities. When the project began, staff emphasized understanding the attributes and circumstances of children at risk (markers of violent behavior, substance abuse, neglect, etc). As the project evolved into building prosocial communities oriented toward promoting normative development, children's roles took on greater importance. Therefore, the project design was continually adjusted to allow the roles of youth to be clarified and strengthened as more was learned about them and the circumstances in which they lived.

Jordanian youth also face conflicting viewpoints on how they should direct their lives as their society wrestles with changes in authoritarian roles. This tension was reflected, for example, in public discussions about the rights of a child or an adult other than the father to report child abuse. Children's premature assumption of adult roles also affected their social development and eventually lowered their educational aspirations. Therefore, the challenge for project staff was to make space for children, allowing them to try out many roles during the school years so they could grow into well-balanced adults. Given the limited geographic mobility of residents of poor urban neighborhoods, it was especially important to treat youth as participants in a community of practice, where they learned how to become competent, respected adolescents (and later adults).

In the ghetto, it was impossible to relate to boys on a totally individual basis. Gang behavior meant that controlling the boys' violence and aggression required reliance on their leaders. In one sense these boys were not integrated in their neighborhood because they lived on the street as part of a special subculture, and adults took great pains to ensure that their children avoided them. Adults also excluded them from activities in the social center because of their antisocial behavior. To resolve this impasse, Questscope planned a summer camp to provide an environment outside the neighborhood where adults responded to children in a civil and responsible manner – for example, no drunkenness, no physical danger from angry adults, no cursing. The camp was based on the simple idea that if adults provided a safe atmosphere, the boys could be "children": able to take instruction, follow rules, control their anger, learn new things, and enjoy new activities.

As a result of this experience, the troubled boys began to behave as partners within the program – a change that lasted after camp was concluded. Thereafter, the camp participants took an interest in what their community offered, and they were aware of being treated as equals in planning activities. Quite simply, they had opinions that they wanted heard and taken seriously. This new form of participation was very different from their customary approach, whereby the loudest shout or the quickest fist was the means to draw attention.

Another significant outcome from the camp experience was cooperation with a national program for youth (14–25 years of age). A member of this organization provided challenging physical activities in the camp program and became interested in how the national program could be adapted to suit disadvantaged street children. He designed novel ways to incorporate the ideas of community service, vocational development, and sports participation into the lives of marginalized youth. The activities that resulted from this initiative have provided young men from the urban neighborhood a chance to be accepted in a broader circle of relationships, thus increasing their role and importance.

One of the community service activities that had a strong rehabilitative effect on the boys involved visiting handicapped children in local institutions. Through individual relationships with these children, the troublesome boys found someone who needed them and to whom they could offer encouragement and help. Increasing their roles as caregivers to others in this way had a significant impact on their own emotional development.

(5) Ineffective Community Institutions. The final aspect of youth's social environment the Questscope project addressed was the problem of ineffective community institutions. Because rapid urbanization and a fast growing youth population created unprecedented social conditions in Jordan, most social development institutions were neither prepared for nor responsive to this change. Furthermore, the viewpoints of "young" urban neighborhoods were not represented in the design and implementation of solutions to emergent social and economic problems.

Before the Questscope project, institutional practices focused on children as offenders. This focus led to growing pressure to increase the capacity of detention facilities. However, because new institutional approaches view children as victims, they respond by establishing shelters for abused youth. The majority of at-risk urban youth were neither offenders (suitable for detention), nor victims (requiring sheltering). Rather, they existed in a continuum between these two publicly identified types. The implication is that children living in marginalized urban neighborhoods had to be seen as important clients whose cooperation was indispensable to help transform their communities into prosocial environments. Otherwise, the numbers of offenders and victims could potentially increase. In short, youth needed to be viewed as the solution rather than the problem.

Residents offered great strengths to build on in developing prosocial community involvement. The traditional relations of trust sustained in social connections are an important aspect of Jordanian sociocultural history that could be bolstered as problems and issues were addressed. Residents realized that creating safe, prosocial environments for youth would require collaborative relationships with "outsiders" – namely, professional experts and institutions that provide assistance and respond to marginalized communities as clients.

Questscope staff assumed that listening to youth would encourage adults to modify their relations with young people. Therefore, project staff anticipated that instead of plans, lectures, and activities based on the authoritarian, adult-centered approaches, the viewpoints and struggles of young people would serve as the starting point to develop solutions. Staff also assumed that organizations were receptive to collaborative approaches that drew on the wealth of professional knowledge and of neighborhood self-knowledge and experience. Thus, professionals, experts, and municipal authorities could build on a solid base of neighborhood experience, with marginalized residents as partners and not just beneficiaries.

In the ghetto, the housing organization was the logical unit to initiate a collaborative process: The social center belonged to them, and the center's staff were community residents. Center staff and neighborhood volunteers had, after all, cooperated successfully during the initial participatory appraisal in 1994–1995 and in creation of a safe place for children equipped with resources for learning (library and computer learning equipment). However, once these physical issues were resolved, the deeper issues of the children's roles (the "troublemakers") in the center remained problematic. Responsible adults in the Center were not prepared to recognize the new roles of children, which eventually led to separation of children's activities from the Center. In fact, Center staff considered that the existing activities (day care, lectures, beauty-salon training, weaving, and embroidery) mandated exclusion of the very youth for whom the new activities were designed.

That adult and youth agendas could not be reconciled in a single facility using a regular staff and volunteers led to an impasse, and activities for troublesome children were excluded from the Center. The housing organization, which had previously decentralized its control over the Center staff, could exert little influence on the dilemma. And the Center staff were determined to maintain their control and compensation as employees. Because of its emphasis on developing an emergent strategy, Questscope itself may also have contributed to misunderstandings by not clarifying for Center staff the potential benefits of changed roles for all parties. The impasse triggered relocation of activities for preadolescent youth from the Center to individual homes and other nearby locations. This exodus of young people had the positive effect of increasing residents' commitment to constructing a supportive neighborhood environment for its youth that allowed them to enact newly emergent roles.

By 1998, Questscope had catalyzed a collaborative relationship between young men in the urban village and a national youth organization with more than 15 years of experience with Jordanian youth. The youth organization was committed to adjusting the principles of the national program to the special needs of troublesome youth from marginalized urban communities. Therefore, the youth program focused on self-reliance, leadership skills, personal development (ranging from literacy to crafts to vocational counseling and training), as well as sports and community service. It included a "wilderness camping" activity to provide challenging experiences that required building trust in others and teamwork. Each of these endeavors was fraught with difficulties, as both youth and providers struggled to learn how to cooperate. However, the program provided a robust model for involving marginalized young people in an existing institution/program in which they worked to build their life skills. The involvement of counselors from a university counseling center in the Questscope pilot sites was another major learning experience for the project because the experts had to modify their approaches to be responsive to the problems faced by marginalized urban youth.

A Vocational Training Center (one of a network of 12 government centers) that participated in the intervention also modified its curriculum for nine boys who were functionally illiterate and accustomed to controlling relationships through violence. Vocational center staff cooperated patiently with Questscope staff to integrate the "troublesome" boys into a special training program in automotive electrical systems. At the end of the 3-month course, the boys graduated with new skills. But more importantly, the Center director learned how to adjust institutional policies and practices to serve disadvantaged young people.

In the urban village, residents maintained their identity and traditional rural practices by insulating themselves from external institutions. Engaging community cooperation required sufficient trust of Questscope to conduct a participatory appraisal their children with community volunteers (Questscope, 1995). Once the community volunteers heard their own youth articulate the hardships and obstacles they faced, they mobilized to establish a small social center for children. Two outcomes resulted from this small initial step. First, the community became confident of its ability to act on behalf of young people. This willingness to improve the condition of youth eventually included cooperation with units outside their bounded neighborhood. Second, in reaching out to external institutions, the local municipal authority acknowledged neighborhood capacity and began to cooperate in providing better facilities and support to the community.

Lessons from the Questscope Program

There were several strengths and limitations of the Questscope program that focused on changing the social environments of poor, socially isolated neighborhoods in the interest of promoting normative youth development. The two-site comparison affords an opportunity to observe similarities in the developmental needs of youth and the diverse strategies devised in the ghetto and the urban village. In the following I describe four main lessons derived from the intervention, with a focus on the implications for youth.

First, new and enriched roles for children and adults were necessary to promote collective participation in choosing and making improvements in their local neighborhoods.

The Questscope program succeeded in achieving a high level of involvement, partnership, and role enrichment within the sites. Particularly among young males (10–18 years), the capacity for self-organization was directed to building positive roles and neighborhood acceptance. "New" lessons learned in the neighborhoods must be incorporated into "old" authority structures in order to be maximally effective. Institutionally, this was most easily facilitated through high-level managers who worked with their middle managers and staff to enhance institutional effectiveness.

However, it is unclear whether the outcomes of this pilot project signal institutional behavior change (policy and procedure). In general, units external to the community did not perceive changes in the roles of the neighborhoods as constituencies whose viewpoints required modifications to institutional policies and practices. The two exceptions to this were the national youth program's intent to adjust their practices to accommodate children from marginalized neighborhoods and the Vocational Training Center's willingness to restructure their programs for uneducated boys. Redirecting resources and refocusing institutional agendas to accommodate the needs of marginalized youth require changes within the institutional culture of organizations. The Questscope pilot project did not address this need because their top priority involved learning from young people to develop a strategy for changing their proximate environment.

That programs for female children were delayed represents a third limitation of the Questscope intervention to promote healthy youth development. Staff *and neighborhood members* assumed involving young girls in programs that took them out of strictly familial relationships would introduce unnecessary complexity to the project. In retrospect, this assumption appears misguided. However, it appeared reasonable on the basis of neighborhood sensitivities that encouraged a focus on boys and young adolescent males in *this early* pilot phase of the work. *In subsequent interventions, the issues of adolescent girls have been successfully approached through centers that serve only female clients.*

A few words of explanation from us about the previous paragraph: Because no organization had worked with these kinds of "at risk" children at the community level, no one knew what to expect as the interventions took place. It was only possible to reach community consensus on approaching children's problems of substance abuse, sexuality, truancy, and so forth, if the work was initiated with males. Once it became clear to everyone involved (local community members, cooperating institutions and their staff, and Questscope staff) that interventions were not disruptive in a basically conservative social environment, then the lessons learned and the success demonstrated could be (and have been) applied to girls. But to start with girls would have led to the immediate closure of the project. The social environment was not ready for work with "at risk" female children. Now such projects with female clients are viable and making progress, but it took a long time and lots of effort to build trust to make this possible. The pilot project with male children provided us with the lessons and "track record" to initiate work with female clients. We do not want to include much detail about this in the chapter, because the focus of the project was on male youth and because we do not want to imply any criticism of the socially conservative nature of the community.

Second, there were characteristics common to both marginalized urban neighborhoods though both sites differed in their strategies to regulate the behavior of young people.

The use of emergent strategy, participatory methodology, and social learning theory created a rich picture of each community, including relations with children and with outside service providers. However, the approach used to learn about the two neighborhoods did not focus on their myriad commonalities. Similarities lend themselves to deriving standard principles that, in turn, can simplify such interventions in the future. Furthermore, the emphasis on participatory learning should be complemented with a broader network of institutional resources to address the needs of several marginalized urban communities simultaneously. The pilot program design did not concentrate on building this broader perspective. Had such a perspective been established, the meaning of community-specific characteristics would have been greatly enhanced.

Third, neighborhood linkages with national providers proved vital to the success of the pilot.

The pilot program established at least four important linkages. First, experts in psychological counseling took seriously the severity of problems in these marginalized neighborhoods. Second, a national program for youth adjusted its operating principles to accommodate the special needs of disadvantaged youth. Third, a national vocational counseling and training center amended its procedures to incorporate children at risk into its programs. And finally, organizations for handicapped persons created opportunities for troublesome boys to volunteer that proved pivotal in helping them discover how to assist other individuals also in need.

Establishment of linkages with individuals who shared ideas for prosocial approaches was relatively straightforward, but such persons were seldom policymakers and decision makers in their institutions. There was always a risk that after a period of successful project work the institutions themselves would curtail the support, or the representative assigned to the project would become overworked as a result of assuming additional responsibilities. Moreover, not all institutions are receptive to allowing youth participation in agenda setting. In only one case – the national youth program – did the organization make it an institutional priority to develop a program responsive to at-risk youth of marginalized urban neighborhoods.

As community members began to trust experts from external organizations, institutional consistency was expected. Once new paradigms involving external organizations were envisioned and new relationships were established, organizational political will and financial resources should have matched the initiatives of residents who were at the forefront of community change. Unfortunately, the organizations involved in linkage relationships often lacked the resources (or did not earmark resources) needed to maintain such consistency. The focus on developing collaborative linkages proved to be a time- and resource-intensive process, and the design of the pilot did not include a strategy to maintain institutional consistency.

> *Fourth, building prosocial communities through fostering vision, capacity, and experience in local neighborhoods; through establishing effective resource collaboration with national providers/experts; and through calling decision makers' attention to their role in eliminating policies and procedures that exclude marginalized youth is crucial to change the landscape and the "peoplescape" of poor urban areas.*

Nongovernment organizations (NGOs) and private volunteer agencies (PVAs) have important roles, along with government organizations, in building prosocial communities. The design of the Questscope pilot capitalized on the ability of an NGO/ PVA to be reflective and reflexive in improvements, understanding the developmental needs of children reared in deprived urban settings during a period of rapid social change. The ideal role for NGOs/PVAs involves taking risks and exploring novel ways to deal with emerging problems. Developing prosocial communities requires building a broad base of consensus at multiple levels in a variety of institutions. But it was more satisfactory in the public eye to reduce the visibility of "problems" by increasing the capacity of detention and reform centers. It was also more socially captivating to individualize problems of "poor youth" by providing shelters and services for abused children, for whom the general public had sympathy and compassion, as long as they were victims. The design of the pilot program did not take into account the necessary options for public and institutional education that would have created public awareness of the variety of prosocial roles marginalized youth can assume. It also did not consider how funding could be obtained and maintained for preventive prosocial initiatives with the majority of disadvantaged urban youth who could not be classified either as offenders or as victims.

Summary and Conclusions

Prosocial approaches to at-risk children were most successful when adults took the time and effort to understand the points of view offered by children about their own circumstances. After all, at-risk youth are the "experts" at succeeding in their neighborhoods. Their behaviors made perfect sense to them, given the pressures they endured.

Adults were responsible for refashioning environments that reinforced children's proactive roles and behaviors. This was accomplished at the neighborhood level as adults responded positively to new roles enacted by their youth. It was accomplished at institutional levels when directors and staff comprehended the needs of young boys to be respected and rewarded for prosocial behavior.

Experts involved in the program were able to suggest interventions that improved the capacities of adults, institutions, and children to cooperate effectively. The emphasis on emergent strategy allowed all parties to observe the effects of "small steps" and to make adjustments that facilitated positive interactions between youths' roles and "outsider" roles.

Neighborhoods required assistance to provide physical facilities and to design and implement activities that reinforced new, positive behaviors of both children and adults. Neighborhood members wanted to understand how to help and encourage their children when they experienced positive responses. As they became more comfortable with their new skills, much volunteer energy was released in both sites. Whereas the pilot program demonstrated the importance of fostering new and enriched roles for both adults and children at the neighborhood level, sustaining role development depended on appropriate institutional responses from actors external to the neighborhood. Although the emergent strategy approach addressed circumstances unique to each community (efficient coverage), it became evident that strategies must also address issues common to all marginalized urban communities (effective coverage).

Another important lesson is that providers external to the neighborhood must strive both for institutional and individual learning. Municipal authorities and government agencies were assisted in establishing relationships that were responsive to children's priorities articulated to cooperating adults. Prosocial community building must ultimately be supported by the highest municipal authorities in order to incorporate local initiatives into policy and practice to alter the urban environment. In the pilot project, such governing agencies became facilitators of local initiatives that originated with children. This was a change from the usual paradigm of agencies' designing urban plans "for" rather than "by" residents of marginalized neighborhoods.

The most encouraging outcome of the Questscope program design and implementation was the emergence of a shared community consciousness in both neighborhoods: that what could be accomplished with children was important and that such efforts would be supported by experts and national agencies. The key to success was returning to the viewpoints and expectations of children as they learned and enacted new roles in their personal lives and in the life of their neighborhood.

REFERENCES

Caincar, L., and Abunimah, A. (1998). *Poverty and Social Exclusion.* Chapin Hall Center for Children at the University of Chicago Report.

Garbarino, J. (1995). *Raising Children in a Socially Toxic Environment.* San Francisco: Jossey-Bass.

Giddens, A. (1990). *The Consequences of Modernity.* Stanford, CA: Stanford University Press.

Hasan, M. (1997). *Children and Youth: A Situational Analysis.* Study commissioned by the General Union of Voluntary Societies, Amman, Jordan.

Questscope. (1995). Urban Community Development with a Focus on the Status of Children in Exceptionally Difficult Circumstance. Phase One. Community Results and Program Directions (unpublished report to UNICEF JORDAN).

Szanton Blanc, C. (1994). *Urban Children in Distress: Global Predicaments and Innovative Strategies.* Yverdon, Switzerland: Gordon and Breach Science Publishers.

Tyler, F. B. (1997). *Urban Settings, Youth Violence and Prosocial Communities.* Paper presented at Urban Childhood Conference, Trondheim, Norway, June 1997. College Park: University of Maryland, Department of Psychology.

IV

WORK, LIFE SKILLS, AND WELL-BEING

10 Work by the Young
The Economic Activity of School-Aged Children

Jim McKechnie and Sandy Hobbs

Throughout the 1990s there was a growing interest in children's economic activity. This was partly driven by the International Labor Organization (ILO), which made this issue the focus of its 1998 meeting in Geneva. The aim was to establish universal principles regarding children's employment and to target "intolerable" forms of work (ILO, 1996b). At the same time "child labor" became the concern of numerous nongovernmental organizations (NGOs) around the world.

In response to this growing interest, two organizations – the International Society for the Prevention of Child Abuse and Neglect (ISPCAN) and Defense for Children International (DCI) – established the International Working Group on Child Labor (IWGCL) to share the experience of researchers and activists from over 30 countries. As authors of the final report of the IWGCL, we came to understand the dilemmas of children at work in the modern city at the beginning of the 21st century (McKechnie and Hobbs, 1998).

One of the themes developed by the IWGCL is that children who work should be able to communicate their experience and influence policy debates relating to child labor. This view builds on provisions in the United Nations Convention on the Rights of the Child, but also on growing interest among academics in reconsideration of concepts of childhood (see, for example, James and Prout, 1990; Corsaro, 1997). Several scholars conclude that to understand childhood we need to draw on the experience of children themselves. Accordingly, the IWGCL report emphasized the value of "listening to children's voices."

Against this background, in this chapter we have three aims. The first is to establish the scale of children's economic activity in both developed and developing nations. The second is to consider the consequences of youth employment, a process that involves challenging the belief that child labor is merely a "problem" of developing countries. A more balanced view of work acknowledges both positive and negative aspects of work for children. Third, we consider the relationship between work and education. Work by children is sometimes viewed negatively, ideally to be replaced by a better alternative, namely, education. However, this either–or approach ignores the possibility of learning through work and assumes that all education is necessarily appropriate to all contexts. We discuss why this conceptualization is overly simplistic.

Given our broad aims, the discussion is perforce selective on coverage. We draw on cross-cultural evidence to demonstrate that the child labor phenomenon is not unique to developing countries. Major debates are also taking place on the causes of child labor, but we shall not pursue that issue here.

Dimensions of Child Labor

On the basis of evidence from about 100 countries in the mid-1990s, the ILO estimated the number of working children between the ages of 10 and 14 years old at approximately 73 million (ILO, 1996a). Aware of the tendentious data on which some of the national figures were derived, the ILO conducted a more detailed study of four developing countries. On the basis of these results, the ILO now estimates that 120 million children work full-time and that if one includes those children who combine work and other activities, such as attending school, the number rises to 250 million (ILO, 1996b).

The number of school-age youth who are not enrolled in school is used as a crude proxy for their labor force activity. The assumption is that if they are not attending school, they are likely to be economically active. The ILO (1996b) estimates that 120 million children worldwide are not attending school, whereas the New Internationalist (1997) puts the figure at 140 million, or approximately 20% of primary age schoolchildren. Nonenrollment by children of secondary school age is estimated at 51%. Taking primary and secondary age groups together, New Internationalist (1997) produces a global estimate of 500 million working children.

The data on the number of children working show considerable variation across continents. The ILO estimate suggests that 61% of working children reside in Asia, 32% in Africa, and 7% in Latin America. However, when the number of workers is derived as a percentage of the child population within each continent, Africa has the highest rate of child workers (ILO, 1996a). The lack of reliable statistics makes it difficult to identify trends. However, several authors argue that the extent of child employment has stabilized in

Southeast Asia and may in some cases be declining. This decline is attributed to increasing per capita income, the spread of basic education, and reduction in family size. By contrast, children's economic activity has increased in Africa and Latin America (ILO, 1996b).

Although the majority of working children are found in these continents, child employment can also be found in Europe and North America. Growing awareness that many children in various parts of Europe are working has generated fairly dependable figures, for example, in Britain (see Cecchetti, 1998). Available evidence suggests that child employment is both an urban and a rural phenomenon. Moreover, dramatic political changes in Central and Eastern European countries have led to an increase in the reported cases of child workers, as in Russia (Mansorov, 1995). In North America, the extent of child and adolescent employment is now well established (see Barling and Kelloway, 1999).

That estimates ranging from 73 million to 500 million can be made in good faith within a year of each other indicates the depth of our ignorance about the pervasiveness of child labor. Both estimates indicate that child employment is a major feature of contemporary society, but the uncertainty about the figures is significant because it stems from two types of causes. One is that there are technical difficulties in enumerating child employment. The other is that there are different views of what should be considered "child labor."

Measurement of Problems

Many estimates of children's working are based on unreliable government figures. In the mid-1990s, the European Union (EU) attempted to compile information on the extent of employment of youth between the ages of 13 and 17 (Heptinstall et al, 1997). Independent national and local studies show far higher levels of employment among 13- to 16-year-olds than the EU figures suggest. For example, Heptinstall and associates (1997) cite a 1976 study that found 106,000 children and young people working illegally in Italy. Because the employment was illegal, such figures would not enter the official government sources. A report released by Italy's largest trade union federation in 1998 revealed that the country, which overtook Great Britain in total wealth in the mid-1980s, employs approximately 300,000 children. The heaviest concentration of these underage workers aid in manufacturing fake designer clothing and apparel in the Naples region (Hooper, 1998). Government officials did not dispute the figure, which may in fact underestimate the true extent of child labor in Italy.

Lavalette argues that inaccurate figures arise from five recurring difficulties (Lavalette, 1994). First, where they exist, national figures are cross-sectional and seldom updated or monitored. Second, many national figures ignore seasonal employment. Third, countries are unlikely to search out and publish information that demonstrates the ineffectiveness of legislation on child employment. Fourth, many of the jobs done by children are not recognized by standard employment classification systems. Finally, most studies tend to focus on children of ages 10 to 14 years, but there is substantial evidence that children younger than 10 years of age also work (ILO, 1996a). Global estimates are also questionable because they tend to focus on developing countries, paying little attention to working children in the developed economies of Europe and North America.

Several theoretical issues also create difficulties in identifying the number of children who work. One is particularly noteworthy, namely, the meaning of the terms *child* and *work*. In common use, chronological age is used to identify a child because in almost every society, "age limits regulate children's activities" (Bellamy, 1997:25). Age limits define when youth may leave school and marry, and how individuals are treated by the legal system. It is thus not surprising that age is also used to define the time when it is acceptable to work. However, age criteria for employment depend on both the nature of work activity under discussion and cross-national characteristics. Age criteria are used to guide the type of work that is acceptable for youth. For example, in Peru the legal minimum age for work in agriculture is 14, in industry 15, in deep sea fishing 16, and in seafaring 18. The ILO has set 15 years as the minimum age for working, and 18 years for hazardous work. More generally, the United Nations Convention on the Rights of the Child defines a child as a person below 18 years of age.

Relying on age as the defining characteristic of childhood is, according to Grootaert and Kanbur (1997), a Western custom that fails to acknowledge how cultural and social factors influence our conception of childhood. Some academics argue that childhood is a social construct because children's roles and statuses are defined not by chronological age, but by social and cultural norms (James and Prout, 1990). Cross-cultural studies lead us to realize that any definition of *child* would also require awareness of the social context. Although this consideration no doubt complicates our attempt to understand childhood, the important point is that such debates have not been reflected in estimates of the numbers of working children. This point bears on how we interpret the work activities of children.

Likewise, the term *work* exists in our everyday language, yet becomes problematic when we attempt to treat it as a meaningful concept in research, which naturally requires a precise definition. One approach to defining child work is to identify activities that involve some sort of production or service for which youth receive compensation. This is relatively straightforward in some cases, such as when a child enters into an arrangement with an employer for payment for services provided in a factory or a shop. How would we view this arrangement if the parent received the money and the child received nothing for the very same arrangement?

Most researchers studying the impact of child employment have failed to consider the differential impacts of varied forms of work. For example, how does working for one's parents compare to working for an employer, in which the relationship is simply one of master and paid servant? Work may be defined not simply by looking at the activity performed, but also by evaluating the nature of the relationship between the employer and employee (Lavalette, 1994). Because many forms of work are "invisible" in the global estimates, we have little idea of the numbers involved or the reality of their working lives (Black, 1997a, 1997b).

To understand fully the idea of youth employment, analysts must comprehend what it is that children do in the labor market. One step toward this goal requires in-depth reviews of child employment in particular countries. Therefore, we examine two countries, one representing the developing economies, Indonesia, and the other representing the developed economies, Great Britain.

Indonesia

In the last few decades Indonesia has witnessed major economic and social changes. Between 1970 and 1991, urban growth increased and agricultural employment fell. By 1990, agricultural employment was below 50% for the first time. Manufacturing employment grew, particularly in the textile, clothing, and footwear sectors. Despite these employment and production shifts, Indonesia is considered a developing country by Western standards.

Indonesia's labor statistics include individuals ages 10 years and over. In 1961, 14% of all 10- to 14-year-olds (1.16 million) were classified as employed, and in 1990, 13% (2.5 million) of youth were so classified. By 1994, youth employment appeared to have fallen, as only 10.5% were employed (2.1 million). However, critics charge that these figures are underestimates because exclusion of children below 10 years of age introduces a questionable bias.

Sastrasuand (cited in White et al., 1997) argues that additional categories of economically active children also need to be combined with the official figures to reflect the numbers who work accurately. If we accept this latter argument, 14.8% or 3.34 million 10- to 14-year-olds would be classified as working. In addition, White and colleagues (1997) note that these figures only refer to children who are working full-time and ignores those who combine education and employment. If one attempts to include this group of working children in estimates, one finds that between 6 and 10 million of Indonesia's children are working.

An ILO study sampled over 4,000 households and 200 enterprises in Indonesia to investigate the kind of work done by 5- to 14-year-olds. This research concluded that 2 to 6 million children were economically active. White and his colleagues suggest the disparity between this and other estimates results because the pilot study took place in a part of Indonesia that is not particularly representative of the whole country.

Rather than focus on the numbers working in Indonesia, more recently academics have looked at the specific character of children's jobs (White, 1994). Given Indonesia's status as a developing country, it is common to find children working in both traditional and new forms of economic activities. Typically they are to be found in both large and small industrial enterprises. Among the traditional areas of employment noted by White and coworkers (1997) are dairy production, sheet metal working, embroidery, rattan furnishing, and footwear. In the factory-based industries they found children employed in the production of electrical fuses, locks, soap, and plastic bags, as well as in plastic recycling.

Children working in family-based enterprises were more likely to combine work with school attendance. Many of the children had consciously decided to leave school in order to work. Presumably this reflects youths' desire to earn money coupled with their perception that committing more time to education would not necessarily result in a better form of employment (White et al., 1997). In the batik and clay pottery industries, it is not uncommon for children to work alongside their parents, learning basic skills of production. This process can start when children are still attending primary school, which they combine with 2 to 4 hours of work per day. Children aged 12 and above are likely to work full-time, abandoning education, since little wage differentiation exists for educational attainment (Haryadi and Tjandraningsih, cited in White et al., 1997).

A variety of different employment patterns are found in the country's export sector. The newer and rapidly growing sectors of footwear and garment production tend to employ youth ages 15 years or over, a trend that is in line with the ILO minimum age for work (ILO, 1996b). In contrast, the traditional export sector of craft goods relies partly on children under 15 years of age. The United States Department of Labor's report (1995) on the use of children in producing American imports claimed that there were "credible allegations" of this practice.

Anti-Slavery International (ASI), which examined child employment in Indonesia's domestic services in the early 1990s, estimated that about one third of the 5 million domestic servants in the country are below 15 years of age, most of them girls (Blagbrough, 1995). Contrary to some portrayals, this is not a benign form of employment. The recent history of Indonesian legislation on the work and education of children has been misrepresented. The "Compulsory Education Program" introduced in 1984 stated that children should attend school from 7 to 12 years of age. However, the program was misleadingly named since no enforcement mechanisms were created. There is also inconsistency on the minimum age at which work is permitted. At the time the Indonesian Republic was established in the late 1940s, the legal minimum age for employment was raised from 12 to 14 years. However, this age limit has never been enforced. Indonesia is not unique in having an ineffective legal framework relating to child employment according to the International Working Group on Child Labor (McKechnie and Hobbs, 1998).

Great Britain

In contrast to Indonesia, Britain is clearly a developed economy that has long since negotiated an industrial revolution and moved from a rural-based economy to an urban one. However, as did the Indonesian government, the British government throughout the 1980s claimed that child employment was not an issue requiring action (Lavalette et al., 1995). This view, which is common in developed economies, sees child employment as a feature of the developing countries. In the developed countries, child employment presumably existed in the past, not the present. This attitude is based on three key myths, namely, that few children work in modern Britain; that children who do work are employed only in "children's jobs"; and that existing legislation is adequate to regulate child employment. Several empirical studies, starting with *The Forgotten Workforce* (Lavalette et al., 1991) and *The Hidden Army* (Pond and Searle, 1991), have helped to dispel these myths.

Let us consider each myth in turn. How many children work in Britain? Our research on the extent of employment among youth ages 14–15 who are in the final years of compulsory schooling suggests that the majority have had part-time employment (Hobbs and McKechnie, 1997). Other studies show that younger children also work (see Hobbs et al., 1996). In contrast to those in Indonesia, employed children were combining full-time education with part-time employment. These figures may underestimate the number of children who had jobs, because there is some evidence linking school withdrawal with employment (Hobbs and McKechnie, 1997); we suspect that some youth absent from school while data were collected may have been working.

When due allowance is made for the varied methodologies employed by researchers, this inference finds support by other investigators (Hibbett and Beatson, 1995; Hobbs and McKechnie, 1998). Using the best estimates from academic research, we estimate that between 1.1 and 1.7 million children may be working in Britain. If we include those who have worked in the past, between 2.2 and 2.6 million children will have had paid employment outside the family before they reach 16 years of age.

The second myth about youth employment relates to the stereotypical idea that British children work only as newspaper deliverers. Although delivery work does account for employment of children, the research evidence shows that children also work in shops, hotels, and restaurants. Other forms of child work include employment as cleaners and telephonists (Hobbs and McKechnie, 1997). Delivery work also includes milk delivery, which can involve starting work at 4:00 A.M., before attending school. A 1998 study in an area of Northern England that revealed children were employed in delivery, shop work, hotel and catering, office work, home working, care work, factory work, farming, and door-to-door sales corroborates these findings (O'Donnell and White, 1998). There are also examples of British children's working in "extreme" types of work. For example, children under 16 years of age are involved in the sex industry working as prostitutes (Lee and O'Brien, 1995; New Internationalist, 1997). Because children work in a wide range of jobs, many of which overlap with the adult labor market, we reject the second myth that youth workers are relegated to benign jobs.

Finally, there is the myth that legislation controls and protects child workers. In Britain, legislation allows children of 13 to 15 years of age to work, reflecting the view that it is acceptable to mix part-time work with education. The law aims to control this experience by setting minimum ages, specifying earliest starting and latest finishing times, stipulating the maximum number of hours that can be worked, prohibiting certain forms of work, and requiring that working children obtain work permits. However, ample research shows that children below the statutory ages are working (O'Donnell and White, 1998). The legislation on start and finish times is also ignored (McKechnie et al., 1994), and very few children obtain the necessary work permits (Hobbs and McKechnie, 1997). The last point is important because the permits are the main protection children have with respect to insurance coverage and also the main source local and central governments use to estimate the number of working children.

Among countries with developed economies, Britain is not unique in terms of the extent of children's economic activity (National Research Council, 1998). In comparing Indonesia and Britain it is apparent that child employment is an issue for both developed and developing economies. We need to accept that children's economic activity is truly a global phenomenon. Despite many variations, similarities exist regarding child employment. Employment tends to be focused in the informal sectors of the economy. Irrespective of the country, the employer–child employee relationship is fundamentally similar, reflecting failure to recognize children's rights and emphasizing their limited ability to change their position in society.

Understanding the nature of children's employment permits a consideration of its consequences. In addition to traditional methods of data collection, there is also a need to listen to the experiences of employed youth and to discover their interpretation of the experience. Such approaches are typically rare, but where they do exist, they challenge any simplistic notion that work and childhood are necessarily mutually exclusive (see Woodhead, 1998).

Understanding the Impact of Work

Debates about the impact of employment on children have been skewed toward examples that highlight the hazardous and exploitative nature of children's work around the world. This emphasis is partly due to the role of the media in directing the public's attention to dramatic cases. It is also an image used by lobbying and advocacy bodies campaigning on the issue (see, for example, Cottingham, 1997). By focusing on such images, the dominant view has been that abolition of child labor is the only appropriate stance.

However, it is conceivable that the abolitionist approach may actually create more problems than it solves (Reddy, 1997). An example illustrates this point. The female employees in a garment factory in Meknes, Morocco, were aged between 12 and 15 years of age. Technically many were employed legally, because they were registered as apprentices. However, they were dismissed after being portrayed as child laborers in a British television program. The IWGCL report highlights the negative impact this action had on the employees and their families (Zalami et al., 1998). Many of the girls had to seek alternative work, which they and their families deemed to be inferior to the factory jobs they had lost.

For many years writers in this field have relied upon the ILO's notion of a distinction between child labor and child work when discussing the impact of youth employment. This distinction, which can be found as early as 1930 in the entry on child labor in the *International Encyclopedia of the Social Sciences* (Fuller, 1930), in which "child labor" is characterized as a social evil that is economically motivated, whereas "child work" is considered part of a child's natural development, and a social good.

How can we apply this distinction to the real world? What criteria distinguish "labor" from "work"? Cottingham (1997) states that child work "can raise a child's self-esteem, teach a trade for the future and help the family." By contrast, child labor "is something else: long hours of hard slog, detrimental to a child's schooling and damaging to his or her emotional, physical and psychological development." Bellamy (1997) argues that we are dealing with exploitative child labor if the work involves the following features:

full-time work at too early an age; too many hours spent working; work that exerts undue physical, social or psychological stress; work and life on the streets in bad conditions; inadequate pay; too much responsibility; work that hampers access to education; work that undermines the child's dignity and self-esteem; work that is detrimental to full social and psychological development.

Bellamy does not clarify whether all of these criteria must be present for the situation to be defined as *child labor* or whether meeting only a few of these criteria is sufficient. However, there are more fundamental problems to be addressed because these criteria are not sufficiently specific to help identify harmful forms of employment. For example, how many hours constitute "too many"? Will this vary depending on the age of the child? What is meant by "too much," and indeed what is meant by "responsibility"? Phrases such as "damaging his or her emotional, physical and psychological development" add a pseudo–social science veneer that may actually hinder rather than help our understanding of the impact of work on youth.

Because such arguments clearly call into question the usefulness of the labor–work distinction, some alternative models have begun to emerge. Before considering them, we acknowledge that the labor–work dichotomy does serve one useful purpose. Implicit in the dichotomy is the idea that employment can be "good" or "bad" for individual youth. This point has been acknowledged in relation to adult employment for some time (see Feather, 1992). However, researchers in the field of child employment have been slow to investigate both the potential costs and the potential benefits of employment for children.

In order to move away from the redundant child labor–child work dichotomy, alternative frameworks are needed. Two approaches that have different emphases but are compatible with each other have emerged to date.

Identifying Key Variables

American researchers have focused on identifying key variables that mediate the impact of employment. The major researchers during the 1980s were Greenberger and Steinberg, who focused on work intensity as the key aspect of work for measuring impact. The definition of *work intensity* is the number of hours that the individual commits to a job.

Several studies show that working excessive hours – usually over 15–20 hours – weekly is more likely to produce deleterious consequences for youth. Because most U.S. research deals with part-time employment, these hours should be treated as additional to the time spent at school. Working excessive hours has been linked in some studies to diminished parental supervision (Greenberger and Steinberg, 1986; Steinberg and Dornbusch, 1991), greater psychological distress and somatic complaints (Greenberger and Steinberg, 1986; Steinberg and Dornbusch, 1991), higher rates of alcohol and drug use (Greenberger et al., 1981; Mortimer et al., 1996), and lower academic achievement, an issue discussed later.

The conclusion one might draw is that curtailing the permissible number of hours worked would reduce the costs that accrue from youth employment. However, some caveats are in order. First, it is unwise to assume a linear relationship between hours worked and the attendant impacts on the employed youth. Some studies show that working a few hours may be more beneficial than not working at all (Bachman and Schulenberg, 1993; Mortimer et al., 1996). It is also necessary to consider *when* those hours are worked (before school, after school, on weekends, in summer). The final caveat is that the findings about hours worked identified in the United States will not necessarily transfer to other countries. Some preliminary work in Britain finds that the negative effects of work emerged if more than 10 hours was worked per week (Hobbs and McKechnie, 1997).

Mortimer and associates (1996) draw attention to the need to go beyond the number of hours worked and attend to the nature of the work undertaken. Because children are employed in a wide range of jobs, it is important to consider the different demands various forms of work make and not to treat all children's jobs as equivalent or simply focus on extreme examples. Furthermore, Mortimer and Finch (1996) challenge the pessimistic view that all youth jobs are boring and mundane. Stern and colleagues (1990) argued that jobs that provide a "quality" experience had a more positive impact on future orientations toward work. In this study Stern and his colleagues defined *quality* by assessing several job features, such as the use of current skills, the development of new skills, and the level of social interaction generated by the job. Other researchers lend support to this interpretation (Finch et al., 1991; Mortimer et al., 1992).

An additional complication arises when addressing the issue of causality. Because most influences about the consequences of youth employment derive from correlational research designs, causal relations cannot be asserted with certainty. Frone (1999) argues that studies on adolescent employment tend to assume that work status is a significant causal variable whose impact can be assessed directly. Less emphasis is placed on the selection process that sorts some youth into the labor market while leaving others to pursue academic activities exclusively (Schoenhals et al., 1998). Rather than employment experiences leading to the development of social skills, it is possible that individuals who are more socially adept select into employment. Schoenhals and coworkers (1998) argue that many of the consequences attributed to working reflect "pre-existing differences among youth who elect to work at various intensities." It is unlikely that the question of causality can be answered simply without longitudinal data.

Theoretical Models
White (1995, 1997) argues that the very terms *child labor* and *child work* have become so confused they should be abandoned. Instead, he proposes an alternative model intended to flesh out the meanings of child employment. As revealed in Figure 10.1, White believes we should think of children's work as a continuum. At one end are the intolerable forms of economic activity in which children around the world are involved. These include bonded labor, child slavery, and prostitution, which are both unacceptable and egregious.

As youth move along the continuum, they reach forms of work that are detrimental or hazardous but that may be susceptible to change, making them less hazardous. For example, the health and safety standards may be improved or the number of hours worked may be reduced. Changes could take the form of combining work with some form of education to improve long-term life chances. *Neutral* work refers to forms of employment that are neither harmful nor potentially beneficial. Opposite to *intolerable* forms of work are the *positive* or beneficial forms of employment, namely, those that foment youth development.

For White, adopting such a model forces a closer look at the nature of children's work while explicitly considering why some forms of work done by children are acceptable and others are not. Ideally, we should be able to identify factors that situate all economic activity along the continuum. However, White recognizes that a set of clear and unambiguous global criteria to

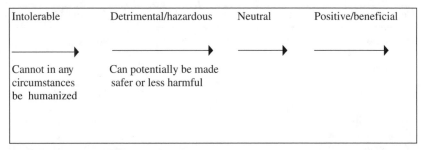

Figure 10.1. White's continuum model.

classify jobs along the continuum is unlikely. Therefore, although the model has universal merit, its application should reflect cultural variations. This conclusion creates problems on the international stage, where the desire to set "universal standards" is strong. White's model raises several questions. Does "neutral" work exist? More importantly, can the extremes of the continuum be defined? If not, White may simply have made a semantic change, replacing "labor–work" with "intolerable–beneficial."

Our model to conceptualize youth employment grew out of a concern about the lack of clarity regarding what is good or bad about work (Hobbs and McKechnie, 1997). For example, numerous references about the impact of work on the "psychosocial" development of the child abound, yet often such terms are left undefined. More generally, understanding the impact of employment on children requires clearer operational definitions of what constitutes a benefit or a cost. Subsequently it then becomes possible to investigate the circumstances under which these costs or benefits may emerge. Beliefs about the positive or negative impact of work remain hypotheses until a particular link with employment is established empirically.

Therefore, drawing on the work of Greenberger and Steinberg, we propose a balance model which permits the study of positive and negative aspects of youth work that may coexist in the same job. Policy interventions may strive to alter the balance of beneficial and detrimental aspects of work to enhance normative youth development. However, as with adult employment, realism requires that we seek to minimize harmful effects rather than eliminate them.

Figure 10.2 incorporates some of the potential costs and benefits that have been associated with youth employment. These are not exhaustive, but merely indicative. Variables such as age, gender, hours worked, time when those hours are worked, and the nature of the job being done warrant explicit consideration, but interactions among these characteristics are highly likely.

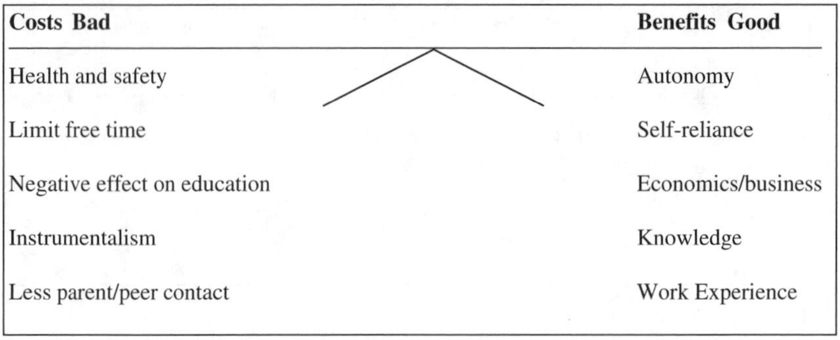

Costs Bad		Benefits Good
Health and safety		Autonomy
Limit free time		Self-reliance
Negative effect on education		Economics/business
Instrumentalism		Knowledge
Less parent/peer contact		Work Experience

Figure 10.2. McKechnie and Hobbs's balance model.

For example, some types of work may be more beneficial to one sex than to the other. Longer working hours may be more harmful in some jobs than in others. Longer hours may also be more harmful if undertaken at particular times of the day or week. The main aim of the balance approach is to ensure that all relevant attributes are given due consideration and defined precisely when assessing the consequences of youth employment

The balance model also acknowledges the cultural and developmental contexts that influence relationships among job and youth attributes. The "balance" cannot exist in a vacuum. As with White's model, the balance concept implies that there are no universal solutions to the problems of child employment. There is a danger that this will be seen as aiding those who wish to justify forms of employment and conditions of work merely on the grounds of ubiquity or wide acceptance within a particular culture. Such cultural relativism justifies many forms of employment under the rubric of tradition. However, the key difference among such arguments, those implicit in the White model, and those of the balance model is that the latter approaches require the evidence of benefits and costs for youth.

Woodhead (1998) maintains that attending to the context does not necessarily exclude using external criteria to identify clearly what transcends acceptability of youth work. For example, any experience that results in pathological problems would be universally recognized as unacceptable (e.g., child prostitution), as would all forms of slavery. Although both models have limitations, both promise to enhance understanding of the potential benefits and costs of the child work experiences. Both models assume that researchers, policymakers, and NGOs must strive to understand the perspective of those who work, by engaging in what the IWGCL termed "listening to children's voices" (see Earls and Carlson, this volume).

The Costs and Benefits of Employment

In the interest of parsimony, we do not undertake an exhaustive review of the research about the costs and benefits of youth employment. For a fuller review readers are directed to Steinberg and Cauffman (1995), Hobbs and McKechnie (1997), and Barling and Kelloway (1999). Instead, we focus on a few issues that are both salient and amenable to intervention.

Health and Safety

One obvious cost of youth employment that has attracted some interest is the potential risk to working children's health and safety. Although detailed empirical evidence across a range of countries is lacking, some research suggests that this issue warrants attention. Studies in the United States clearly show that many children who are employed sustain work-related injuries (see, for example, Knight et al., 1995; Castillo, 1999). In addition to documenting the prevalence of such injuries, there is a pressing need to uncover the causes and the consequences of such injury. These problems are being investigated in Britain, where between 18% and 36% of working children sustain some form of injury at work. Little attention is given to the long-term impact of employment on the child's development. For example, many of the supposedly acceptable delivery jobs children do require them to lift heavy loads, but there is no research on the long-term impacts of this phenomenon.

That accidental injury occurs on a significant scale among employed children in the developed countries, where effective regulation is assumed, leads us to suspect a more worrisome scenario in developing countries. Unfortunately, inadequate evidence limits our ability to draw firm conclusions. However, it is apparent that many children are at risk as a result of the types of environments in which they work and the tasks they carry out. Forastieri (1997) argues that international agencies have tended to ignore the health implications of child employment. This is an arena ripe for international and domestic policy intervention.

Autonomy

Research in the 1980s explored work as a means by which individuals achieve some sense of autonomy. However, terms such as *autonomy* and *independence* are used rather loosely in this context. In the developed economies, the majority of child employees are effectively in the developmental stage of adolescence, when youth begin to display moves toward independence (see Steinberg, 1993; Coleman and Hendry, 1998). In these circumstances employment may facilitate youth development (Heaven, 1994). Cole (1980) claims that by finding and holding on to a job, youth gain important skills; further, having some earning power permits them to establish their partial independence from parents. Empirical work by Finch and associates (1991) lends some support for this view in showing that work experience influences a youth's sense of control over events in his or her life. Finch demonstrates that the benefits of employment in this area derive not from the work status itself, but from the nature of the work experience. For example, males are more likely to develop a sense of mastery if they perceive their work as providing long-term opportunities for them.

Steinberg and associates (1981) show that part-time employment experience can also foster a sense of personal responsibility. Employed youth exhibit dependability, self-reliance, and orientation toward work. However, such gains are greater for girls than for boys either because of the different jobs they perform or because of different interpretations they place on such work experience.

More recent studies suggest that the link between work and development of psychosocial functioning may be modest, at best (Steinberg and Dornbusch, 1991; Steinberg and Cauffman, 1995). Several studies show little, if any, impact of youth employment on outcomes such as self-esteem, locus of control, personal responsibility, or self-reliance (Steinberg and Cauffman, 1995). One possible explanation is that many of these studies consider the number of hours worked as the key explanatory variable. Others argue that the type of work and the experience of employment are more important (Mortimer and Finch, 1996).

Vocational Development
If early work experience improves youth's acquisition of skills and abilities, we might expect that child workers will be more likely to be employed as adults than their agemates who did not work. Meyer and Wise (cited in Mortimer and Finch, 1986) found that youth with work experience were more likely to secure jobs after completing their education. Moreover, the hourly earning rate of youth with substantial work experience was higher than that of those with limited or no such work experience.

Greenberger (1983) maintains that such effects may in fact be limited to the short term, however. Academic attainment, rather than early work experience, may be a more critical determinant of long-term employment benefits. However, Carr and coworkers (1996) demonstrate that early employment experience had a positive impact on work status and income 12 years later. It is worth recalling that these studies are based on youth experiences in a developed economy, where educational achievement can be reflected in employment opportunities. All economies do not value educational qualifications uniformly.

Steinberg and Cauffman (1995) acknowledge that research does support the view that practical skills and work habits can be gained from employment that may not be attained through traditional education systems. They include interpersonal skills, such as how to deal with customers, as well as knowledge about how to get a job and how business works. Other researchers question whether or not early work experience of this sort will necessarily have a positive influence. Greenberger and Steinberg (1986) claim that the "dead-end" nature of many children's jobs encourages negative work values. For example, Steinberg and associates (1981) argue that low-skill, poorly paid jobs undertaken by children produce "occupational cynicism."

Stern and coworkers (1990) find that the quality of the employment experience also affects individuals' motivation. Challenging employment that provides the potential to learn is associated with high levels of motivation, especially if the work draws on skills that are learned elsewhere, such as at school.

Work and Education

This section considers child labor in relation to school, and in particular, the educational consequences of youth employment. Because schooling is the model activity of children and youth, the fact that many children and adolescents work while enrolled or leave school in order to work raises myriad questions about the long-term consequences of child labor. This issue is relevant to both developing and developed nations, albeit in different ways.

Faced with morally intolerable forms of child labor, many child advocates understandably argue that work should be regarded as an adult experience, from which children should be "saved." Associated with the view that childhood is a period for learning and play is a belief that education is the dominant means of combating children's economic activity. Several prominent activists take this position. According to the ILO, "compulsory education has historically been one of the most effective instruments in eliminating child labor in practice" (ILO, 1996b:35). UNICEF also argues that education must be at the heart of any comprehensive strategy to tackle the issue of working children (Bellamy, 1997). Typically, Britain or the United States is cited as an example for these claims (Bequele and Myers, 1995). In both cases the legislative history establishing universal education parallels the decline of child labor. This experience provides the basis for urging developing countries to adopt similar policies as a way of reducing the labor force activity of children. Weiner (1991) is an advocate of this position, claiming that if children must attend school, they are unavailable for work. Weiner does not accept claims that a country's level of poverty is, in and of itself, an adequate justification for failure to introduce compulsory education. He cites Japan as an example where compulsory education was introduced in the 1870s, when it was still a poor country.

However, the causal relationship between education and levels of youth employment is not clear. Analyzing the economic and social changes in 19th-century Britain, Lavalette (1994) argues that compulsory education in Britain did not remove children from the labor market. Rather, education changed the nature of the youth employment: Compulsory education meant that most economic activity shifted to part-time work. Moreover, because some jobs were defined as "children's jobs" carried out for "pocket money," employment came to be viewed as a benign activity.

The introduction of compulsory education and the removal of children from the workplace redefined childhood as a period for learning (Corsaro, 1997; Lavalette, 1994). This fomented an idealized construction of childhood, which was viewed as a period of innocence that warranted protection and nurturing. School allows children to move into adulthood in a safe environment while effectively socializing them.

Are these views of childhood and compulsory education uniformly applicable cross-culturally? Although there are some universal human needs for normative development, it is unwise to assume that historical patterns identified in the 19th century in developed countries are solutions to problems in presently developing countries. Moreover, notions of educational content and skills are not uniform cross-nationally. In fact, initially, the introduction of formal education systems may clash with traditional views of the child's role (Corsaro, 1997).

Simply welding an educational system onto a culture without attending to the child's role in that society may solve some problems, while creating others. Different expectations of childhood need to be considered to appreciate the significance of universalizing compulsory education. In the last few years there has been a growing interest in this issue. Social policy debates are being reformulated to take account of the contextualizing of childhood (James and Prout, 1990; Lavalette, 1994; Corsaro, 1997; James, Jenks and Prout, 1998).

A similar debate is emerging within psychology. Burman (1994, 1996) has raised concerns about the treatment of norms of development as "culturally neutral" constructs, particularly if they become the models upon which international policies are based. Bequele and Myers (1995:140) suggest,

"It is worth remembering that today's concept of 'basic education'...
includes education in life skills useful in their particular economic, social
and cultural context." In addition to critically examining the content of educational programs, it is equally important to examine the value of work
experience – in both economic and social terms.

Once again, Britain and Indonesia provide a useful comparison. In Britain
the requirement of compulsory education is largely complied with and children attend school full-time up to the age of 16. However, the majority of
enrolled youth combine schooling with paid employment of some kind.
It is the minority of school students who will not work and simply attend
school. In Indonesia a compulsory education system is only notionally in
place because, White and colleagues (1997) note, there is no legal mechanism to compel children to attend school. Some children work full-time,
some combine work and school, and others attend school full-time.

Compulsory education has become such an accepted part of the social
structure of developed economies that we tend to take it for granted. Educational institutions have a number of functions: to socialize, to teach literacy
and numeracy, and to prepare the child for adulthood and for the world of
work. This last function is particularly relevant to the present discussion,
since there are "work experience" programs within schools in developed
countries. These programs are designed to allow youth to learn about the
realities of work through short-term placement programs. By implication
they acknowledge the educational potential of the workplace (Saunders,
Stoney, and Weston, 1997; Pettitt, 1998).

By adopting a broader definition of education that includes both academic and life skill goals, it is possible to argue that work has the potential
to contribute to education. In fact, several studies suggest that employment
may have a positive impact on a range of cognitive skills. Greenberger (1983)
demonstrated that children who worked performed better on tests relating to
economic and consumer behavior. Such results suggest the need to consider
the transferability of knowledge between work and school. It is conceivable that knowledge gained in employment may improve understanding of
concepts dealt with in school, and vice versa. Steinberg and associates (1981)
claim that work may have a positive impact on youth's sociocognitive development. In his study, working children had a greater understanding of
social relationships and showed a greater sensitivity to other people's moods
and temperament. However, he failed to consider whether more sensitive
children were more likely to be employed than less sensitive children.

In one of the few studies in this area outside the United States, Saxe
(1988) investigated Brazilian street vendors ages 10 to 12 who had little or

no school experience. Saxe argues that their everyday experience of street vending provided them with the capacity to solve mathematical problems. The important point for Saxe is that nonworking children with little or no education are unable to solve such problems, a belief that suggests that the work experience had contributed to the development of the children's mathematical knowledge. Providing further support for this claim, Carraher (1986) shows that job experience is related to the ability to deal with mathematical problems in meaningful settings. Adult construction workers with little formal education were better able to solve mathematical problems involving proportions than school students, the workplace was their learning environment. Price-Williams and colleagues (1969), who compared young children from potters' families with children from nonpotters' families, showed that the former were more likely to have developed the cognitive ability to conserve. The experience of potterymaking enhanced the child's cognitive growth, allowing skills to be developed in meaningful settings.

Being taught a work skill compares favorably with having formal lessons (Boyden, 1994), but these are not perfect substitutes by any means. A number of researchers have looked at the nature of the relationship between the tutor and the tutee and related it to the novice–expert comparison (Rogoff, 1984, 1990). Greenfield (1984) highlights the way that weaving skills are acquired through the transmission of information from adults (experts) to children (novices). By providing appropriate scaffolding, adults allow for the individual child to attain specific skills. However, we must beware of overstating the role of work in learning. That very few studies have compared work-based learning with schooling over a range of types of learning limits our ability to answer our original question.

In some parts of Africa where education in formal school settings is not well established, the child's work is central to the social integration, socialization, and transmission of relevant skills and knowledge. In a study of the sociocognitive competence of children in Cameroon, Nsamang, and Lamb (1993:438) suggest, "Child 'work' is an indigenous mechanism for social integration – a strategy which keeps children in contact with existential realities and the activities of daily life."

The statements of children who work also suggest that they perceive their jobs as providing them with skills and training (Woodhead, 1998). Although work may have the *potential* to provide learning, it cannot be assumed that this will occur in all circumstances. For example, there exist apprenticeship systems that do not provide effective training (Bequele and Myers, 1995; Zalami et al., 1998). Furthermore, such basic skills as literacy and numeracy may require more structured tutoring and resources for effective learning.

In short, work cannot be treated as a complete alternative to schooling, but perhaps as a strong complement in settings when compulsory education is not the norm.

Education System Failures. At the First International Meeting of Working Children held in Kundapur in 1996, representatives of working children came together to discuss common problems. One priority expressed by these children was "an education system with methods and contents adapted to our reality" (IWGCL, 1996). From the perspective of these working children, the available education systems were failing them. One source of dissatisfaction with current education systems is that they are driven by an inappropriate model. Many apply a curriculum that has not been planned to make schooling relevant to children's life circumstances. The Kundapur Declaration suggests that working children require a pragmatic approach to knowledge.

In developing countries, about one in three children drops out of primary school after enrollment. This dropout rate varies among countries and does not consider those who never enroll (Bellamy, 1997). Why do children not enroll in school? Why do children drop out? Poverty is the most frequently cited reason for children's working while enrolled in school. Research in Brazil found that one third of families were totally or partially dependent on children's earnings. A study in Bangalore, India, found that 19% of family income was earned by children. In Egypt male children contributed one fourth of family income. In Nepal, 23% of children working on a tea estate claimed to be the sole earners in the families (Boyden 1994; Bequele and Myers, 1995). Many children carry out unpaid work within the family, such as child care duties, releasing parents to work (Bequele and Myers, 1995).

However, the cost of school attendance cannot be measured simply in terms of lost income to the family. Schooling also incurs significant costs for books, supplies, clothes, and transportation. Alarcan reported that children in Lima worked to put themselves through school and to provide funds to supplement the teachers' salaries (cited in Boyden, 1994). One of the reasons given by Indonesian children for dropping out of school was the difficulty of paying the school fees (White et al., 1997).

Poverty is not the sole force that influences children's participation in school. At times traditional social norms require children to work. In such circumstances the value attached to education must rise to supersede the tradition of requiring children to work. In other countries, unequal sex roles contribute to low school attendance. For example, in India the belief that it is more important to educate male children remains widespread.

In Nigeria, school enrollment rates are higher for male than for female children. If fewer girls are in school, presumably more are available for work. However, in some parts of eastern Nigeria it is primarily girls who attend school, since boys are working (Oloko, 1995). There are also sex differences in the type of work done by children. Just as adult women carry out "dual roles" of domestic worker and paid employee, female child workers may fill triple roles: work, school, and domestic duties. In addition, sex differences in adult employment also influence the perceived value of education for male and female children.

For education to succeed, both parents and youth must be engaged. In the IWGCL report on Egypt, for example, it was apparent that some poor families saw education as their means of changing the opportunities for their children. Yet children reported that their main reason for not attending school was the lack of parental support (Abdalla, 1995). Other children report that they do not attend school because their experience is not positive. If school is dull or perceived as irrelevant, work can emerge as a ready alternative to achieve satisfaction and immediate financial rewards. Teaching methods and teacher attitudes also play a role in influencing choices between education or work. Sudhir, an 11-year-old in India, says:

> In school teachers would not teach well. If we ask them to teach us alphabets, they would beat us. They would sleep in the class. . . . Even if we did not understand, they would not teach us. So I dropped out of school. (Bellamy, 1997:29)

The IWGCL report contains an account of Manju, a tribal boy from Ullar in India. While he attended school for more than 5 years he was humiliated by other pupils and teachers for belonging to a tribe and wearing his hair long, as was the custom in his community. He eventually started to work, and the monetary and self-esteem rewards gained from work finally led him to leave school (McKechnie and Hobbs, 1998). Historically, schools have not always been welcoming places to children who work (Stadum, 1995). One of the key problems faced by children who combine work and school is creating the time to carry out both tasks. Bequele and Myers (1995) argue that schools need to adopt flexible approaches to make access to education viable for working children. Some are wary of this approach on grounds that it may simply perpetuate child employment. However, Bequele and Myers suggest that legislative demands that force employers to provide education for working children may reduce the demand for child employees since they can create problems in adjusting production processes.

Boyden (1994) notes the advantages in many countries that have adopted flexible education systems that provide access to school in morning, afternoon, and evening shifts. However, she also believes there is a need to appreciate the drawbacks, notably whether children in different shifts are being disadvantaged. In one example in Brazil, children in the evening school shift complain of fatigue. Clearly, there is a need for careful evaluation of the costs and benefits of such programs.

Educational Consequences of Youth Employment. We have already alluded to the effect work may have on educational performance. Since most of the research in this area has taken place within the developed economies, the dangers of generalizing across cultural boundaries should be stressed. Marsh (1991) proposed that two models have emerged to consider the impact of work, the zero sum and the developmental. Whereas the developmental model considers the benefits of work for the individual's development, the zero sum model assumes that debates about the impact of work should take place in the educational arena. This definition of childhood views education as the "work" of the child. This model assumes that given the limited time that children have, work will detract from education.

In testing this hypothesis researchers have focused on the number of hours that school students work. The findings from such research have been mixed. Steinberg and Cauffman (1995) argue that students who work in excess of 20 hours per week perform worse in school than student-workers who spend less time on the job. In a more recent review, Frone (1999) notes that some findings are contradictory but acknowledges that working excessive hours is associated with negative attitudes to education. Some preliminary findings in Britain suggest that the negative effects of work on education may emerge if students work more than 10 hours per week (Hobbs and McKechnie, 1997). This lower figure may reflect the different education systems in these countries.

We cannot be sure that working long hours "causes" children to lose their interest in schooling. An equally plausible interpretation is that academic failure leads children to opt out of education, by reducing their commitment and effort, and to seek work as an alternative source of immediate rewards (Steinberg and Cauffman, 1995; Hobbs and McKechnie, 1997). Some of the research evidence currently available suggests that both processes are at work (Mortimer and Finch, 1986; Steinberg et al., 1993). Steinberg and Cauffman (1995) suggest that three different mechanisms may be operating. First, through work, school students disengage from school and lose their emotional investment in it and its tasks. Second, work has a negative effect on health, for example, inducing high fatigue levels, and this affects school performance. Third, employed students lose their motivation to succeed in education because concrete short-term rewards from work are more tangible than long-term rewards from education that youth cannot envision. Although there is a generalized consensus that increases in the number of hours worked are associated with higher risk of deleterious outcomes, it is also the case that no work at all is not necessarily better than 1–5 hours of work per week (Bachman and Schulenberg, 1993:231). Such findings, supported by Mortimer and coworkers (1996), Schoenhals and associates (1998), and Hobbs and McKechnie (1997), suggest that education may benefit from some work experience, provided the hours worked are not excessive.

Markel and Frone (1998) argue that the "quality of employment" also needs to be considered to appreciate the value of youth employment. For example, forms of work that draw on skills taught in school may reinforce each other, allowing benefits to be realized. Boyden (1994) reports some preliminary findings for other countries, noting that street workers in Asuncion were behind their normal age group in terms of educational attainment and were concentrated in primary grades of school. This finding implies inadequate progression and grade repetition. A study by Oloko (1995) in Nigeria also finds that academic performance was adversely affected by working. However, working children were more advanced than nonworkers in areas of moral values and leadership abilities. Clearly there is a need for more research in developed and developing countries. What emerges from the available evidence offers support for the view that working does have an impact on schooling, although we should not assume this will only be a negative influence.

Conclusion

We set out with a number of specific aims, including to identify the scale of "child labor," assess its impact, and determine the relationship between work and education. In each of these areas, there is a shortage of reliable information, but especially in developing countries. By failing to clarify children's economic roles we leave them invisible in policy debates. Although everyone will condemn exploitative and harmful work practices, some employment has the potential to provide youth benefits, both socially and financially. Our review demonstrates that no single variable can explain fully the diverse impacts of youth employment.

The final challenge from this overview of child employment is that there is a clear need to reconceptualize the work–education relationship. Education is important in terms of individual development and economic well-being.

However, no single "education model" fits all circumstances. There is an urgent need to consider the alternative means by which relevant and accessible education can be made available, particularly for youth in developing countries. That such options are viable has been shown in India, Colombia, and the Philippines (Bordia, 1991; Bequele and Myers, 1995; Bellamy, 1997). If we set as our goal the attainment of skills in both the work and educational domains, we may achieve an additional benefit, namely, acknowledging the value that children see in their work. This will require a change in traditional views in which childhood is naturally seen as a time for school rather than work.

REFERENCES

Abdalla, A. (1995). *Child Labor in Egypt: An Overview and an Exploratory Study of the Child Labor Triangle of Masr Al-Qadeema (Old Cairo)*. Amsterdam: International Working Group on Child Labor.

Bachman, J. G., and Schulenberg, J. (1993). How Part-Time Work Intensity Relates to Drug Use, Problem Behavior, Time Use and Satisfaction among High School Students: Are These Consequences or Merely Correlates? *Developmental Psychology*, 29, 220–235.

Barling, J., and Kelloway, E. K. (1999). *Young Workers: Varieties of Experience*. Washington, DC: American Psychological Association.

Bellamy, C. (Ed.) (1997). *The State of the World's Children*. Oxford: Oxford University Press.

Bequele, A., and Myers, W. (1995). *First Things First in Child Labor: Eliminating Work Detrimental to Children*. Geneva: ILO.

Black, M. (1997a). *Child Domestic Workers: A Handbook for Research and Action*. London: Anti-Slavery International.

Black, M. (1997b). Caged Birds, Silent Song. *New Internationalist*, 292, 15–17.

Blagbrough, J. (1995). *Child Domestic Work in Indonesia: A Preliminary Situation Analysis*. London: Anti-Slavery International.

Bordia, A. (1991). Education for Working Children in India. In W. Myers (Ed.), *Protecting Working Children*, pp. 121–130. London: Zed Books.

Boyden, J. (1994). *The Relationship between Education and Child Work*. Innocenti Occasional Papers, Child Right Series No. 9, Florence: UNICEF.

Burman, E. (1994). *Deconstructing Developmental Psychology*. London: Routledge.

Burman, E. (1996). Local, Global or Lobalized? Child Development and International Child Rights Legislation. *Childhood*, 3, 45–67.

Carr, R. V., Wright, J. D., and Brody, C. J. (1996). Effects of High School Work Experience a Decade Later: Evidence from the National Longitudinal Survey. *Sociology of Education*, 69, 66–81.

Carraher, T. N. (1986). From Drawings to Buildings: Working with Mathematical Scales. *International Journal of Behavioural Development*, 9, 527–544.

Castillo, D. N. (1999). Occupational Safety and Health in Young People. In J. Barling and E. K. Kelloway (Eds.), *Young Workers: Varieties of Experience*, pp. 159–200. Washington, DC: American Psychological Association.

Cecchetti, R. (1998). *Children Who Work in Europe.* Brussels: European Forum for Child Welfare.

Cole, S. (1980). Send Our Children to Work? *Psychology Today,* 13, 44–47.

Coleman, J. C., and Hendry, L. (1998). *The Nature of Adolescence,* 3rd ed. New York: Routledge.

Corsaro, W. A. (1997). *The Sociology of Childhood.* Thousand Oaks, CA: Pine Forge Press.

Cottingham, M. (1997). *A Sporting Chance.* London: Christian Aid.

Feather, N. T. (1992). *The Psychological Impact of Unemployment.* New York: Springer Verlag.

Finch, M. D., Shanan, M. J., Mortimer, J. T., and Ryu, S. (1991). Work Experience and Control Orientation in Adolescence. *American Sociological Review,* 56, 597–611.

Forastieri, V. (1997). *Children at Work: Health and Safety Risks.* Geneva: ILO.

Frone, M. (1999). Developmental Consequences of Youth Employment. In J. Barling and E. K. Kelloway (Eds.), *Young Workers: Varieties of Experience,* pp. 89–128. Washington, DC: American Psychological Association.

Fuller, R. G. (1930). Child Labor. In E. R. A. Seligman (Ed.), *Encyclopedia of the Social Sciences,* Volume III, pp. 412–424. New York: Macmillan.

Fyfe, A. (1989). *Child Labor.* Cambridge: Polity Press.

Greenberger, E., (1983). A Researcher in the Policy Arena: The Case of Child Labor. *American Psychologist,* 38, 104–110.

Greenberger, E., and Steinberg, L. (1986). *When Teenagers Work: The Psychological and Social Costs of Adolescent Employment.* New York: Basic Books.

Greenberger, E., Steinberg, L., and Vaux, A. (1981). Adolescents Who Work: Health and Behavioral Consequences of Job Stress. *Developmental Psychology,* 17, 691–703.

Greenfield, P. M. (1984). A Theory of the Teacher in the Learning Activities of Everyday Life. In B. Rogoff and J. Lave (Eds.), *Everyday Cognition: Its Development in Social Context,* pp. 117–138. Cambridge, MA.: Harvard University Press.

Grootaert, C., and Kanbur, R. (1997). Confronting Child Labor: A Gradualist Approach. In J. Gugler (Ed.), *Cities in the Developing World,* pp. 189–195. Oxford: Oxford University Press.

Heaven, P. C. L. (1994). *Contemporary Adolescence: A Social Psychological Approach.* South Melbourne: Macmillan Education.

Heptinstall, E., Jewitt, K., and Sherriff, C. (1997). *Young Workers and Their Accidents.* London: Child Accident Prevention Trust.

Hibbett, A., and Beatson, M. (1995). Young People at Work. *Employment Gazette,* 103, 169–177.

Hobbs, S., Lindsay, S., and McKechnie, J. (1996). The Extent of Child Employment in Britain. *British Journal of Education and Work,* 9, 5–16.

Hobbs, S., and McKechnie, J. (1997). *Child Employment in Britain: A Social and Psychological Analysis.* Edinburgh: The Stationery Office.

Hobbs, S., and McKechnie, J. (1998). Children at Work in the UK: The Evidence. In B. Pettitt (Ed.), *Children and Work in the UK,* pp. 8–21. London: Child Poverty Action Group.

Hooper, J. (1998). Child Labour Figures Put Rich Italy to Shame: Victims of Jobs Market. *The Guardian,* 8 January, 13.

International Labor Organization. (1996a). *Child Labor: What Is to Be Done?* Geneva: ILO.

International Labor Organization. (1996b). *Child Labor: Targeting the Intolerable.* Geneva: ILO.

IWGCL. (1996). *First International Meeting of Working Children* (Working Paper). Kundapur: International Working Group on Child Labor.

James, A., Jenks, C., and Prout, A. (1998). *Theorizing Childhood.* Cambridge: Polity Press.

James, A., and Prout, A. (1990). *Constructing and Reconstructing Childhood.* Basingstoke: Falmer Press.

Knight, E. B., Castillo, D. N., and Layne, L. A. (1995). A Detailed Analysis of Work Related Injury among Youth Treated in Emergency Departments. *American Journal of Industrial Medicine,* 27, 793–805.

Lavalette, M. (1994). *Child Employment in the Capitalist Labor Market.* Aldershot: Avebury.

Lavalette, M., Hobbs, S., Lindsay, S., and McKechnie, J. (1995). Child Employment in Britain: Policy, Myth and Reality. *Youth and Policy,* 47, 1–15.

Lavalette, M., McKechnie, J., and Hobbs, S. (1991). *The Forgotten Workforce: Scottish Children at Work.* Glasgow: Scottish Low Pay Unit.

Lee, M., and O'Brien, R. (1995). *The Game's Up: Redefining Child Prostitution.* London: The Children's Society.

Mansurov, V. A. (1995). *Supplementary Country Report: Russia.* Amsterdam: International Working Group on Child Labor.

Markel, K. S. and Frone, M. R. (1998). Job Characteristics, Work–School Conflict, and School Outcomes among Adolescents: Testing a Structural Model. *Journal of Applied Psychology,* 83, 277–287.

Marsh, H. W. (1991). Employment during High School: Character Building or a Subversion of Academic Goals? *Sociology of Education,* 64, 172–189.

McKechnie, J., and Hobbs, S., (1998). *Working Children: Reconsidering the Debates.* Amsterdam: Defense for Children International.

McKechnie, J., Lindsay, S., and Hobbs, S. (1994). *Child Employment in Dumfries and Galloway.* Glasgow: Scottish Low Pay Unit.

Mortimer, J. T., and Finch, M. D. (1986). The Effects of Part-Time Work on Self-Concept and Achievement. In K. Borman and J. Reisman (Eds.), *Becoming a Worker,* pp. 66–89. Norwood, NJ: Ablex.

Mortimer, J. T., and Finch, M. D. (1996). *Adolescents, Work, and Family: An Intergenerational Developmental Analysis.* Thousand Oaks, CA: Sage.

Mortimer, J. T., Finch, M. D., Ryu, S., Shanahan, M. J., and Call, K. T. (1996). The Effects of Work Intensity on Adolescent Mental Health, Achievement and Behavioral Adjustment: New Evidence from a Prospective Study. *Child Development,* 67, 1243–1261.

Mortimer, J. T., Finch, M. D., Shanahan, M., and Ryu, S. (1992). Work Experience, Mental Health and Behavioral Adjustment in Adolescence. *Journal of Research on Adolescence,* 2, 25–57.

National Research Council. (1998). *Protecting Youth at Work.* Washington, DC: National Academy Press

New Internationalist. (1997). *Child Labor.* No. 292, July (whole issue).

Nsamenang, A. B. and Lamb, M. E. (1993). The Acquisition of Socio-cognitive Competence by Nso Children in the Bamenda Grassfields of Northwest Cameroon. *International Journal of Behavioral Development,* 16(3), 429–441.

O'Donnell, C., and White, L. (1998). *Child Employment in North Tyneside*. London: Low Pay Unit.

Oloko, S. B. A. (1995). *In Depth Country Report: Nigeria*. Amsterdam: International Working Group on Child Labor.

Pettitt, B. (1998). Work Experience or Experience of Work? In B. Pettit (Ed.), *Children and Work in the UK*, pp. 107–123. London: Child Poverty Action Group.

Pond, C., and Searle, A. (1991). *The Hidden Army: Children at Work in the 1990s*. London: Low Pay Unit.

Price-Williams, D., Gordon, W., and Ramirez, M. (1969). Skill and Conservation: A Study of Pottery Making Children. *Developmental Psychology*, 1(6), 769.

Reddy, N. (1997). Child Work in India: Lessons for the Developed and Developing World. In S. McCloskey (Ed.), *No Time to Play: Local and Global Perspectives on Child Employment*, pp. 29–46. Belfast: One World Center for Northern Ireland.

Rogoff, B. (1984). Introduction: Thinking and Learning in Social Context. In B. Rogoff and J. Lave (Eds.), *Everyday Cognition: Its Development in Social Context*, pp. 1–8. Cambridge, MA: Harvard University Press.

Rogoff, B. (1990). *Apprenticeship in Thinking: Cognitive Development in Social Context*. New York: Oxford University Press.

Saunders, L., Stoney, S., and Weston, P. (1997). The Impact of the Work-Related Curriculum on 14- to 16-Year-Olds. *Journal of Education and Work*, 10, 151–167.

Saxe, G. (1988). The Mathematics of Child Street Vendors. *Child Development*, 39, 1415–1425.

Schoenhals, M., Tienda, M., and Schneider, B. (1998). The Educational and Personal Consequences of Adolescent Employment. *Social Forces*, 77(2), 723–762.

Stadum, B. (1995). The Dilemma in Saving Children from Child Labor: Reform and Casework at Odds with Families' Needs, 1900–1938. *Child Welfare*, 74, 33–55.

Steinberg, L. (1993). *Adolescence*. New York: McGraw-Hill.

Steinberg, L., and Cauffman, E. (1995). The Impact of Employment on Adolescent Development. *Annals of Child Development*, 11, 131–166.

Steinberg, L., and Dornbusch, S. M. (1991). Negative Correlates of Part-Time Employment during Adolescence: Replication and Elaboration. *Developmental Psychology*, 27, 299–317.

Steinberg, L., Fegley, S., and Dornbusch, S. M. (1993). Negative Impact of Part-Time Work on Adolescent Adjustment: Evidence from a Longitudinal Study. *Developmental Psychology*, 29, 171–180.

Steinberg, L., Greenberger, E., Vaux, A., and Ruggiero, M. (1981). Early Work Experience: Effects on Adolescent Occupational Socialization. *Youth and Society*, 12, 403–422.

Stern, D., Stone, J. R. III, Hopkins, C., and McMillion, M. (1990). Quality of Students' Work Experience and Orientation toward Work. *Youth and Society*, 22, 263–282.

U.S. Department of Labor. (1995). *By the Sweat and Toil of Children*. Vol. 1. *The Use of Child Labor in American Imports*. Washington, DC: U.S. Department of Labor.

Weiner, M. (1991). *The Child and the State in India*. Delhi: Oxford University Press.

White, B. (1994). Children, Work and "Child Labor": Changing Responses to the Employment of Children. *Development and Change*, 25, 849–878.

White, B. (1995). *Globalization and the Problem of Child Labor*. International Working Group on Child Labor, Working Paper. Amsterdam: Defence for Children International.

White, B. (1997). Child Labor in the International Context. In S. McCloskey (Ed.), *No Time to Play: Local and Global Perspectives on Child Employment*, pp. 11–28. Belfast: One World Center.

White, B., Tjandraningsih, I., and Haryadi, D. (1997). *Child Workers in Indonesia*. Amsterdam: International Working Group on Child Labor.

Woodhead, M. (1998). *Children's Perspectives on Their Working Lives: A Participatory Study in Bangladesh, Ethiopia, the Philippines, Guatemala, El Salvador and Nicaragua*. Stockholm: Radda Barnen.

Zalami, F. B., Reddy, N., Lynch, M. A., and Feinstein, S. (1998). *Forgotten on the Pyjama Trail*. Amsterdam: Defense for Children International.

11 Life Skills for Ugandan Youth

Fred Ogwal-Oyee

Introduction

The normative development of young people poses challenges to most societies, but especially those with limited resources to invest for the benefit of their youth. There are many reasons why such underinvestment occurs, and civil strife and armed struggles greatly complicate the goal of investing in youth. The case of civil war and political upheaval in Uganda during the 1970s and 1980s illustrates how a generation of youth lost opportunities for normative development; the present predicament of that generation requires major attention.

This chapter examines Uganda's troubled history of nearly two decades of civil strife, combined with severe abuse of human rights, economic mismanagement, and the general destruction of basic services to illustrate how these factors undermined options for the current generation of young people. These young people have been denied educational opportunities; some are struggling to earn a living from the streets; many more are orphans or laborers doing odd jobs with minimal pay. Large numbers of young people are infected with human immunodeficiency virus / acquired immunodeficiency syndrome (HIV/AIDS) or affected by it because their close relatives suffer from AIDS. Young girls are particularly disadvantaged as they face additional challenges related to sexual and physical abuse.

Several supportive programs have been established by subsequent Ugandan governments to rehabilitate the country and its people in the aftermath of the lost decades. One is the Life Skills Intervention for Young People, which recognizes that different categories of Ugandan youth missed opportunities for growth in a normal environment. The program serves youth who found themselves prematurely exposed to an environment in which they could not cope on their own and in which adults were ill equipped to offer them meaningful support.

The Life Skills Program offers young Ugandans the opportunity to recover through the acquisition of psychosocial skills both within formal school for enrolled youth and through outreach services for those not attending school. The government of Uganda has taken the lead in addressing the problems facing young people, but nongovernmental organizations (NGOs) operating in the country have been useful allies in implementing the program. In the main, implementation of the Life Skills Program has been smooth, though some structural problems have been encountered. Most of these are related to shortcomings of institutions, which are just beginning to regain shape. The lessons learned from the implementation of the Life Skills Program in Uganda provide many examples for policymakers interested in improving the lives of youth who missed opportunities for normative development and in preparing them for useful future adult roles.

In what follows, I provide a background for the Life Skills Program by setting the sociohistorical context and outlining the condition of Ugandan youth. After describing the program and its accomplishments, I assess the strengths and limitations of the program and conclude with research and policy implications.

Background

Uganda is a landlocked country lying astride the equator, sharing its international borders with Kenya in the east, Tanzania and Rwanda in the south, Democratic Republic of Congo in the west, and Sudan in the north. Its population of 22 million (1998 estimates) consists of 40 clearly distinct ethnic groupings. The Bantu tribes live in the central, south, and western parts of the country; the Nilotic and Nilo-Hamatic tribes are found in the north and east, with cultural linkages to groups in the Sahelian regions and the Horn of Africa. The country is probably one of the least urbanized in Africa, with about 90% of the population living in rural areas. Endowed with favorable climatic conditions and generous arable land, Uganda has long been considered the potential granary of East Africa. Early visitors to the continent named it the "Pearl of Africa" in recognition of this potential. Yet, in spite of this bounteous endowment, Uganda's political history since independence from Britain in 1962 has caused great hardships for young people.

During the colonial era and the immediate period after independence, Uganda was on the right track to development. Its education system was one of the best in East and Central Africa, as Makerere University produced highly qualified professionals for the entire region. The health system was based on a well-distributed network of hospitals and health centers, making the quality of medical services among the best in Africa. Expectations for sustained economic growth were high. Between 1963 and 1971 for example, the gross domestic product (GDP) grew at an annual average rate of 4.5%. Because this growth rate exceeded population increase, real per capita income rose. The excellent road and railway infrastructure facilitated the marketing of rural farm produce and enabled most rural populations to send their children to school and to afford medical treatment from the health centers and hospitals.

This period of sustained growth ended abruptly in January 1971, when the democratically elected government was overthrown in a military coup, led by General Idi Amin. Between 1971 and 1980, economic mismanagement accompanied civil wars and professional standards deteriorated rapidly as skilled personnel either were killed or fled the country for fear of their lives. Uganda's GDP declined by about 25%, exports by 60%, and import volumes by close to 50%. Inflation skyrocketed to unmanageable levels. Low levels of cash crop production and a limited capacity to pay and collect taxes meant meager public revenue. This situation was aggravated by large increases in defense expenditures and corruption. Ironically, the weapons were to butcher the country's own citizens, making the Ugandan government one of the leading abusers of human rights.

The education sector largely collapsed, as most of the educated Ugandans sought safe havens by fleeing to exile. The health sector also came to a near-standstill. The government hospital infrastructure and many health centers were destroyed, leaving most health care in the hands of the voluntary non-government bodies. For example, in 1970 approximately 70% of the target population was reached by health programs, but this share plummeted to 15%–25% by 1980 (Statistisches Bundesamt, 1992). Funding for the health sector virtually disappeared, and many health personnel abandoned government employment or fled to neighboring countries. This loss of personnel combined with grinding poverty left the health sector with half of its employed staff untrained.

To compound social damage, the government tried to control the economy and generate political support through expulsion from Uganda of the Indian community, who controlled the booming commercial sector, and through nationalization schemes. These actions generated an immediate shortage of essential commodities, coupled with a massive expansion of the public sector from an estimated 50,000 employees in 1970 to 250,000 in the early 1980s. The bloated bureaucracy, in tandem with corrupt policies and a passive population overwhelmed by years of political violence, contributed to the near-collapse of the economy (Macrae and Birungi, 1993). This situation continued until 1979, when a force of exiled Ugandans ousted the military junta, with support from neighboring Tanzania.[1] The new government, ushered in through an election in 1980, immediately ran into trouble with the accusation of rigging elections. Uganda had to face yet another guerrilla war that made it difficult to carry out any meaningful economic rehabilitation.

Uganda's legacy of nearly two decades of civil strife and severe abuses of human rights not only dehumanized its people in the eyes of the international community, but also impoverished most Ugandans. The poorest segments of society were particularly hard hit, as most of them were unable to escape the devastation of the war and lost their sources of livelihood when agricultural inputs became unavailable and government subsidy was withdrawn. The lucky few turned to petty trade to eke out a living. Children born to these families lacked basic life necessities (food, shelter, and clothing) and access to basic social services, including education and health care. They experienced a sense of helplessness, isolation, and social exclusion in an atmosphere beset by violence and abject poverty. The majority of Uganda's young people fit this profile.

By 1986 when the guerrilla-turned-liberation-army National Resistance Army took over the government, the economy was in shambles and social services largely destroyed. Expenditures in real terms on education and health, for example, amounted to only 27% and 9%, respectively, of the levels enjoyed in 1970 (World Bank, 1993). For young people who survived the period of violence, their past has a strong bearing on their ability to cope with challenges associated with the transition to adulthood.

The Profile of Today's Ugandan Youth

The 1991 census put the Uganda population at 16.7 million people, with about 50% below the age of 15 years and 19% below 5 years. At the present annual growth rate of about 2.5%, the population at the turn of the 21st century is estimated at about 22 million. Children born around 1978, at the height of the Amin military regime, and around 1986, when the present government came to power, are between 12 and 20 years old. The Life Skills Program in Uganda is targeting this population, which features a wide variety of disadvantages.

---

[1] Tanzania had itself become a target of the military regime war-mongering policy.

The Out of School Youth

The majority of young people found in Uganda today have been disadvantaged in several ways. The two decades of civil strife led to a virtual dismantling of the education sector. The education system, especially the primary school, consisting of Grades 1 to 7, which usually enrolls children between the ages of 6 and 14 years, failed to achieve its goals. By 1990, quality was poor, with 49% of the teachers untrained and enrollment of less than 50% of eligible children. The attrition rate was equally high, at 50%, and completion rate for primary education at Grade 7, particularly for girls, was as low as 9%. Parents' contributions to primary schools accounted for 50% to 75% of all expenses, yet many could not afford the high cost of educating their children as they progressed to the next levels. In addition, a rigid primary school system and timetable prevented children involved in petty trade or household activities, especially in urban areas, from attending school. Yet such income-generating activities were essential for sustaining their families. The net result was that most youth discontinued their education and now contribute to the increasing number of Ugandans who can hardly read or write. This situation has serious implications for their participation in development and contributions to their society.

The Street Youth

Several of the children who lost their parents, and others whose parents could not meet their needs, found themselves joining the ever-rising number of street children. The problem of street children, previously confined to the capital city of Kampala, is now widespread in all the major urban centers. Parental death is not the only reason for children's living on their own. According to NGOs working with street children, economic hardship is also a major contributing factor. Some children are actually sent to the street by their parents or guardians to earn their living. For example, girls as young as age 6 are sent from city slums to the market to collect beans and other foodstuffs that might have fallen from lorries or under the stalls, which are then resold at a cheaper price.

A small survey in Kampala revealed that about two thirds of street children are in regular contact with at least one parent, or a guardian, and often contribute money to the household; only 37% were completely on their own and slept in the streets (Natukunda and Kamya, 1993). The 1991 population census put the number of street children at 4,000, but this estimate has been increasing at an alarming rate every year. This situation is not unique to Uganda, as children's living on their own is a common phenomenon in postwar situations. Finding themselves violently separated from their families and not knowing where to go, or finding the family unable to fend for them, abandoned children head to the cities and major towns in search of survival.

Young People with Disability
Young people with one form of disability or another are common in Uganda. This is partly a direct consequence of the civil war, but also the result of inadequate access to health care. The number of young people who are disabled in Uganda could well be as high as 1.5 million, of the total population of about 20 million (Tuhaise, 1992). In 1997, the World Health Organization (WHO) estimated that 10% of the Ugandan population was disabled, and that continuing violence and the breakdown of immunization programs are largely responsible for the increase. The National Union of Disabled People of Uganda (NUDPU), an umbrella organization for NGOs operating in this area, estimates the percentage to be around 17%, excluding the emotionally disabled. It is easy to imagine that the horrors of the civil wars have seriously traumatized large numbers of people, who are now unable to lead normal productive lives. The young disabled people require different and more specialized kinds of skills to enable them to contribute to the development of their societies. Because programs that promote such skills are largely unavailable, these youngsters end up with no skills and continue to live in perpetual dependency, poverty, and frustration. Hence, the majority of children living on the street trying to survive by begging are also socially disabled.

Young Laborers
Child labor is a major social problem as most underage youth who work offer their labor in exchange for less than minimum wage or for something to eat. About 83% of working children labor within their families, an arrangement that is not recognized as work; 9% are self-employed; and only 3% are salaried employees (Government of Uganda, 1998). The most common forms of youth work in cities and towns involve bicycle or motorcycle transportation (*boda boda*), domestic work, small-scale industry, odd jobs related to portage and packaging, cross-border smuggling, and commercial work. According to the Sentinel Community Surveillance Fifth Study Cycle completed in March 1997, child work was the third major cause of school abandonment. Irregular attendance due to lack of money for school fees and parental indifference to the educational needs of their children also contributed to youth withdrawal from school. Because most employed children lack basic skills, including skills for negotiation for pay, they are the lowest paid and continue to live in poverty.

Orphaned Youth
Orphans constitute yet another category of poor and vulnerable youth in Uganda. The 1991 population census estimated that about 1.2 million children in Uganda lost one or both parents as a result of civil unrest and the HIV/AIDS epidemic. The number was projected to increase to 1.5 million around the year 2010. The 1995 Demographic and Health Survey reports that 25% of all families surveyed were looking after at least one foster child (Republic of Uganda, 1995). When foster families could not afford basic necessities for their own children, the foster children fared poorly. If the family was confronted with decisions on which child should go to school, for example, the foster child usually remained at home.

Girls as a Special Group
Girls constitute another group of young people in Uganda who face unique challenges. Young girls contribute significantly to Uganda's high fertility rate, which is one of the highest in the world. In 1995, the rate of teenage pregnancies was very high, as 43% of young girls already were pregnant or had a first child. As gender-related inequalities continue to affect girls' enrollment and persistence in school, cultural practices and norms deprive them of needed protection and opportunities for normal development. Social norms keep young girls in submissive roles throughout their development. The practice of early marriage is common to secure a bride price that meets the immediate needs of families. These marriage arrangements put heavy domestic and parental responsibilities on young girls at the time when they are least prepared to assume familial responsibilities and also take them away from school.

Youth Living in Conflict Areas
Rebel forces continue to wreak havoc on the population in the northern part of the country. These residents continue to suffer as warring factions destroy schools, hospitals, and residences and conscript young men and women into their ranks. Young girls are often the victims of rape and sexual abuse. The majority of the children in northern Uganda do not attend school, and social service facilities either are nonexistent or are in ruins. Young people living in areas fraught with armed conflict confront a set of challenges different from those their peers living in more peaceful areas face.

   These Ugandan youth experience a wide variety of vulnerabilities. Youth are finding themselves prematurely exposed to situations they are ill equipped to manage, with adults unable to provide necessary support. Even youth who have the opportunity to attend school experience developmental challenges that warrant immediate attention and intervention. The government, in its quest for sustainable development of its young people, has underscored the critical need for policies and programs that can improve household incomes and ensure access to basic resources and social services for both the rural and urban areas. This is seen as the first step in addressing the inequalities. Support from international donors, nongovernmental organizations, individuals, and the civil society has been and continues to be critical in this endeavor. However, critical to addressing the challenges faced by young people are interventions that can assure their healthy development and provide the skills necessary for both their present lives and their future adult roles. The Life Skills Program was designed with these broad objectives in mind. It recognizes that the majority of young people in Uganda have missed opportunities to participate in national development and to develop to their full potential. The guiding premise is that possibilities exist to recover these losses to some reasonable degree.

The Life Skills Program in Uganda

Rationale

Concerned about the impact the country's past had on the health and development of the young Ugandans, the government in 1987 designed the School Health Education Program (SHEP) to be implemented in all primary schools throughout the country. The strategy was to use the primary school infrastructure – which miraculously remained fairly intact during a period of misrule in the 1970s and 1980s – to reach out to young people. SHEP used health-promoting approaches and provided basic health services, including immunization and first aid. The emergence of HIV/AIDS as a major threat to the health of young people reinforced the urgent need for health education.

Health education aimed to achieve three important objectives: to increase the knowledge of children and adolescents about health issues, thereby promoting normal development; to help children and adolescents adopt healthy life-styles through behavior change; and to encourage children to take the health messages to their peers who were not attending school, their families, and the community in which they lived. Such messages focused on prevention of common diseases arising from poor sanitation, poor living environments, and sometimes pure neglect. In essence, both the children and their teachers were designated agents of change within their communities. Health education was incorporated into the primary school curriculum, and activities like drama employed health-related themes. Teachers from all the primary schools were trained to teach health education. Relevant teaching and learning materials were developed and distributed to the schools. Reference books for students and health kits formed part of the materials developed. Education inspectors made several visits to schools to ensure that health education received the required attention in the school timetable.

By 1993, 6 years after the implementation of SHEP, a process evaluation identified two particularly important findings (Government of Uganda, 1993). The first was that children participating in the program were knowledgeable about the health issues they confronted. For example, over 70% of the children interviewed in the upper primary classes (Grades 5 to 7) could recite more than 60% of the common diseases found in their communities. Virtually all knew what caused malaria and how it could be prevented. Over 90% of the girls could identify one or two dangers associated with teenage pregnancy, and both boys and girls knew that HIV/AIDS was mainly spread through sexual intercourse. Over 80% of the children interviewed associated the incidence of diarrhea with unclean conditions and lack of latrines in the homes.

However, when the evaluation team investigated how this high level of awareness was being translated to actual practice, they found substantial disparities. For instance, although the children knew the connection between mosquitoes and malaria, most did nothing to protect themselves from mosquito bites. In fact, the team found ample evidence of absenteeism from school associated with incidence of malaria. There was empirical evidence, at least from reported cases of teen pregnancy, that despite the awareness of the spread of HIV through unprotected sex, unsafe sex was widely practiced. When the team visited the school latrines, there was no provision for washing hands, despite a chorus recitation by children to wash hands after using the toilet. Most of the schools visited had no provision for waste disposal, yet youth had responded knowledgeably when asked to explain how to keep the school compound clean.

There was also evidence that members of the community were participating as audience in some of the cocurricular activities conducted by their children at school. Such activities included drama organized as part of HIV/AIDS awareness, games, sports, and other periodic events. Children not attending school also enjoyed such functions. However, these activities seemed to signal a weakening of such school–community interactions. Not a single teacher interviewed had organized any community development work. In one of the schools, a nearby water source was shared with the community. However, stagnant water and muddy and bushy surroundings littered with animal droppings were common sights. The teachers, their families, and schoolchildren drew water from the same source every day. This was clear evidence that the teachers were not practicing what they taught in class and the students were not conveying to the community what they learned in school.

On the basis of these findings, the evaluation team concluded that there was a wide gap between the health knowledge and awareness of young people, on the one hand, and actual behaviors and practices, on the other. Several explanations were discussed in the report, including the lack of resources in the schools, poor facilities both at home and in school, failure of most teachers to provide role modeling, and traditional attitudes of adults about children. The strong recommendation from this assessment was the need to implement a program that would narrow if not eliminate the gap between the knowledge and practice. Life skills education was identified as "the missing link."

The findings of the SHEP evaluation were corroborated by the 1994 Situation Analysis of Children and Adolescents, which indicated that young people accorded high priority to their social and emotional needs, peer relations, and recreation (GOU/NCC, 1994). It identified the main problems facing young people as inadequate education, poor parenting, risky sexual activity, poverty and unemployment, inadequate adult guidance, and failure of young people to develop life goals. The same analysis reported that young people in Uganda generally felt ill equipped to handle these challenges.

These findings were supported by studies done elsewhere. For example, Life Skills Programs are known to contribute to improved teacher and student relationships, better behavior in the classrooms (Parsons et al., 1998), increased school attendance, and improved academic performance (Caplan et al., 1992). Life Skills Programs were also demonstrated to improve interpersonal and communication skills among young people (Rossouw, 1990). If properly designed and implemented, programs would also improve their creativity and negotiation skills. In the area of HIV/AIDS prevention, earlier findings indicate that strategies that include the promotion of life skills were more effective than those excluding life skills (Gold, 1991; McLean, 1994).

Objectives. The Life Skills Program sought to equip Ugandan children and adolescents with skills that would enable them to deal effectively with the demands and challenges of everyday life. The program emphasizes helping young people to develop the personal and social competencies needed to keep them safe and to enable them to become responsible citizens. Specific program aims include promoting the abilities of young people to make positive health choices and informed decisions, practice healthy behaviors, and recognize and avoid risky situations and behaviors. The program aims to link knowledge to practical application of skills that enable young people to become confident and competent individuals. The skills would not be taught in isolation, but as an integral part of other ongoing programs.

Program Strategies
The initial strategy to implement the Life Skills Program in Uganda involved organizing a high-level policy seminar in which participants identified and discussed challenges facing young people with regard to their health, education, social interactions, and developmental concerns. Representatives of various youth groups were given the opportunity to expound on issues emanating from the 1994 Situation Analysis. In addition, the youth representatives demanded increased access to reliable information about the challenges they face growing up. They also requested support to set up facilities where they would express themselves freely and communicate effectively with each other.

The second step was to generate baseline information by documenting the level of life skills of children and adolescents in their present setting. Initially, two baseline studies were conducted; they were followed by studies conducted in primary and secondary schools. In primary schools (for children between 6 and 13 years), the study was conducted in 5 of 45 districts, with six schools selected from each district representing urban/rural settings, performance in national examinations, and gender differences. Questionnaires were developed and administered to pupils, school management, and community leaders. The questionnaire placed most of its emphasis on skills related to behavior development, behavior change, and interaction, and to a lesser degree on vocational and other practical skills. The skills included self-knowledge, because young people build their self-esteem and self-confidence largely on personal assessments of what they can and cannot do. The same set of skills would also lead to self-control, enabling young people to cope with their emotions and stresses arising from difficult situations, including loss of parents, peers, and even poverty. Questions related to decision making and problem solving were also included.

The baseline study in primary schools confirmed that the life skills of primary school pupils were generally poor (averaging 2 on a 1 to 5 scale developed by the study group). However, teaching styles and learning environments also did not promote the acquisition of the life skills. Teachers mostly used the instructor-centered methods, which allowed limited or no student participation (Cele et al., 1997). Teachers' responses revealed that the majority were insensitive to the varied needs of different groups attending their classes, such as girls, orphans, and the disabled. Community leaders participating in focus group discussions also revealed very limited involvement in supporting the development of young people beyond paying school fees.

The secondary school baseline study recognized that older students confronted different challenges from primary school youth, which also differed between urban and rural coeducational schools. Questionnaires similar to those of the primary school study were used and were supplemented by various other sources of information, including focus group discussions with community leaders. We found that 13- to 18-year-olds were weak in most life skills (Opolot et al., 1997). The students rarely discussed among themselves issues related to their health or social development except during structured academic discussions, which were usually supervised by a teacher. Most were unconcerned about events in other parts of the country. Parents and teachers were mainly concerned with whether their children would pass the national examinations. Schools lacked resources to assist teen mothers; rather, girls who became pregnant faced threats of beating and expulsion. School authorities paid no specific attention to orphans or children with disabilities. Community leaders around the schools had only vague ideas about what transpired in the schools on a day to day basis. Their interaction with the school management stopped at parent meetings, usually held once or twice a year, when mostly financial issues were discussed.

The two school-based studies concluded that if young people were to learn and internalize life skills, more interactive and participatory, learner-centered approaches had to be employed. Specifically, students require exposure to learning experiences that both enable them to gain knowledge and provoke them to think and interpret how knowledge gained applies to their lives. Exposure to frank discussion of real life situations, practical games, role-playing, case studies, and songs and debates are relevant strategies to translate knowledge into practical life skills. Furthermore, teachers must serve as role models through development of specific skills. Finally, community leaders are also critical to the promotion of life skills because of the central role they occupy within their communities, including organizing community activities for young people.

Two additional studies about life skills were conducted. One explored education managers' awareness of the need for life skills education for young people. Although education managers were generally aware of the need to promote such skills, it was unclear whether they made conscious efforts to promote skill development at their institutions (Ogwal-Oyee, 1997). The second study documented the circumstances of nonenrolled youth, knowing that several nongovernmental organizations were dedicated to life skills development for some groups of nonenrolled youth. However, we learned that most NGOs focused their attention on specific aspects of life skills, such as health or social problems addressed by their programs. The study revealed the need to integrate life skills training to address the specific problems facing young people. For example, youth living in northern Uganda needed counseling services and psychosocial support to cope with the trauma of war.

The third step involved developing a Life Skills Program that would address specific problems identified in the situation analysis of 1994 and in the various baseline studies. For example, skills to cope with emotion enable young people to come to terms with the loss of parents and friends. This was a common occurrence in the war-ravaged north and as a consequence of the HIV/AIDS epidemic. The skills for decision making and problem solving were emphasized because they are required for most situations, including sexual relations, career choices, and most personal decisions. Many of these decisions would have serious implications for the health and development of young people, such as hygiene and alcohol consumption. Negotiation skills are equally important, especially for young girls, who must manage difficult situations, such as the possibility of rape or physical assault by aggressive peers. Due attention also was given to health-promoting skills, emphasizing activities that emphasized critical thinking, self-awareness, problem-solving, and assertiveness, which are skills that young people required the most both at school and in the home.

The fourth step involved identification and categorization of schools, which were based both on the importance they accorded to certain life skills, and their operational constraints due to location, resource base, or category of children served. Urban schools, for example, would promote skills that protect their students from exposure to information and entertainment facilities unsuitable for young people. Rural schools emphasized skills that enabled youth to cope with limited access to basic services and promote information sharing because most of the schools lacked media and other information resources. Mixed schools, perhaps more than single-sex schools, would ensure the promotion of skills that helped the students understand fully their relations with the opposite sex, and gender sensitivity.

Step five entailed building strategic alliances with both new initiatives and established countrywide programs to promote life skills for young people. A similar alliance was also envisaged with nongovernmental organizations. All efforts to develop a life skills program for youth ensured active participation of young people from the planning stage to the actual implementation of the skills-promoting activities. Teachers and other facilitators of programs for young people were given priority focus in the life skills program.

Activities and Accomplishments of the Program
Implementation of the Life Skills program started in July 1996 with advocacy, training, and the development of materials. Fifteen writers and educators were selected and trained in the concept of life skills and strategies for their inclusion in the formal school curriculum. The trainers were selected from the National Curriculum Development Center; the Institute of Teacher Education; the National Examinations Board; the Ministries of Education, Health, Gender, and Community Development; primary and secondary schools, and NGOs. The 3 week training strengthened their grasp of the subject matter, prepared them to write the training manuals, conduct field tests, and do subsequent training of manual users. Two training manuals were written: one for primary school trainers, the other for secondary schools. A handbook for facilitators was also written to accompany the manuals.

In August 1996, 40 trainers from the Departments of School Inspection, Curriculum Development, Examination, Health, Education, and Community Development and NGOs participated in an orientation training as preparation to field test the manuals. The field test was conducted in four districts in September and October. Suggestions for improvement were incorporated in the final drafts. Twenty thousand copies of the primary school manual and 10,000 of the secondary school manuals were produced and distributed among the trainers. In February 1997, 45 national facilitators were trained to instruct tutors in teacher training colleges. By February 1998, 1,500 tutors in 50 of the 64 primary teacher colleges throughout Uganda had attended the 10-day intensive life skills training program. The national facilitators instructed trainers to become district-based facilitators. By the end of March 1998, 900 trainers from 30 of 45 districts were certified instructors in the Life Skills Program.

For the NGOs, a training manual was developed to facilitate the integration of life skills into their educational activities. The manual recognized the diverse needs of nonenrolled youth as including those living on the street, those living in conflict areas, orphans, and the disabled. Young people working under hazardous and exploitative conditions, those who were sexually exploited and abused, and children who witnessed atrocities (especially in conflict areas) were also targeted. Appropriate life skills topics and activities were developed for their varied needs. By the end of April 1998, three trainers each from 30 NGOs that worked directly with youth had attended a 10-day training program and were certified to promote life skills for their respective target groups.

In addition to the systematic integration of life skills activities into formal teacher-training programs and NGO activities, the skills are also being promoted through school clubs, debates, drama, and role-playing. In early 1997, as part of this initiative, the program trained 70 Scouts leaders and Girl Guides from 20 districts as life skills promoters, taking advantage of the existing Scouts and Guides network and discipline. These leaders have now embarked on life skills training for their peers throughout the country.

Recognizing the power of communication in influencing the behavior of young people, the program targeted different communication groups, religious institutions, and other community groups to develop initiatives for young people. The Straight Talk Foundation, which produces newsprint for young people, was funded to promote specific life skills messages and activities. *The Straight Talk Newsletter* reaches more than 500,000 adolescents and adults each month and serves as an effective communication vehicle for adolescent health and development issues. For example, it conveys sexual health information to young people in a style and language to which they relate. It also provides a forum where youth are able to discuss and debate sexual health and social issues, such as teenage pregnancy and substance abuse, and can offer suggestions for skills that would enable them to meet such challenges.

The HIV/AIDS Communication Initiative, started in 1995, works to encourage behavior change by utilizing HIV-infected volunteers to share their life experiences. The volunteers are trained in communication skills, which improve the effectiveness of their messages, and work with target groups of young people in schools as well as with nonenrolled youth. The Life Skills Program has supported this organization by providing training materials as well as technical and financial assistance. This support has enabled the organization to traverse the countryside and urban centers with very effective behavior-change messages.

The Sara Communication Initiative, aimed at promoting the status and potential of girls in eastern and southern Africa, also complements the promotion of life skills. This initiative supports social mobilization processes designed to enable female adolescents to realize their potential and to foster their participation in development. It also seeks to raise awareness of and advocacy for the reduction of existing disparities in the status and treatment of girls. Through an animated character, an adolescent girl named Sara, the Initiative has produced a positive symbol and dynamic role model for girls through which they can acquire self-esteem and learn life skills for empowerment. The Initiative also promotes communication information regarding survival, protection, and development of young people, especially girls, with specific messages on education, health, nutrition, and other social concerns. The initiative builds on the power of the media to raise awareness, generate discussion, and thereby increase knowledge about such themes such as sexual abuse, school dropout, and discrimination against female children. The Life Skills Program has incorporated themes and illustrations from the Initiative in its materials to promote specific life skills for young girls.

In 1994, the government began the Complementary Opportunity for Primary Education (COPE) in response to alarming statistics that almost half of Uganda's eligible school-aged children were not attending school. Some had never been to school at all; others, especially girls, had dropped out. Although it was previously assumed that prohibitive schooling costs were the major reason for nonattendance, the 1994 Situation Analysis showed other reasons to be equally strong. These included the loss of household labor and other "opportunity costs," social and cultural values that negatively affect girls, and rigid and largely irrelevant curriculum (GOU/NCC, 1994). The Ministry of Education, in collaboration with UNICEF, then designed the COPE program to provide minimum basic education at an accelerated pace to children between 8 and 14 years of age. This accelerated program enabled youth to achieve basic literacy and numeracy within 3 years and thereafter to continue with their education to the fifth grade in the formal school system if they wished to do so. The Life Skills Program took advantage of the COPE initiative to incorporate life skills concepts and activities in the COPE pedagogical materials. Through this collaboration, about 5,000 adolescents had received training in life skills by the end of 1997.

An Analysis of Opportunities and Constraints

An emphasis on teacher training is based on the understanding that life skills–promoting activities in school provide several opportunities to practice those skills. However, this is only possible if teachers allow young people latitude to organize themselves and to decide what tasks to conduct. It also means that life skills are promoted through a social learning process involving observation, practice, and application. Classroom methods would include group work, role-playing, brainstorming, debates, and open discussion (WHO, 1993). Such opportunities enable students to interact, thus improving on their communication and negotiation skills, their critical thinking as they carry out tasks they choose, and self-awareness as they come to understand each other's role in undertaking tasks. Students improve their self-esteem as they manage activities better over time. However, this is not an easy process, as the trainers have discovered. Although the teachers appreciated the program, as reflected in their evaluation of the training they received, most are uncomfortable with interactive and learner-centered methods required to promote acquisition of life skills. Partly because of the examination-driven curriculum, many teachers have difficulties in adopting what they see as time-consuming methods. One solution to this problem involves restructuring schools and school curricula to take account of the time needed for teachers to carry out demonstration of life skills activities. Absent this, the Life Skills Program will need time to achieve the desired results.

It became evident that several cultural practices in Uganda continue to hinder the development of important skills required by young people. Most discourage youth's assertiveness, especially among girls, insisting that it promotes lack of respect and discipline. These societies are accustomed to children being submissive. Skills related to sexual behavior are especially difficult to promote because many parents oppose discussing sexual topics at home, even when they support sex education in public forums. This means young people are unable to practice the skills they learn at school, partly defeating the purpose of the program. It is therefore important to buttress school-based life skills promotion with community-based efforts. In a country such as Uganda, where about 50% of the adult population are illiterate and poor, this is not an easy task.

Working with local NGOs also poses many challenges. NGOs are scattered geographically and usually reluctant to share information and experiences. Poor documentation of success and challenges pertaining to interventions and best practices are widespread. For example, it is not easy to find information on the number of young people benefiting from interventions of a particular NGO or the profile of such beneficiaries. This affects evaluations that seek to determine whether such interventions actually make a difference in the lives of young people. Sometimes the will to collaborate at the national level is apparent, but local collaboration points are not pursued and adequately exploited.

Lack of comprehensive data on young people also is a significant impediment to the design of effective interventions. The most recent population census, from 1991, is the most comprehensive source of information on young people. Likewise, the Situation Analysis Report on Children and Adolescents in Uganda, produced in 1994, provides only scanty information on young people. Many believe that the number of street children is increasing rapidly, but there is little concrete documentation to that effect. It is also known that youth are dropping out of school at high rates, but there is virtually no information on their fate once they are out of school. Lack of data is compounded by the fact that targeting young people with specific interventions is a relatively new development in Uganda; thus there are limited institutional data and a weak policy framework for the provision of services specifically designed for young people. This anomaly, if not addressed, will continue to undermine genuine efforts to develop and implement programs specifically designed for youth.

As internal conflict persists in the various parts of the country, contact with young people in those areas remains limited and risky. Yet the conditions prevailing there put young people at very high risk and increase the urgency of preparing them to meet the challenges associated with armed conflicts. Presently, this task is entirely in the hands of NGOs, whose limitations, outlined previously, call for urgent government participation to complement their work.

Concluding Remarks and Issues for Policy and Research

The implementation of the Life Skills Program in Uganda has provided important lessons and raised issues of interest to policymakers and researchers. Promoting interactive and participatory methods and adopting approaches centered on young people are crucial for the success of programs that aim to change behavior of young people and enhance their development. Teachers are key actors in understanding and promoting educational change (Fullan and Stiegelbauer, 1991). Although there is evidence that teaching is becoming increasingly participatory in Ugandan schools, sustaining this positive approach in the face of rigid curriculum- and examination-driven school programs remains a formidable challenge to policymakers. Certainly the teachers and managers of programs for young people must be assisted to understand that unless they provide opportunities for children to learn interactively and to practice life skills, the practical aspects of learning will never be acquired and used.

The Life Skills Program is designed to address interrelated needs and problems of young people within the constraints of the school and other service providers. Some of the skills address prevention issues (e.g., teenage pregnancy and HIV infection); some aim to empower young people to look after themselves, the community, and the environment; others focus on the development of healthy and sociable behavior, thereby enabling young people to reach their full potential. Although it is not easy to measure behavior change, Life Skills Programs should produce observable outcomes by which they can be assessed (Manoncourt, 1998). It should not be very difficult, for example, to observe whether young people who participate in the program practice healthy life-styles, solve conflicts among themselves in a peaceful manner, or behave in ways that display self-esteem, respect for each other, and gender sensitivity. It is also possible to assess whether and how young people change as a result of increased access to particular services, and how these impact them. Four years after its implementation, the Life Skills Program continued to present challenges to policymakers and researchers.

The mass media in Uganda have become more aggressive in recent years, since their liberalization and increased privatization. Frequency modulated (FM) stations have mushroomed in most urban areas, and their broadcasts are received in most rural areas as well. Most of these stations are quite popular with young people, although some of the programs may not always be suitable for them. Providing information and stimulating debate on issues affecting young people are most effective when young people are given a platform and supported in expressing their views. The FM stations could, therefore, be encouraged and supported to design sustainable programs for young people that deliver messages that encourage healthy life-styles and behavior. The opportunity to make the best use of these radio stations should be explored.

Uganda's government is a signatory to the United Nations Convention on the Rights of the Child (CRC). The fundamental principles of the CRC focus on the best interests of the child, respect for her or his views, the right to survival and development, and nondiscrimination. These principles are supported by the national youth policy in Uganda, which is being formulated. One strategy to implement Uganda's youth policy is to adopt the rights-based approach that clearly specifies the rights and obligations of young people. The Life Skills Program is playing an important role to enable youth to develop, as enshrined in the CRC. Herein lies the framework for the government to provide the best development opportunity for its young population to fulfill its national and international obligations.

To conclude, this discussion on Uganda brings into sharp focus several issues regarding a generation of youth lost to underinvestment during the 1970s and 1980s as a result of conflict and political disarray. Several countries in the developing world have witnessed similar experiences, albeit with varied results. As a result of recent events in Angola, Liberia, Sierra Leone, the Balkans, and the former Soviet Republics, it is possible that many more countries may find themselves in the same dire circumstances. One clear lesson from Uganda's experience is that what young people endure in their lives as they develop has long-lasting consequences for their adult lives. What young people see today and how they are treated will determine what kind of societies they will build as adults.

The strategies adopted by Uganda's Life Skills Program are primarily supportive, educational, and preventive. They recognize that young people's disadvantaged position can be attenuated and overcome by well thought out interventions that make a lasting difference in their lives. The positive lessons from Uganda may help improve the lives of young people in similar situations elsewhere. The Life Skills Program in Uganda may prove that, after all, something good can be done for young people even where resources are limited. What are essential are the will and the commitment of society as a whole to provide for its future generations.

REFERENCES

Caplan, M., Weissberg, R. P., Grober, J. S., and Jackoby, C. (1992). Social Competence Promotion with Inner City and Sub-Urban Young Adolescents: Effects on Social Adjustment and Alcohol Use. *Journal of Consulting and Clinical Psychology*, 60(1), 56–63.

Cele, C. I., Eriko, Z., Kamya, H., and Oguttu, J. (1997). Baseline Study on the Level of Life Skills of Uganda's Primary School Children (Unpublished). Kampala: UNICEF.

Fullan, M., and Stiegelbauer, S. (1991). *The New Meaning of Educational Change*, 2nd ed. New York: Teachers College Press.

Gold, R. S. (1991). Cultural Sensitivity in AIDS Education: A Misunderstood Concept. *Evaluation and Program Planning*, 14(4), 221–231.

Government of Uganda/National Council of Children (1994). *Equity and Vulnerability: A Situation Analysis of Women, Adolescents and Children in Uganda*. Kampala: National Council of Children.

Government of Uganda/UNICEF. (1993). HEN/SHEP Process Evaluation (unpublished). Kampala: UNICEF.

Government of Uganda/UNICEF. (1998). 1997 Annual Report on Basic Education, Child Care and Adolescent Development Programme. (Unpublished). Kampala: UNICEF.

Macrae, J. A., and Birungi, H. (1993). *A Healthy Peace: Rehabilitation and Development of the Health Sector in a Post-conflict Situation – the Case of Uganda: A Pilot Study: Health Economics and Financial Program*. London: Health Policy Unit, London School of Hygiene and Tropical Medicine.

Manoncourt, E. (1998). Communication for Behavior Change (unpublished). New York: UNICEF.

McLean, D. A. (1994). A model for HIV risk reduction and prevention among African-American college students. *Journal of American Health*, 42(5), 220–223.

Natukunda, E., and Kamya, S. (1993). Operational Research on the Situation of Orphans within Family and Community Context (unpublished). Kampala: UNICEF/UCOBAC.

Ogwal-Oyee, F. (1997). Education Managers and Their Awareness of Life Skills: A Research Report (unpublished). Kampala: UNICEF.

Opolot, J. A., Cele.C. I., and Jehopio, P. J. (1997). The Level of Life Skills of Uganda's Secondary School Students: A Baseline Study (unpublished). Kampala: UNICEF.

Parsons, C., Hunter, D., and Warne, Y. (1988). *Skills for Adolescents: An Analysis of Project Material, Training and Implementation.* London: Christ Church College, Evaluation Unit.

Republic of Uganda. (1995). *Uganda Demographic and Health Survey.* Kampala: Ministry of Health.

Republic of Uganda. (1996). *Statistical Abstract.* Entebbe: Ministry of Finance and Economic Planning.

Rossouw, D. J. (1990). What Industry Demands of Science Educators: A Survey. *Onderwys Education Bulletin,* 34(1).

Tuhaise, C. (1992). Need for Foster Care in Uganda. *Vulnerable Child (UCOBAC) Newsletter,* 1, 3–4.

UNDP Uganda. (1997).*Uganda Human Development Report.* Kampala: Print World Limited.

UNICEF/NCC. (1994). Equity and Vulnerability: A Situation Analysis of Women, Adolescents and Children (unpublished). Kampala: Uganda.

World Bank. (1993). *Uganda: Growing Out of Poverty.* Washington DC: The World Bank.

World Health Organization. (1993). *Training Workshops for the Development and Implementation of Life Skills Programs* (WHO/MNH/PSF/93.7B. Rev.1). Geneva: World Health Organization.

V

PROSPECT AND RETROSPECT

12 Prospect and Retrospect

Options for Healthy Youth Development in Changing Urban Worlds

Marta Tienda and William Julius Wilson

Both rich and poor countries face formidable challenges in adhering to the terms of the UN Convention on the Rights of the Child. Global economic, demographic, and social trends have undermined many of the traditional social support systems that protected young people and gave them a sense of belonging, self-worth, and purpose. These challenges are especially acute for developing countries, where intense rural–urban migration coupled with high demographic growth rates strain the capacity of existing urban institutional structures to accommodate the rapidly changing needs of urban youth. In industrialized countries as well, economic restructuring has accentuated the economic marginalization and social isolation of inner-city youth. The expansion of a technology-based service economy has decreased the relative demand for low-skilled labor and contributed to the rise in concentrated urban poverty in highly segregated cities.

As a consequence of these macroeconomic trends, the divide between the middle class and the poor has widened in both developed and developing countries, particularly in urban areas, where the effects of economic restructuring on social differentiation are most acute. Urban youth throughout the world are adversely affected when national economies contract and result in realigned fiscal priorities that give lower priority to youth-serving organizations. Young people are both agents and victims of social and economic transformations that rearrange their life options because they must not only master the major developmental tasks during adolescence, but also find their place in an order that is in constant flux.

The social and economic isolation of adults is inextricably linked to the destitution of youth and, coincidentally, their abnormal psychosocial development. At best, children and adolescents assume the adult roles at early ages; at worst, they experience hardships that thwart any semblance of a normal transition to adulthood, if they survive adolescence. The accumulation of negative life experiences through childhood and adolescence has a profound effect on youth's prospects for prosocial adjustment and can have myriad deleterious consequences that last a lifetime.

In addition, the effects of concentrated poverty stymie aspirations and inculcate a sense of hopelessness about the future. These circumstances challenge researchers to continue assembling insights from case studies to ferret proximate causes from distal causes of abnormal development carefully and to incorporate context-specific situations in the design of intervention programs intended to ensure that all youth enjoy the protections specified in the UN Convention on the Rights of the Child. Although addressed to national governments as representatives of their citizenry, the Convention explicitly asserts that *all* members of society share responsibility for protecting the basic human rights of *all* children and youth. That is, the standards and guidelines of the Convention can be fully realized only when universally respected – by parents, professionals, political and community leaders, and youth advocates working in public and private institutions.

The chapters included in this volume, several of which are inspired by the Convention, document the social conditions of urban youth from a cross-national perspective and examine intervention programs aimed at alleviating or reversing the debilitating effects of acute child poverty. Despite the highly diverse social and cultural contexts of urban youth worldwide, their requirements to mature into healthy, emotionally stable, and socially productive adults are remarkably similar. These essential needs include safety and security, a sense of acceptance and belonging, a reasonable degree of predictability in their lives, and access to caring adults, preferably in intact families. Other essential shared requirements for maturing into healthy adulthood are access to high-quality education and age-appropriate income generating opportunities, supportive communities, public institutions that value and respect youth, and, as illustrated in several chapters, opportunities to use creative strategies in managing environmental risks.

Although young people's basic requirements for healthy, normative development are similar, societies vary in the routes they take to ensure their physical, emotional, and social well-being. In many countries public policy to enhance youth development is virtually nonexistent. Indeed, one of the most important challenges facing groups and institutions that work to promote healthy youth development is convincing local and national governments to invest in young people. As White and Prothrow-Stith point out, media sensationalism that emphasizes atypical and transgressive behavior reinforces stereotypes that make authorities and adults in general fearful and suspicious of young people.

It would appear that in some countries nothing short of a national campaign by coalitions of youth advocates is needed to overcome and reverse political postures that view youth as burdens rather than assets. This campaign ought to have two main goals: to raise the public awareness of the value of young people to their families, their communities, and society at large, and, as suggested by several case studies reported in this volume, to educate political leaders on how to capitalize on and cultivate the myriad assets youth embody.

It is reasonable to assume that increased public awareness of the value of young people will result in greater support for conditions that promote and enhance youth development. Field studies and practitioner experiences provide several lessons for policymakers and concerned citizens wishing to improve the overall conditions of youth. In the following sections we summarize several overarching lessons based on the cross-cultural evidence that draws from both research insights and the concrete experience of practitioners.

Prioritizing Needs of Children and Youth

Poverty has devastating long-term effects on the well-being of children and youth; therefore, political leaders must recognize that strong antipoverty policy is strong youth development policy. Antipoverty policy is also an investment for future economic growth and national prosperity. Accordingly, promoters of social policies to expand employment income generating opportunities and redistribute wealth ought to acknowledge the close connection between material conditions and psychosocial well-being of adults and children. Why? Because a country's future economic prospects depend crucially on current investments in youth – its future leaders.

Of course, raising incomes of poor families is a necessary, but insufficient condition to meet all requirements for healthy normative development of poor urban youth. As emphasized in the Convention, access to high-quality education is a basic human right no child should be denied. Providing universal access to high-quality education must be at the forefront of every national agenda. Not only is formal schooling the building block upon which the successful development of children and adolescents is grounded, but education is essential for preparing young people to become engaged social actors, productive citizens, and architects of new democratic societies. It also provides them the skills to behave in socially responsible ways and to manage adversity creatively as they mature.

Because schools play an important role in the cultural and social development of children, it behooves administrators to incorporate life skills in standard curricula, particularly in resource-poor urban settings. And because many children must contribute to their family's economic support, McKechnie and Hobbs recommend flexible scholastic schedules that permit youth to remain enrolled while they work. Low-income countries especially require innovative pedagogical approaches that allow young people to study if they have to work. Given that many youth become discouraged or overwhelmed as they assume the double burden of student and worker, flexible scholastic schedules may help them retain the desire to learn and envision a better future.

Responsive and Supportive Adults

The emotional and social supports of strong kinship networks are essential for normative development of youth. But, as Ogwal-Oyee relates, in countries torn by civil strife and ravaged by acquired immunodeficiency syndrome (AIDS), the high rates of adult mortality produce some of the highest rates of orphanhood in the world, thereby depriving many youth of parents and relatives at very young ages. In circumstances in which kinship networks are either unsupportive or potentially damaging to youth, or indeed are nonexistent (as when parents die), the attachment of a responsible, caring adult is crucial for helping youth succeed. South African and Brazilian programs that target homeless street children and shelter them from the dangers of the street are guided by this fundamental principle. As Rizzini, Barker, and Cassaniga illustrate, program interventions that provide for the stabilizing influence of benevolent adults are an important step toward fulfilling the emotional and social development needs of street children.

The importance of strong and caring adults is also clearly revealed in Earls and Carlson's practical application of their theory of adolescent development, namely, a Chicago project that examines young people's characterization of their own well-being. Conversations with the youth who participate in this project clearly revealed the important role of caring adults, including teachers and project staff, in providing both the structure and the motivation for improving their social and material circumstances.

Youth as Stakeholders

Voicelessness is particularly egregious for poor young people who are doubly marginalized because of their economic status and their age. Accordingly, the Convention on the Rights of the Child stresses the importance of respecting children's right to express their views. Several of the preceding chapters illustrate age-appropriate strategies to channel young people's ideas in the design of interventions and policies that can improve their immediate and future life circumstances while not compromising the human rights or responsibilities of others.

Most youth development experts agree that young people should be afforded a significant voice in the design of policies and programs that affect their lives, and the Convention so stipulates. Several chapters in this volume illustrated how youth can convert punitive adult-centered problem-resolution approaches to more effective child-centered strategies. White's contrast of the developmental and punitive approaches to youth deviance is a compelling testimonial, but so too are Prothrow-Stith's descriptions of the various public health approaches to youth violence.

Nevertheless, opinions on the nature and extent of participation that enhances both collective betterment and individual youth development vary. The domains in which youth involvement in decisions that potentially affect their future have not been clearly delineated in a coherent and synthetic document, although specific illustrations are scattered throughout studies on youth development. Of course, the domains of youth participation will necessarily evolve according to the age of the participants and differences in local and national settings. Furthermore, there is a lack of consensus on the mechanisms through which young people can and should participate in policy and program design. Therefore, a major challenge for both practitioners and researchers is to formulate guidelines not only on the participation of youth in various activities and decisions that directly impact their futures, but also on age-appropriate venues to give young people a voice.

Because causes of poverty are so complex, it is not obvious that youth are best positioned to propose solutions to ameliorate its consequences. However, the evidence provided by several of the authors in this volume suggests that youth involvement in the development and implementation of programs to serve them is productive in two ways. It can help adults understand and value child-centered perspectives, and it can identify strategies that may enhance the likelihood of success in the design of effective problem-solving interventions. Nonetheless, Rhodes, Mihyar, and Abu El-Rous emphasize, as do Earls and Carlson, that giving youth a voice in decision making and program design must be done in the context of adult supervision.

Approaches to youth empowerment must extend beyond the designing of policies and programs that affect the lives of young people to involve the broader processes of political and social mobilization. Whereas many countries, especially the lowest-income developing societies, often impose cultural constraints that require youth to assume a passive or nonconfrontational role and therefore refrain from collective action, there are several clear examples of youth-organized initiatives that have profoundly altered the course of social change at both local and national levels. For example, at the local level, Rhodes and his colleagues illustrate how the organized voices of young people in Lebanon made neighborhoods more youth-friendly. At the national level, Ramphele describes how the collective action of youth in South Africa's Black Consciousness Movement help Black adults overcome feelings of inferiority and attitudes of fatalism generated by the apartheid system of racism.

Thus whether the focus is on the implementation of local youth programs or on collective action to bring about social change in the broader society, the authors in this volume provide compelling support based on concrete field evidence for the need for a broader vision of strategies to promote healthy youth development. This is a vision that both recognizes the importance of youth as stakeholders in bringing about change to enhance their lives and acknowledges the need for serious discussions on how best to involve young people in program implementation and strategies of social change.

Understanding the Roles of Government

The state's definition and perception of low-income populations are important components in proposing economic or social interventions to alleviate their material and social disadvantages. Satisfying some of the basic needs for healthy youth development does not require large fiscal outlays by governmental units. What are perhaps more important than fiscal resources are the political will and commitment to honor the terms of the international Convention on the Rights of the Child. Rich countries obviously have greater resources to invest in their children and adolescents, yet as noted in Chapter 1 and illustrated by Heitmeyer, Prothrow-Stith, and Earls and Carlson, residing in a high-income country does not guarantee that the basic needs and human rights of young people are respected.

But countries where most of the world's poor urban youth reside lack the resources or organizational infrastructure to realize some or all of these goals in the short term. Poor communities in low-income countries often rely on innovative demonstration programs to create incremental changes in the lives of youth rather than wait for national commitments on behalf of children and adolescents. However, even in resource-poor environments, coordination among existing local and private community and government organizations can go a long way toward improving opportunities for normative youth development.

As Rizzini and her collaborators discuss for Brazil, and Rhodes and his colleagues elaborate for Lebanon, in many situations, grass-roots organizations or a small group of dedicated workers can provide marginalized youth with productive opportunities and healthy choices that promote a successful transition from adolescence to adulthood. For many of these interventions, outreach in the form of a caring adult who can shield young people from the physical and emotional ravages of poverty is a crucial first step in the battle against youth disenfranchisement.

Although all members of society ought to share responsibility for promoting the human rights of children and adolescents, a theme running throughout this volume is the urgent need to generate a greater commitment among governments around the world to uphold the principles set by the UN Convention on the Rights of the Child and to support youth programs that impact significant segments of the population. How to do this is unclear, but one strategy to begin this process is to create a focal point for youth within the United Nations, just as has been done for women with relative success. Unfortunately, the pitch and range of children's voices have not yet reached the highest levels of the UN bureaucracy to initiate this action.

Evaluating Intervention Strategies

The specific circumstances in which poverty delimits opportunities and undermines the requirements for normative adolescent development warrant consideration in the design and implementation of youth programs. Although no cookbook method is available for delineating all of the components of interventions that successfully mediate the pernicious effects of poverty on youth, well-formulated evaluation designs are essential for program development. The foregoing chapters provide numerous examples of interventions that are successful in promoting some aspects of healthy youth development and in ameliorating the deleterious effects of poverty and social isolation. Nevertheless, the demonstration of *how* a specific program or intervention produces its desired effect or *what components* of the intervention are critical to the success of the process is generally vague, making replication and generalization difficult.

In many instances the crucial ingredient of a successful program is the involvement of a charismatic or caring individual who can connect with marginalized youth. In other instances, success is attained through coalitions of caring organizations that are able to combine resources to address a wide constellation of interrelated problems that undermine healthy youth development. Understanding of the different features of programs and the ways they are implemented is essential in evaluation designs for deciding which activities should be brought to scale with government (local or national) support and under what circumstances. Context-specific circumstances also dictate the necessary and sufficient ingredients for successful interventions. Therefore, evaluation designs should also be sensitive to the complexities of the concrete conditions in which youth navigate their developmental tasks, and sufficiently sophisticated to identify both the intended and the unintended consequences of an intervention.

Even the best-intentioned programs can exacerbate an already onerous situation if unintended consequences are not carefully anticipated. For example, as McKechnie and Hobbs explain, by ignoring the precarious income generating strategies of poor families, policies that prohibit all forms of youth employment may actually aggravate the material deprivation of children by depriving the family of crucial means of support. Thus, flexibility is required in devising policies to protect the economic status of young people while creating opportunities to enhance their development into productive adults.

Where from Here? Next Steps

Two of the main reasons for convening a highly diverse group of researchers and practitioners to discuss the challenges of promoting normative development in the context of urban poverty were to highlight the complexities of the problem and to illustrate successful approaches that simultaneously adhere to the guiding principles of the UN Convention on the Rights of the Child. The overriding message is that urgent action is needed at international, national, and community levels to curb the escalating problem of acute urban poverty and its attendant maladies. Delineating how urban youth experience the ravages of poverty and illustrating successful intervention strategies in localized settings from a cross-cultural perspective are but first steps in creating an action agenda for change.

An accurate gauge of the limits of national policies or top-down approaches to youth development requires an understanding of country-specific priorities in the measurement, documentation, and alleviation of poverty and in the assessment of the political, social, and economic climate. Community-initiated approaches to establishing supportive networks for youth development require a keen awareness of available resources and the degree to which the community options are constrained by national economic conditions. In situations in which national initiatives are lacking, community awareness of economic and social constraints can provide program planners with an inventory of available support networks that can be used to enhance youth development. The building blocks for the successful mobilization of limited resources to create youth-friendly environments are essentially the collective energies of dedicated groups and individuals, including neighborhood residents, faith-based organizations, and public sector agencies.

Extended family networks also play a critical role in the monitoring, socialization, and normative development of youth and are the first line of defense against external sources of risk. The essential elements of the familial bond always need to be protected and sustained, but youth need to be connected immediately to functional substitutes, such as extended relatives or unrelated caring adults, when parents are unavailable. The living arrangements of youth can provide immediate protection for managing risk and adversity that young people inevitably confront in impoverished urban settings. Interventions that involve entire families in one way or another, forestall children's premature assumption of adult roles, and provide young people the opportunity to master age-appropriate developmental tasks in their path to adulthood should be showcased and brought to scale whenever possible.

Finally, when all other support mechanisms fail, or when social forces are such that children become the unwitting victims of war, family dissolution, or community dislocation, individualized and targeted interventions aimed at stabilizing and reconnecting youth with mainstream society are imperative. Although usually quite resilient, youth who suffer from the mental or physical abuse of self or a loved one require a great deal of caring and strategically directed support to affect a positive change in their lives. And, although the UN Convention on the Rights of the Child has clearly delineated the guidelines for ensuring that all youth reach their maximum potential, without the political commitment of strong leaders to broker on behalf of youth, nations will continue to compromise their economic potential by underinvesting in their most precious resource – young people.

Index